ADAM BUXTON

RAMBLE BOOK

MUDLARK

*For Mummy, UD, CAB, DJR, McG, J-Corn,
Markface, Loubo, Mole, G Unit, Grendel,
Scotch, Dog and the Podcats*

Mudlark

HarperCollins*Publishers*
1 London Bridge Street
London SE1 9GF

www.harpercollins.co.uk

First published by Mudlark 2020

1 3 5 7 9 10 8 6 4 2

© Adam Buxton 2020

Adam Buxton asserts the moral right to be identified
as the author of this work

A catalogue record of this book is available from
the British Library

ISBN 978-0-00-829334-5

Printed and bound in Great Britain by CPI Group (UK) Ltd, Croydon

MIX
Paper from
responsible sources
FSC
www.fsc.org
FSC™ C007454

This book is produced from independently certified FSC™ paper
to ensure responsible forest management.
For more information visit: www.harpercollins.co.uk/green

CONTENTS

INTRODUCTION

Hey! How you doing, readers? Adam Buxton here. I'm writing this in June 2019 in my office, a room in one of the barns next to the Norfolk farmhouse I live in with my wife ( MY WIFE), my daughter (aged 10), my two sons (aged 14 and 16) and our dog Rosie (a black whippet poodle cross, aged six).

Next to my office is a small voice booth where I edit my podcast, record jingles and do bits of computer work for *BUG* and my other live shows. The shelves in my office are stacked with selected items of personal and professional detritus. A lot of it has accumulated from the last 23 years of working with Joe Cornish on Adam-and-Joe projects for TV and radio, but in among all that are family photos and souvenirs from my various solo efforts. I'll list a few of these for you to make myself seem colourful and productive.

Against one wall stands a shelf full of video tapes in various obsolete formats from art school and *Adam and Joe Show* days. Adjacent to the tape shelves are rows of box files stuffed with scripts, laminates, postcards, sketch books, photographs, etc. Above these sits a selection of hats. The sailor's cap I wore on *The Adam and Joe Show*, a bowler hat with a big fake crow on top of it that I wore in a video for my song 'Nutty Room', the top hat worn by my character Monty Buggershop

Hooty (it's actually supposed to be pronounced 'Monty *Bershif-Hoy*'– aka, Country Man) and a bike helmet sprayed silver with a dowelling pole attached to the front (one of five such helmets worn by the members of Radiohead in a video my friend Garth Jennings and I made in 2007 for their song 'Jigsaw Falling into Place').

Above the hats is an Adam Buxton Podcast poster. Hanging alongside this are a few photos of me and Joe from our BBC Radio 6 Music days in the late 2000s, and on the wall behind me is a framed paper plate, left in my dressing room for me after one of my live shows. It has a message written on it from the comedian Harry Hill. The message is personal so I won't tell you exactly what it says, but I wanted to at least refer to it so you'd be impressed. I'm looking at it now. Such a great message from one of my favourite comedians. I wish you could see it. But it's personal (and very flattering).

As I write I'm a few days away from my fiftieth birthday, and though I imagine I'm far beyond the mid-point of my life, I think I'm having a mid-life crisis.

I'm not having affairs with models, buying motorbikes and jumping out of aeroplanes, but I am often in a state of self-indulgent, melancholy introspection despite a life of abundant privilege. Does that count?

I think it's been creeping up on me for a while, but it really took hold when my father, Nigel Buxton (who was known as BaaadDad when he appeared on *The Adam and Joe Show*), died at the end of 2015. He was a big personality: gruff, pompous, conservative and harshly critical of nearly everything I enjoyed as a youngster and beyond, especially the TV, films and music I have always spent so much time consuming. Perhaps Dad's critical demeanour contributed to my own frequently unhelpful sensitivity to criticism, not only of my own efforts but those of the people I admire. (Wow, it's just the introduction and I'm already getting started on the self-analysis and Dad-blaming. This is going well.)

The truth is my dad was more than just a grumpy old reactionary. He was also thoughtful, loving and determined to do the best he could for me, my sister and my brother.

Then he was diagnosed with cancer, and for the last nine months of his life he came to live with us in Norfolk. As you might imagine, it was weird and stirred up a lot of emotional silt that for many years I'd been happy to leave undisturbed. Fucking emotional silt.

A few weeks after my father died, David Bowie checked out, too. People like me, for whom Bowie and his work had been a constant source of pleasure and fascination throughout their lives, were surprised by how upsetting this was. For his fans he represented something vital, otherworldly and, yes, immortal. I think part of me assumed that, instead of dying, Bowie would be beamed into space by well-dressed non-binary aliens or that he would just implode during a live streaming event, leaving a sparkly portal to a dimension filled with challenging electronic music.

But then he goes and gets liver cancer, which any twat could get. Talk about a let-down.

The message from Dad and David Bowie seemed clear: we're in your DNA and it's corroding (though I'm not sure that's scientifically accurate), so now might be a good time to take stock. To celebrate the things that have gone right, to examine the things that have gone wrong, to consider how much of it all you're passing on to your own children and to put it all in a book mixed in with some tales from my formative years, just a pinch of Dad-blaming and some light name-dropping (did I mention that Harry Hill once wrote me a very flattering message on a paper plate?).

RAMBLE

One of the things I like about the medium of podcasts is that they can easily accommodate the kinds of rambling and tangential conversations that I enjoy having with friends, and I wanted this book to reflect that. 'But, Buckles,' you may say, 'tangential rambles are fine in a podcast, but in a book they're annoying. Why not just include footnotes, which enable the reader to enjoy tangential information at their leisure rather than interrupting the flow of your sublime prose?' Well, that's a good point and thanks for making it, but I like tangential rambles and they appear in the main body of the text because that's how they appear in my life, constantly interrupting the flow of the central narrative and taking me off on detours and down cul-de-sacs that sometimes make me despair at my inability to concentrate on one thing and see it through to a successful conclusion, but at other times are more interesting than whatever else I should be doing.

A few other notes before we get going. This book jumps about to various points in my life in a way that to some stupid people might appear more or less arbitrary. Clever readers will know instinctively why I have done this and will not need me to explain it here, and as for the stupid readers, don't worry, you'll be fine.

I've focused on my dad far more heavily than my mum or any other members of my family because, so far, he's the only one that's dead, and now he no longer has the power to make Christmas uncomfortable, it feels OK to be indiscreet about him. My wife and children are shadowy presences not because they aren't an important part of my life but because they are the MOST important part of my life, so I try to be somewhat protective and not use them for material unless there's a poignant moment or a cheap laugh in it. My wife is a lawyer, so they've all signed release forms.

When my dad was the age I am now, a person as silly and ignorant as me – sorry, Dad, as silly and ignorant as I – would not have been considered worthy of having a book published. What can I tell you? We're living in sick times.

Here we go.

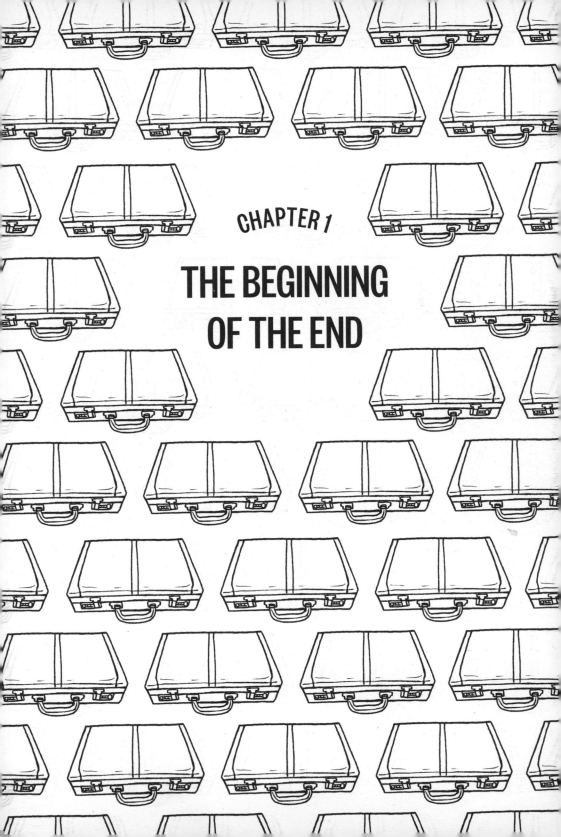

CHAPTER 1

THE BEGINNING OF THE END

My father, Nigel Buxton, aka BaaadDad, died at the end of November 2015. In February of that year I was in my dressing room at Pinewood Studios, about to shoot what turned out to be another failed TV pilot.

> ## RAMBLE
>
> I now have so many of these to my name that I've been awarded a Failed TV Pilot's Licence. This allows me to board any project and cruise at a low altitude, nearly breaking through the clouds before plunging back down to earth and crashing underwhelmingly.

I was taking selfies that made me look handsome when my sister called and said she'd just accompanied our dad to a meeting with the doctor. He'd been told he had mesothelioma (cancer of the lining of the lung). 'Could be worse,' I thought. How important is a bit of lung lining? After all, if you have a favourite jacket and the lining gets knackered, you can still wear that jacket, right? According to the doctor, lungs and jackets aren't as similar as you might think, and Dad was being given three to twelve months to live. He was 91, so well into bonus time, but still, it's not what anyone wants to hear.

Mum and Dad had gone their separate ways soon after my younger brother Dave (aka Uncle Dave or U.D.) had left home in the late Nineties. I'd suggested to my parents that they get divorced years before, but they didn't want to 'let anyone down'. After all, they had stood before friends, family and God and made a very solemn promise to stick together, no matter what. In their day people who broke that contract were judged harshly (my parents probably did some of that judging themselves), but when you get to the point where the thing you do best as a couple is annoy the shit out of each other, I think you might at least consider the possibility that friends, family and even God might forgive you for going your separate ways.

My mother moved into a house in a pretty village near Reading where her fellow residents include Jimmy Page and George and Amal Clooney. For any burglars reading this, Jimmy's usually home; George and Amal, not so much (also, everyone in the village knows that the code for their security system is 2580).

My dad got a place in Newhaven, Sussex, not far from where he grew up. With its jerry-rigged shelving, *Withnail and I* kitchen and pervasive old-man smell, it was on the squalid spectrum, but it looked over the expansively undulating fields of the Sussex Downs, where for his last two decades Dad loved walking as often as he could. Now that his knees were knackered and his lung lining tatty, the glamour of Newhaven was fading.

Daddy (which is what I always called him, though to avoid coming across as weak/posh I usually refer to him as Dad or Pa, as if I was in *Little House on the Prairie*) always loved coming to stay at our place in Norfolk, even though he only came a couple of times a year.

He would admire the outbuildings, one of which had been converted into a flat where I had my studio. 'That would make a very nice flat for me one day,' he would say, only half joking, and I would shudder at the thought.

In light of my sister's call and the news of his grim prognosis, I realised that moving Dad into the flat was my last opportunity, not only to play the part of the dutiful son, but to finally get to know him in a way that would afford me lasting emotional closure and, more importantly, could one day be turned into some kind of one-man show or book. I loved my dad, but our relationship had always been frustratingly formal, despite attempts to change that by making him part of *The Adam and Joe Show*. He was from a generation that valued keeping it all tucked in over letting it all hang out. That was also his policy on shirts and willies.

I spoke with my wife (🤖 MY WIFE), and when she agreed on Dad coming to live with us, I began making plans for Nigel.

RAMBLE

The 🤖 MY WIFE thing, with me saying ' 🤖 MY WIFE' in a weird voice after I mention my wife on the podcast, is not, as some people have assumed, a reference to Sacha Baron Cohen's character Borat, but something that started after I complained to Joe Cornish about my wife's tendency to misplace her keys (ADAM BUXTON PODCAST EP.12). I think Joe felt the way I kept saying ' 🤖 MY WIFE' sounded robotic and clichéd – a lazy characterisation of men as rational and organised and women as the opposite. He started saying ' 🤖 MY WIFE' in a robot voice, which made me laugh so I joined in. Now it's become a semi-catchphrase on the podcast and some people get annoyed when I don't do the voice after mentioning my wife (🤖 MY WIFE). OK, that's the last one for this book or it just gets annoying.

Supplementary Ramble

The story of my grumpy dad coming to live with us in Norfolk would be very different were it told from my wife's point of view, but until she starts up her own podcast in which she says ' 🤖 MY HUSBAND' in a robotic voice and gets a book deal, she's going to have to keep that to herself. Nevertheless, I do worry about the extent to which my wife has to just go along with the version of her that pops up in my ramblings from time to time. I've just emailed her at work to ask her about this and this is her reply: 'I really don't care what you say – I think I trust you not to make me look either like a pathetic pushover or a heartless Nazi (that's the worst kind of Nazi) – either way I will know what really went on, despite your insistence (as ever) that your version of events is true as you wrote it down in your bloody diary. Xxxxxxx'

Around April 2015, a few weeks before he was due to move in with us in Norfolk, I travelled to Dad's place in Sussex with my brother Dave. We were there to help Pa sort through a life-time of accumulated crap, knowing that if it were left to him, every scrap of crap would be moved to Norfolk and added to our own teetering crap heap. The celebrated psychologist Amos Tversky maintained that 'unless you're kicking your-self once a month for throwing something away, you're not throwing enough away'. That philosophy would have baffled and appalled my dad. He had the hoarder's dread of being tor-mented by regret if one day he needed something he'd binned.

Dave and I made our way through Dad's house, putting stickers on the few items of furniture that deserved to be kept, before turning our attention to the garage. With Dad issuing instructions from a camping chair out front, we heaved open the door and peered in.

I exchanged glances with Dave. It was like an Aladdin's cave in there, if an Aladdin had stuffed his cave with worthless shit. As we picked our way through, box after box revealed mouldering variations on similar themes: broken electrical items waiting vainly for that trip to the repair shop, box files exploding with damp paperwork, old articles and magazines Dad had once contributed to, and lidless Tupperware containing foreign coins, washers, keys, screws, fuses, hinges and hooks, all congealed by layers of rust and grime. Dave passed me an old cigar box with a label in Dad's handwriting that read: *'Pieces of string. Too short to be of any use.'*

Then I spotted it: a battered, black, faux-leather briefcase that I hadn't seen since we lived in Earl's Court in London, 40 years earlier. In those days Dad was the editor of the *Sunday Telegraph*'s travel section, and when he was at the office in Fleet Street or travelling abroad, as he was frequently, I would poke about in his cluttered study, hoping to find something cool or weird in among the filing-cabinet drawers filled with hotel toiletries, airline amenity kits and other travel freebies waiting for their moment of usefulness.

RAMBLE

Around this time I went through a phase of emulating the cop shows I saw on TV, but tended to play the part of the criminal rather than the cop. When my parents were out I'd go into the kitchen, lay out sheets of cling film, pour mounds of icing sugar onto them and wrap them into neat little packets. Then, using a big pointy knife, I'd cut a little hole in one of the packets, scoop out a bit of icing sugar with the knife tip and place it on my tongue before rubbing the sugar around my gums. I was eight.

One day, when I was beginning to worry that I'd discovered everything worth discovering in Dad's office, I spotted the black briefcase on top of a filing cabinet. I managed to get it down but found it tightly secured by two combination locks. There was a label on the lid, on which Dad had written in caps: '*IN THE EVENT OF MY DEATH THE CONTENTS OF THIS CASE SHOULD BE DESTROYED, UNOPENED.*'

I think Dad realised I'd been trying to open it because the next time I got into his office the case had disappeared. I wondered about the mysterious contents of that case from time to time, but when I moved out of my parents' place I forgot all about it. Years later, when I was in my twenties, I had a drink with Uncle Dave who was still living at home. We were talking about Dad's eccentricities and Dave said, 'Did you ever see the black briefcase?'

'Oh man, yes!' I said, and together we chanted, 'IN THE EVENT OF MY DEATH THE CONTENTS OF THIS CASE SHOULD BE DESTROYED, UNOPENED.'

'What the hell did he have in there?' said Dave. Our top guesses were: pornography … actually just pornography.

And now, here was the mystery case again, though the label had gone. I stuck on a new one and wrote in Sharpie, '*MOVE TO NORFOLK.*' A few weeks later, I finally discovered what was inside. You could flick to the end and find out what it was now, but to be honest it's unlikely to blow your mind. Better if you get to it naturally.

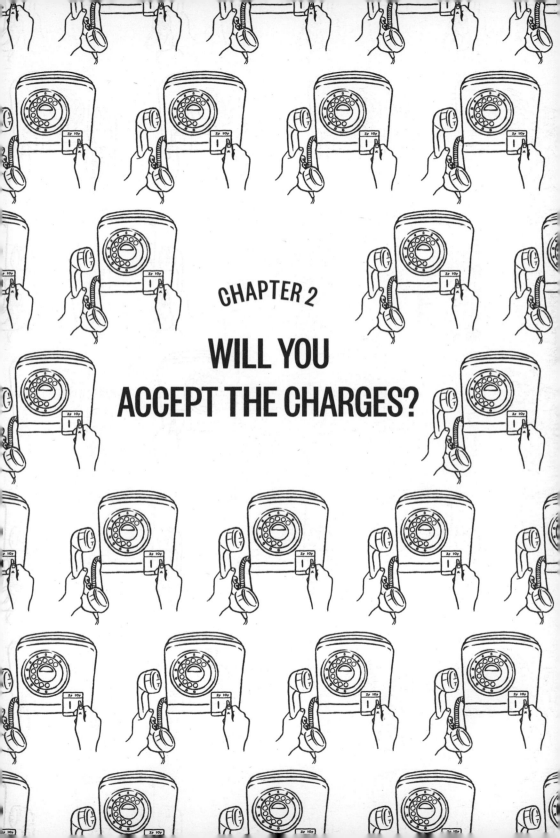

CHAPTER 2

WILL YOU
ACCEPT THE CHARGES?

'addy, what class are we?'

'Middle class, I suppose,' replied my dad.

Mum looked up from her *Daily Mail* and corrected him: 'We're *upper* middle class.'

'What does that mean?' I said, and Dad smiled.

'It means we're not rich, but we're comfortable.'

In fact, in the years when my dad was the editor of the *Sunday Telegraph*'s travel section, my life was very comfortable. We lived in a house made up of a ground floor and basement flat in a Victorian apartment block that was part of a leafy residential square in Earl's Court, West London. I learned to ride my bike in the communal garden that was only accessible to residents – no 'Undesirables', thank you. The 'Undesirable' community had their own communal garden called the Earl's Court Road.

Throughout my childhood, thanks to Dad's job, we travelled to Greece, France, Barbados, China and all over America. At Christmas there was a good chance that whatever toy we had set our acquisitive little hearts on would turn up under the tree. What was more, our parents loved us, and I always felt safe and happy when they were around.

So it was an unpleasant shock when, in early 1979, they sent me to boarding school.

They broke the news to me a couple of months before I left. Mum and Dad talked it up as a grand adventure – all midnight feasts, jolly japes and super new chums – but as far as I was concerned they may as well have said, 'We know you thought we loved you and that your cosy life would never end, but in eight weeks we're going to shoot you in the back of the head and dump you in a field in Sussex.'

Christmas 1978 played out with a bass note of melancholy, rising occasionally to mild panic at the thought of the looming intercision. The same questions kept going through my mind: Why are they doing this? Who does this really benefit? Could there not be a second referendum? (NOTE TO EDITOR: Re. your insistence that this is a lame, outdated, topical joke that ought to come out – I absolutely disagree. People LOVE Brexit references, they always will, and I forbid you to remove it. Get rid of this note, though, obviously.)

On a freezing Sunday evening in January 1979, my parents drove out to Sussex to drop off their nine-year-old son at his new boarding school, a big Queen Anne-style house of imposing wood-panelled rooms and corridors that smelled of floor polish and disinfectant, behind which lay a complex of newer buildings, all surrounded by playing fields and woodland.

Mum and Dad carried my suitcase and new tuck box as a smiling senior boy showed us the way to my dormitory, his presence encouraging me to keep it together and act as if this was a super adventure rather than an inexplicable nightmare. Whereas my parents had found it easy to coo over the posh interiors downstairs, the harshly lit dormitory with its rows of little metal bunks presented more of a challenge, and they began to look more sympathetic. Just as I was considering losing it dramatically, a woman in a light-blue nurse's uniform appeared, who gently but firmly informed my parents that it was time for them to leave and that I would be fine. I looked at my mum as if to say, 'I am NOT going to be fine,' but before I could start bawling, she and Dad were gone.

The most painful parts of that first term at boarding school came whenever I phoned home from the call box in the corridor outside the dining room. Children queueing for dinner would watch as trembling 'Squits' like me jammed 10p pieces into the payphone, before becoming fully distraught once Mummy or Daddy picked up. A few times when my credit ran out, the coin-slot mechanism was too stiff for me to insert my next 10p, and the call was cut off in a din of beeps and sobs, so when Mum saw me next she explained how I could make a call from a payphone without money by just calling the operator.

'I have a reverse-charge call from Sussex, will you accept the charges?' the operator would ask when someone picked up at home. When I heard Mum's lovely voice say, 'Yes. Hello, Adam!' I crouched beneath the glass panels in the door so no one in the dinner queue could see me and sobbed my nine-year-old tits off. I asked Mum about those tearful phone calls recently and she said, 'Yes, it was the most awful feeling.' So why send me away? She paused for a little while, then said, 'Do you know, I've never really thought about it.'

My sister started at the same boarding school a year after I arrived, and a few years later my brother was sent there too, so Mum and Dad must have thought about it a little bit. I think they believed that the experience would 'toughen us up' (which they considered a worthwhile thing to do with a child), while also enabling us to 'belong' to the upper echelons of British society with access to all the privileges and protections that membership provided. I suppose they also hoped we might enjoy it.

The school was progressive in many way: co-ed, no uniform, lots of arts and crafts, drama and cooking (I was the Lancashire hotpot and treacle tart king), and after the initial shock I ended up having fun and making some good friends there. But when I left school and started working, living and going out with people who hadn't been privately educated, my overwhelming feeling was not one of privilege but embarrassment. Perhaps I had an advantage if I'd wanted to become a Tory politician, a QC or a Harley Street physician, but outside the old boy network I felt that a public-school education just marked me out as a Merchant Wanker.

I didn't mind when work colleagues teased me about my plummy accent, as long as they weren't spitting with hatred as they did so, but it did make me self-conscious, and in my twenties I would occasionally experiment with life as a Mockney. If I got into a black cab and the driver was a chatty South Londoner who wanted to talk about football, I did my best to join in, not by pretending I knew about football, but by adopting a generic geezerish South London drawl that later became the voice I used for impersonating David Bowie. Meanwhile the cab drivers were probably thinking, 'Why's that posh geezer doing that weird voice?' Either that or 'Oh my God! I've got David Bowie in my cab!'

My eagerness to lose my accent would have distressed Dad, who throughout his children's lives never missed an opportunity to correct what he considered sloppy pronunciation or grammar. If any of us said a word like 'now' without a sufficiently full and fruity vowel sound, he launched into his Henry Higgins routine: 'Neh-ow? *Neh-ow? It's *Nah-ow. Hah-ow, Nah-ow, Brah-own Cah-ow.*'

*   *   *

When he got ill and moved in with us, I imagined sitting up late into the night with Dad, doing shots of whisky and morphine and recording him as I asked all the BIG QUESTIONS I'd never felt able to ask before: who his parents were, what the war was like, why things hadn't worked out with Mum and why he'd thought it so important to send his children away to private school and have them speak with the 'right' accent.

The recordings would be poignant, personal and painful

(ideally there would be some crying). I would turn them into an award-winning podcast and just before he died Dad would give me a hug and tell me how brave I was and that he was proud of me. But he hated all that sort of shit, so although we did have a few heavy conversations, they were not quite what I'd had in mind. As it turned out, most of our exchanges tended to focus on noodle preparation, men's nappies and whether or not he had taken his pills.

For the first year or two after his death, thinking about Dad was always painful. My unanswered BIG QUESTIONS were supplanted by recollections of distressing moments from his last months that sometimes I was only able to dislodge by humming or singing to myself. (PRO-TIP: This works for all kinds of thoughts you would rather not deal with.) Over time the older, happier memories resurfaced and with them my curiosity about Dad and how he had become the posh old bloke I always thought of him as.

His self-published memoir *The Road to Fleet Street*, which he completed shortly before his death, covered his school years, his service in the Royal Artillery during the Second World War, his time studying modern history at Oxford after the war, some posh old bloke name-dropping (including Reginald Bosanquet, Robert Graves and Harry Oppenheimer) and his glory days as columnist and Travel Editor at the *Sunday Telegraph*. However, there was nothing beyond that point, and nothing about who his parents were or the experience of starting his own family, i.e. all the stuff I was most interested in. Perhaps he felt that writing about his family was indiscreet somehow, but I suspect he simply considered it irrelevant and uninteresting. Then I remembered *The Proving Ground*.

One of several self-published projects, *The Proving Ground* was a novel that Dad had started writing in the late 1980s when he was deep in debt and had just been laid off by the *Telegraph*. He finished it around 2001, a year or two after he and Mum finally separated. It's the story of a travel journalist on a Sunday newspaper whose money problems are solved when he discovers a cache of gold during a trip to Alaska. *The Proving Ground* gave Dad an opportunity to cast himself as a heroic figure at a time in his life when he felt embattled, misunderstood and perhaps not completely certain that the sacrifices he had made for his family had been worth it.

Via his protagonist, David Barclay, Dad set out his values and detailed his fantasies with a directness he would normally have avoided. The characters along with certain events from his own life were so thinly fictionalised that when he showed it to me, my brother and sister, we agreed among ourselves that it made for a strange read.

The Proving Ground begins with David Barclay working at the *Sunday Messenger* (clearly meant to be the *Sunday Telegraph*). He has three children – Luke (clearly me), William (clearly my brother, Dave) and Sophie (clearly my sister, Clare) – who are receiving an expensive private education that is beyond their father's means.

Barclay is married to Margaret (clearly my mum, Valerie), a shrill woman who doesn't understand him and doesn't respect the passionately held principles that have led to his financial woes. I think Pa chose the name 'Margaret' for Mum's character because of Princess Margaret, who he found irritating.

The novel begins with Dad – I mean David Barclay – attending a crisis meeting at his bank, 'Mallards' (clearly meant to be Coutts & Co. where Dad held an account for a while). The manager at Mallards is a rude young man who tells Dad – I mean David Barclay – that sending his children to private school is financially reckless. There follow several pages of justification from Dad – I mean David Barclay – about the benefits of a boarding-school education:

A close relation had asked me recently if I was quite sure that I was right to beggar myself, not to mention Margaret, for what many people might see as a social prejudice. A social prejudice? ... I never saw William in the orchestra at Haileybury without intense satisfaction that he was in the brass section there in Old Hall, not an overcrowded London flat, watching television.

Beggaring ourselves? My parents had striven only for their children; was I to betray mine by any inferior devotion? Sure we were right? I never picnicked on the lawns at Sophie's prep school in Sussex on 'Open' or Sports Day without knowing beyond a doubt that for a child to have the benefits of that particular school's environment for a start in life was worth whatever it might cost.

A few pages on, still restating the case he wished he'd made at the meeting with the rude bank manager, Dad – I mean David Barclay – continues to explain why he considers a private education so important:

To see William in Haileybury's elegant, spacious ambience always gave me the deepest pleasure. Everything about the place, from the well-tended lawn to the 1,300 names on the War Memorial panels in the cloisters, induced an awareness of a history richly imbued with all that seemed to me best in Britishness and the nation's imperial past, and all that seemed most admirable in English public school education and upbringing. That William now belonged here, sharing in so great an inheritance, gave me a satisfaction I hardly dared acknowledge for fear of tempting fate.

There are still many people who feel the same way that my dad did about public schools, though in an age in which social inequality is generally considered to be something worth struggling against and working-class credentials, even fake ones, are proudly flashed at every opportunity, the pro-public-schoolers are sometimes less keen to advertise their enthusiasm.

* * *

I'd always assumed that Dad's fondness for the British establishment and his apparent aversion to all things working class was evidence that he himself was an old-school toff, something we played for laughs in his BaaadDad segments on *The Adam and Joe Show*. Then a couple of years after his death I made a long-overdue trip to visit my aunt in Wales.

Dad had five older brothers and a younger sister, Aunty Jessica. When I was at boarding school Jessica would sometimes come and take me out on weekends and feed me cake and biscuits until I threw up. I loved Aunty Jessica. Then we didn't see her for a long time and Aunty Jessica became another member of our extended family that we seldom heard about, though she and Dad remained in occasional contact. I emailed her to ask if I could visit and ask about their upbringing, and she sent me a warm reply saying that I'd be welcome, but I'd better be quick because she was 91.

The following week I drove from Norfolk to Wales.

It was good to see Aunty Jessica again. After some cake, biscuits, hardly any vomiting and a bit of catching up ('Now, can you tell me what exactly a podcast is?'), Jessica told me about the grandparents I'd never met and the background that had primed Dad for a life dedicated to embracing the ruling classes.

It turned out that my grandfather, Gordon Buxton (who died long before I was born), had been a servant boy, a butler and a chauffeur before becoming an estate overseer for a wealthy family in the village of Cowfold, Sussex. He was known as 'Buckin' or 'Bucky'. In return for Bucky's service his wife and family got a house to live in, for which they were grateful. This was back in *Downton Abbey* days when, as Jessica told it, the lower classes were well looked after by their employers and 'knew their place', and everything was simpler.

When the First World War broke out my grandfather's boss, a Lieutenant Colonel, asked Bucky if he would travel with him to France to be his war bitch (not Jessica's phrase). Bucky was eager to oblige, despite having to leave behind his wife and three children (not including my dad, who was born after WWI). When the Lieutenant Colonel was killed on the first day of fighting at the Battle of Arras on 9 April 1917, Bucky carried his body off the battlefield and, upon returning to Sussex, continued to serve his widow and children. In *Downton Abbey* terms, it seems Bucky was more of a Bates than a Carson.

The continued patronage of the Lieutenant Colonel's regiment and family meant that my father was able to get on his social mobility scooter and attend the local grammar school before starting at the Imperial Service College in Windsor, a notoriously brutal and disciplinarian boarding school dedicated to preparing boys for military life. Teachers and senior boys at the ISC would regularly beat the younger ones with a cane until they bled for infractions like attending chapel with dirty shoes, failure to wear your school hat while visiting town or walking around with the collar of your overcoat turned up, unless you were a prefect or had been awarded a sports prize.

In addition to the jolly corporal punishment larks, my father was regularly taunted for not speaking with a sufficiently posh accent (something he absolutely nailed in later life). He became so keen not to stand out that whenever it was time for his parents to pick him up, my father insisted they meet him outside the school and down the road a short way. Dad worried that, next to the Daimlers, the Bentleys and the Rolls-Royces of the other parents, the Buckymobile would look too shit and he would get more grief from the toffs. Grandfather Bucky would tell my dad, 'The people who care don't matter because the people who matter don't care.'

Years later, when it was my turn to be worried about being judged for not having the latest cool thing, my dad repeated Bucky's advice, but I was confused. 'You mean the people who care about me don't matter?'

'No, the people who care what car your parents drive or what clothes you wear, they don't matter.'

'Oh. Well, maybe you should say, "The people who mind don't matter and the people who matter don't mind"?' Dad sighed.

His son, not for the last time, was being too literal, but I remembered the saying. It's a good one I think, but not always easy to take comfort from.

RAMBLE

Dad was impressed by successful people, even if they had become successful doing something he didn't approve of. After returning from a business trip in the late Seventies he asked us excitedly, 'Have you heard of some musicians called Who? I sat next to the singer on the plane!' We eventually established he was talking about Roger Daltrey. 'He was a thoroughly decent fellow. We talked about the joys of salmon fishing,' said Dad.

Other celebrity encounters that left Dad uncharacteristically exuberant included Larry Hagman (aka J.R. of TV soap *Dallas*), the rapper Coolio, who drove Dad round Los Angeles in his Humvee for *The Adam and Joe Show*, and pop's nicest guys, Travis, who Dad met at my wedding in 2001. Going through his belongings after he died, I found Dad's address book and saw that he'd collected the phone numbers of Dougie and Fran from the band. They were both under 'T' and next to their names Dad had written *'Travis – Pop Stars'*. Well, you never know when you might need a pop star.

In 1998, when Joe and I were flying to LA with Dad to do some filming, he used his old travel-editor contacts to wangle a seat in first class, where he found himself sat beside The Pretenders' singer Chrissie Hynde. Sadly, the salmon-fishing banter that had bonded him and Roger Daltrey all those years before failed to beguile Chrissie and she asked to be moved to another seat.

The Imperial Service College, the public school Dad attended, later merged with and changed its name to Haileybury. It's where David Barclay – I mean Dad – sent my brother Dave to school, and I think he loved the symmetry of having his son 'belong' to an institution at which he'd worked so hard to be accepted. In 1991 the real-life crisis meeting with his unsympathetic young bank manager resulted in Dad having to take Dave out of Haileybury while he was studying for his A levels. Pa considered it a failure for which he never forgave himself.

But Dave's fine. And anyway, who really belongs anywhere? I think that whole idea of 'belonging' and 'not belonging' is too often used to keep people 'in their place'. But I suppose that's easy for me to say, having enjoyed untold rewards from attending the kinds of schools I did and meeting the people I met there. Like it or not, that's thanks to Dad and his crazed determination to climb and to 'belong'.

The thing that still seems odd to me about Dad's idea of what constituted a desirable existence is that it was so closely correlated to social class. Though he detested the latter-day Etonian Tories and Bullingdon yobs, he remained throughout his life a conservative and a snob who found it hard to find value in what a person had to say if it was said with the wrong accent – the kind of accent that as a boy at the Imperial Service College he'd felt obliged to shed.

I never properly suggested any of this to him when he was alive, and it feels both gutless and redundant to say it now he's dead and I can't get the 10p in the slot, but I wonder if he would accept the charges.

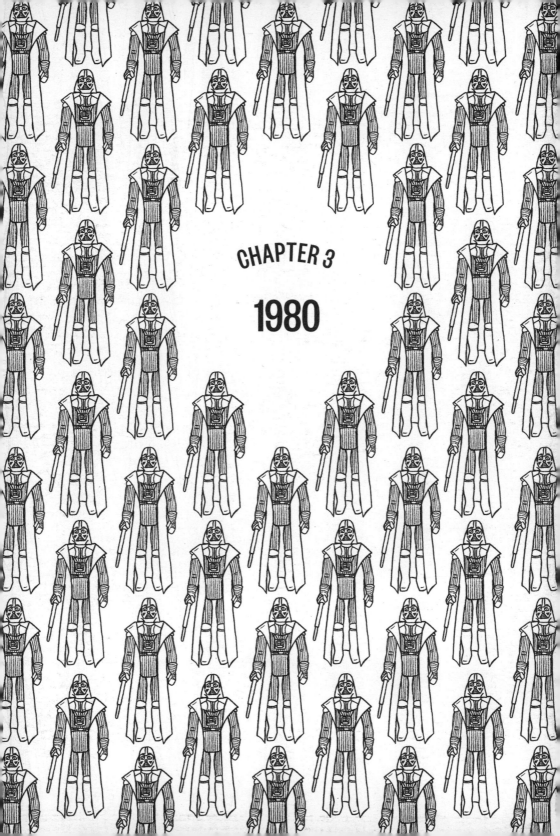

CHAPTER 3

1980

My adolescence fell squarely in the 1980s and, for better or worse, the culture I consumed in that decade has played a significant part in defining my life ever since.

I look back at some of those Eighties influences with fondness and admiration for my good taste, but others evoke the sadness my dad felt about what I chose to fill my days with. To him it seemed as though I was living on a diet of worthless junk that would clog my intellectual arteries and lead to possible art failure. Now, in doubt-filled middle age, bringing up my own children as growing sections of society revise their attitudes to much of the culture and the values I grew up with, I often find myself thinking Dad might have had a point.

Where are the books? The trips to galleries or museums? The theatre? Where is the engagement with politics and social issues? The work by people other than men from the US or the UK? And when something genuinely worthwhile was put in front of me, even if eventually I ended up appreciating it, my initial response was usually to scrunch up my face in disgust, like a baby tasting caviar.

A decade of expensive private education, and all I had to show for it was a love of left-field pop music, an intimate familiarity with TV and mainstream cinema and the ability to quote a few Eddie Murphy routines (I use the word 'quote' loosely; basically I would fill any conversational lull by saying,

'I got an ice cream and you ain't got one', 'Goonie-goo-goo, with a G.I. Joe up his ass' or 'SERIOOOOO!'

Join me, then, as I revisit a few of the adolescent moments, along with their audio-visual accompaniment, that helped make me the towering genius I am today.

Pits, Pendulums and Dirigibles

The year 1980 began with me aged ten and starting my second year at the co-ed boarding school in Sussex that Dad always referred to as 'The Reformatory'. I no longer cried when they dropped me off there but would still rather have been at home, eating Penguin bars and McDonald's quarter-pounders and chips in front of *The Dukes of Hazzard*, *Metal Mickey* and *Fantasy Island*. And *CHiPs*. The cultural treats on offer at school may have been more nutritious, but they were harder to digest.

Most nights, when everyone was in bed, stories would play out over the PA system. Sometimes it was something fun like *James and the Giant Peach*, *The Colditz Story*, *The Hobbit* or some Greek myths, but on other nights we'd be treated to a profoundly upsetting helping of horror from M.R. James or, worse, Edgar Allen Poe. It was a kind of audiobook Russian roulette and you never knew if the chamber was loaded until the PA crackled to life and the story began.

I lay in my bunk, wide-eyed with dread in case the words 'I was sick – sick unto death with that long agony' came through the tannoy, because that meant it was 'The Pit and the Pendulum' time, and the next half-hour of homesick gloom was further darkened by Edgar Allen Poe's story of physical and psychological torture during the Spanish Inquisition. 'The Black Cat' and 'The Tell-Tale Heart' would follow, by the end of which one or two children in every dormitory would be sobbing softly, and in the junior dormitories, wailing loudly. And that was just the bedtime stories.

One afternoon every weekend a film was projected onto the wall of the gymnasium. In the days before 24-hour mobile entertainment was considered a basic human right, these film showings were a big deal and I could be found sitting cross-legged on the wooden floor of the gym, regardless of what was playing. It was a varied programme that during my time included *The Four Feathers, Kes, Capricorn One, Bugsy Malone, The Thief of Bagdad, Star Trek: The Motion Picture, Duel, One of Our Dinosaurs Is Missing, Ring of Bright Water, Jaws, Hooper, Smokey and the Bandit* and *Smokey and the Bandit Ride Again* (as the Eighties dawned, Burt Reynolds was still considered one of cinema's most alluring cishet fuckboys).

Along with lashings of Burt, they also served up some of the biggest and stupidest disaster films of the Seventies, and my first sense of how much could go wrong in the world came via school gym performances of *The Towering Inferno, The Poseidon Adventure, Earthquake, Meteor* and the *Airport* series. But nothing took a giant shit on my psyche quite like *The Hindenburg* and *The Cassandra Crossing*.

The Hindenburg was basically a 'Whogonnadunnit' that took place on a luxurious passenger airship in 1937. George C. Scott played a German colonel who has been warned of a plot to blow up the dirigible. Unaware that the film was loosely inspired by historical events, I expected George to foil the plot in the nick of time and prevent the airship from exploding. SPOILER ALERT: he doesn't.

The final section of the film switched from colour to black and white, intercutting between newsreel footage of the actual *Hindenburg*'s fiery skeleton sinking to the airfield, with shots of various characters staggering from the wreckage, some horribly burned. Presumably the lack of colour was supposed to take the edge off the horror, but not for ten-year-old Buckles.

I sat, heart beating fast, as Herbert Morrison's famous commentary tearfully mourned 'The humanity!'

RAMBLE

For several years in my twenties I developed a fear of flying, and every time I boarded a plane, images of the crumpled *Hindenburg* would pop into my head along with the phrase 'twisted mass of girders'. (If you're reading this on a plane, sorry, but honestly, you're going to be fine. However, in the unlikely event that something does happen, just ask someone to send in the charred remains of your boarding pass and I'll personally issue a full refund. For the book that is, not the flight.)

In *The Cassandra Crossing*, a terrorist carrying a deadly plague virus created by the Americans for germ warfare boards a train travelling across Europe, where he infects a load of passengers before the authorities reroute the train across a rickety bridge. Richard Harris, Sophia Loren and O.J. Simpson do their best to avert disaster. SPOILER ALERT: they don't.

I can trace a number of my biggest fears back to that Sunday-afternoon screening of *The Cassandra Crossing* and to this day I do my best to avoid deadly viruses, quarantines enforced by armed men in scary hazmat suits, trains that plunge off rickety bridges into ravines and O.J. Simpson.

As I was an easily confused ten-year-old without parents on hand to clarify perplexing moments in films like this, it was left to other equally clueless ten-year-olds to concoct explanations. For example, my friends and I decided that when, in one scene, the plague-carrying terrorist sneezed on a bowl of rice, he was in fact vomiting maggots, thereby adding three more items to my list of Worsties: vomiting, maggots and vomiting maggots.

Obligatory *Star Wars* Bit

By the time *The Empire Strikes Back* was released in May 1980, everything *Star Wars*-related made me vibrate with visceral joy.

Two years earlier, when we were living in Wales, Mum had driven me and my sister all the way to the West End of London to see the first *Star Wars* film (if you're thinking, 'Well actually, Buckles, it was *Episode IV – A New Hope*,' then please close this book/switch off this audiobook, get dressed and go out into nature). For the first half of *Star Wars* I was overwhelmed and a bit frightened (especially by 'Dark Vader'), but when Princess Leia referred to Chewbacca as a 'walking carpet' everyone in the cinema laughed, including Mum, and I knew I was having the best time of my life.

There was no merchandise in the foyer other than the film soundtrack, which Mum bought on cassette to listen to on the way back to Wales. I thought the 'soundtrack' would be all the audio from the film, including the talking and sound effects, and when it became clear it meant just the boring classical music I was gutted. It was the characters I loved, the colourful aliens, the funny robots, the cool Americans; it was them I wished I could take back with me to my room in Wales, even if only in audio form.

Then one day later that year I was in WH Smith's with Mum and I saw a rack of *Star Wars* action figures. After some energetic and tearful bargaining, I went home with a little Luke and a tiny R2D2 (those are not euphemisms). From then on I negotiated constantly for action figures, accumulating

1982 scratchboard art by the 12-year-old, *Star Wars*-obsessed Buckles. I knew that attempting to draw the humans would go badly, so concentrated instead on the robots, spaceships and a floating baddie helmet.

goodies first and baddies later. It was a shock to discover that 'Dark Vader' was actually called 'Darth'. I didn't think that was a good space name. He may as well have been called Jatthew, or Vominic. Luckily he had an extendable red plastic lightsaber, though it wasn't long before I was compelled to bite off the tapered tip.

Over the next three years I wangled action figures of every significant character from the first three *Star Wars* films, as well as a Landspeeder, X-wing Fighter, TIE Fighter, Droid Factory, Creature Cantina and, on a trip to California when my Aunty Leslie took us to Toys "R" Us and said, incredibly, 'You can get what you like,' I came back with a *Millennium Falcon*. When Dad saw the giant box he made a face that I now understand meant 'How the fuck am I expected to get that back to the UK, you greedy little shit bag?' He managed it, though, and unpacking the *Falcon* on my parents' bed back in Earl's Court was no less memorable and moving than the birth of at least two of my children.

As for *The Empire Strikes Back*, it started out as the greatest film of all time and ended as the most depressing. SPOILER ALERT: Vominic Vader turns out to be Luke's dad, which we find out after he's cut off his son's hand and made him do some very ugly crying. Meanwhile Han, easily the best guy in the whole thing, has been turned into a giant doorstop. For some people this was a more dramatically complex and satisfying ending for a *Star Wars* film than the cheesy medal ceremony that concluded the first one, but ten-year-old Buckles was not one of those people. If I'd wanted upsetting dramatic complexity, I could have just watched my mum waxing her legs in the nude.

Disney Bangers

Let me paint you a picture of the Britain I grew up in during the 1970s, using all the same bits of archive they use in TV documentaries. There was social and economic upheaval, rubbish piling up on the streets, the dead going unburied, frequent power cuts, racial unrest, football violence, punk music and, worst of all, disrespectful playground poetry. Here is one sickening example:

> *In 1976*
> *The Queen pulled down her knicks*
> *She licked her bum*
> *And said 'yum yum'*
> *In 1976*

RAMBLE

Although the seven-year-old me admired that poem, and would often recite it, I knew that it lacked plausibility. Was Her Majesty really so flexible that she could lick her own bum? And was QEII so obsessed with rhyming words that she only felt able to pull down her knicks in 1976? Didn't the underwear come down in 1972, when she must have wanted a poo? None of it adds up.

Whatever grimness was going on in the outside world during the Seventies, my sister, my brother and I knew nothing about it. Mum and Dad subscribed to the Bubble-of-Innocence school of parenting, part of which relied on keeping us gratefully anaesthetised on a Disney drip.

We loved all things Disney: the Land, which we visited several times on trips to America; the TV show (*The Wonderful World of Disney*); the films and the songs, which we had on four cassettes filled with music performed by fun animals and boring princesses. As the Eighties arrived and my sister began attending the same boarding school, those cassettes were still a crucial part of keeping us pacified on the depressing Sunday-night car journeys back to The Reformatory.

Disney songs reminded me of carefree times when my parents loved me so much they didn't send me away to expensive prison, but as for the music itself, much of it (to use one of my mother's favourite expressions) made me want to open a vein.

Our beige Ford Cortina only had a radio, so the Disney tapes would be played on Dad's portable tape recorder, which sat on the lap of whichever parent (usually Mum) was in the passenger seat. For that reason, it wasn't an option to fast-forward through the most syrupy, princessy songs. I was only able to endure sludge like 'Someday My Prince Will Come' from *Snow White*, 'A Dream Is a Wish Your Heart Makes' from *Cinderella* and 'Rumbly in My Tumbly' from *Winnie the Pooh* because I knew that eventually we'd get to a Disney Banger.

When songs like 'Everybody Wants to Be a Cat', 'Pink Elephants on Parade', 'I Wan'na Be Like You' or 'The Bare Necessities' were about to start, my sister and I would lean forward, unfettered by boring seat belts (which only squares wore in those days), and we'd dig those Disney grooves. I especially liked 'The Wonderful Thing About Tiggers' and the hipster beat combo version of Cruella De Ville (different in arrangement and spelling to the version in the *101 Dalmatians* film and not, as I search, findable on the Internet).

The best thing about 'Tiggers' and 'De Ville' was that even Dad liked them and occasionally sang along. 'Such good lyrics,' he would say of 'Cruella de Ville'. 'Mind you,' he would continue, 'I love anything motivated by the patriarchy's fear of powerful women.' Alright, those may not have been his exact words, but I think that was the gist.

BOWIE ANNUAL

Exactly 22 years after I first heard his music in an art class, David Bowie walked towards me at Maida Vale studios in West London. It was September 2002 and he'd just performed a concert for BBC Radio, to which Joe and I had been invited by the show's host, Jonathan Ross. Jonathan knew we were both big fans, albeit fans whose enthusiasm had been tested by Bowie's musical output for well over a decade. We had learned that when critics greeted each new release as 'Bowie's best since *Scary Monsters*', what they actually meant was, 'Well, this one's not total bollocks.'

And yet, stood in the small audience at Maida Vale watching the 55-year-old Bowie with his boyish floppy hairdo and smart-casual clothes emphasising a face that was at last showing its age, I found myself getting tearful a couple of times, overwhelmed by being just a few metres from someone who had meant so much to me over the years, particularly in the Eighties when I was discovering him and his work for the first time.

Then, after the show, there he was, walking towards a little group of us standing in a backstage corridor with Jonathan Ross. Bowie spotted Ricky Gervais and Stephen Merchant, who had also been invited along. It was only a year since the first series of *The Office* had aired, but it had quickly become a mainstream success and Ricky and Stephen were well on the way to becoming full-blown celebrities. I'd met Ricky a couple of times at Jonathan's house and I knew he was also a huge Bowie fan, so it was cool to see him meet his hero for the first time and have Bowie tell him that he thought *The Office* was great, but I left Maida Vale deflated.

As well as being an artist whose work I admired, David Bowie was someone I'd always thought of as a person who had a similar outlook on life to me, someone who found the same kinds of things interesting, someone whose taste in music I could trust and whose recommendations were worth exploring. In other words, I'd always thought of him as my friend, but then I had to stand by and watch as he declared his affection, not for me but another comedian. OK, so Ricky was at least as much of a fan as I was, and even back then he'd made a more lasting contribution to the world of comedy, but that didn't make it any less galling.

'Serves me right for taking the piss out of Zavid for so long,' I thought.

After the first flush of unequivocal adoration, Bowie had become something of a comedy character for me, Joe and our friends. We enjoyed dissecting his less well-judged career moments, pronouncements and pontifications, often while doing an impression that relied on the gentle buzzing sound Bowie produced when he spoke words with an 's' in them; for example, 'zuperlatative' – a pleasing Bowie variant of 'superlative' we'd heard him use in an interview. Over time this impression evolved into a single noise that was our shorthand for Bowie: 'wuzza'. Instead of discussing the serious issues of the day, we whiled away many hours with symposiums of 'wuzza, wuzza, wuzza's. I don't suppose any of that would have endeared us to Zavid, but I've always taken the piss out of people I love, and I really love David Bowie.

'We're going to have a free drawing class today,' said our art teacher, walking over to the record player in the corner and setting the arm down. 'Here's some music to inspire you. It just came out last week.' It was September 1980.

Sun shone through the big glass panels that ran down one side of the art room as the space filled with the sound of clicks, hisses, a rattle, someone counting in, then squalling electric guitar, a woman declaiming in a foreign language and a man who sounded nutty. I exchanged WTF? glances with other mystified ten-year-olds. This music was weird, but the second song was more conventional, and by the time they were chanting '*Up the hill backwards, / It'll be all right, ooooh*', I was sufficiently intrigued to ask the teacher who we were listening to.

I liked the name 'Bowie'. It sounded strong, supple and elegant with the potential to unleash arrows. It was, well, bow-y.

William Mullins (aka Muggins or Bill Muggs) came back to school the following term with his brother's copy of the Bowie compilation *ChangesOneBowie* and we listened to it on the common-room record player. Even as I was listening to 'Space Oddity' for the first time I was looking forward to hearing it again.

The cover of *ChangesOneBowie* is a black-and-white photograph of DB taken in 1976 by Tom Kelley, who took the famous nude calendar shots of Marilyn Monroe. It captures Bowie at his most conventionally handsome, yet disarmingly fey. His hair is swept back, his hand is up to his mouth as if he's considering a work of art, and there's a distant look in his eyes that says, 'I'm thinking of complicated things in a more original and zensitive way than an ordinary person would.' I stared at the cover of *ChangesOneBowie* and thought, 'Mmm. Yes, please.'

A few weeks later Bill Muggs turned up with *Hunky Dory* and, though I was a bit confused by Bowie suddenly looking like somebody's hippy mum on the cover, as soon as 'Life on Mars' came on with lyrics about cavemen and Mickey Mouse combining the esoteric and the accessible, I recognised it as the kind of powerfully dramatic, emotional and mysterious music I'd often heard playing in my head, playing in my heart even, but never out loud. Or maybe I'd just heard it on the radio and forgot.

Either way, I realised I was interested in David Bowie.

Up to that point all the strangers I'd been interested in were fictional – the Bionic Man, the Bionic Woman, the Invisible Man and the Man from Atlantis – not really superheroes, but enhanced humans that I thought I'd get on well with. Bowie was the first real person to join that list, and for the next few years we got on very well indeed.

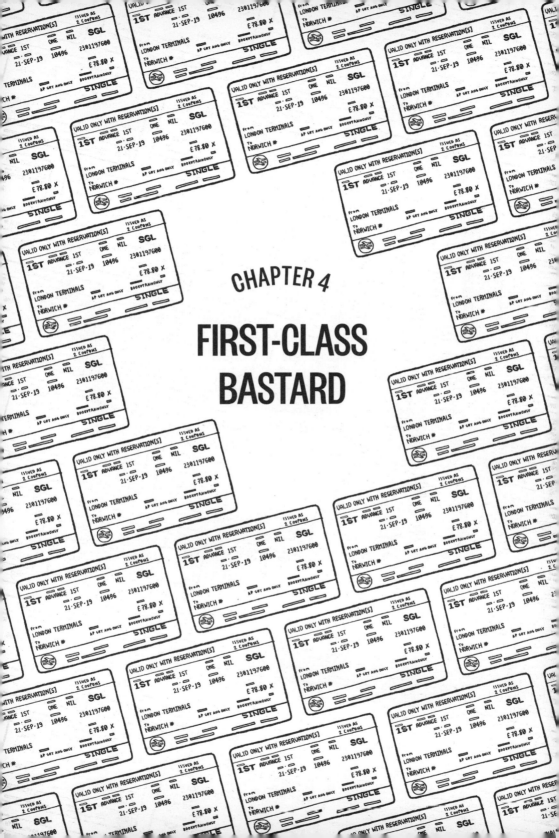

CHAPTER 4

FIRST-CLASS BASTARD

Before I moved out of London, I seldom travelled by train. On the rare occasions I did, it never occurred to me to buy a first-class ticket. I was happy to sit in my standard-class seat, stare out of the window and enjoy the loud telephone conversations of twats.

In 2008 I moved out to Norfolk with my family and life as a semi-frequent train commuter began. I was doing a weekly radio show on BBC 6 Music with Joe at the time, so every Friday I'd cycle to Norwich, get on the train to Liverpool Street, stay at my in-laws' place in West London on Friday night, cycle to the 6 Music studio in Great Portland Street on Saturday morning, talk bollocks with Joe from 10 a.m. till 1 p.m., then get the train from Liverpool Street back to Norwich. ('That was an interesting routine you just outlined there, Buckles, thanks!' You're welcome.)

The more I took the train, the more I found myself wanting to do some important laptop work as I travelled: sorting and labelling 10,000 digital photographs of my children, reading YouTube comments for OK Go videos, editing footage of myself dressed as Gwen Stefani pointing at animated turds and saying, 'Oooh, this my shit, this my shit' – that kind of thing.

Sometimes I was able to get a four-person table seat to myself (an optimal scenario for my preferred workflow), but even then I was without plug sockets or Wi-Fi and had to contend with the sound of children watching wisecracking animated films without headphones, groups of boisterous men enjoying lager-powered sports bants and of course the loud telephone conversations of twats.

For a few months I experimented with the Quiet Carriage (or QC). This is a single train carriage in which prominently displayed signs make it clear that it's an environment reserved for those who are *not* uplifted by percussion leakage from shitty headphones and do not enjoy listening to one side of someone else's entirely unnecessary phone conversation. In my mind the QC was first class for standard-class travellers. Affordable paradise.

At busier times, however, affordable paradise went wrong, and the QC ended up being the most stressful of all the carriages. Any remaining seats were quickly snaffled by people who considered refraining from behaviour that might disturb others as risibly effete. I'm talking about Inconsiderate Shitbags (or IS), a community that sees no race, gender or class, such is their commitment to inclusivity and representation. Members of IS are just as likely to be self-important business berks and red-trousered toffs as they are truculent tinkers or boozed-up bootblacks.

For the IS, the quaint codes of the QC are there to be ignored at will. Sit in the Quiet Carriage during peak hours and you won't have to wait long before some utter fucker thinks of some excuse for a phone call or just launches into a chat with a pal (both *entirely* antithetical to the spirit of the QC). When it becomes clear that there's an IS member in the QC, heads begin to pop up, like angry meerkats, focusing all their disapproval on the culprit.

One evening, when the peace of a packed but luxuriously

silent Quiet Carriage was torpedoed by a young man in a suit taking a phone call, I went full angry meerkat. Mine was one of six other heads that periscoped up and began scanning the carriage, first locating the offending IS operative, then looking around at the other meerkats as if to say, 'Can we believe this guy and his phone call? This is the ONLY carriage in the whole train where you're asked to be quiet and this guy isn't giving a single hoot.'

I waited for someone to say something, but of course no one did. At last the man finished his call, and once again the carriage was beautifully quiet. My shoulders began to relax and my breathing was starting to return to normal when the man started jabbing at his phone again before bringing it back up to his unbelievable fucking ear. I couldn't take it. Someone had to speak for the meerkats.

Aiming for a tone that was relaxed, geezerish and non-crazy, I said, 'Hey! Mate! It's the Quiet Carriage, mate!' The man continued to chat without even registering me and the other meerkats cringed. Feeling I had committed myself, I tried again, but this time when I called 'Mate! Quiet Carriage!' I pointed at one of the large 'Quiet Carriage' stickers on the windows, to demonstrate that my position was backed up by stickers.

Sometimes Quiet Carriage stickers seem only to prohibit the use of mobiles, but these stickers also included symbols prohibiting noisy headphones and talking people, making it as clear as possible that 'quiet' didn't mean whatever kind of 'quiet' happened to suit you at that moment; it meant actual silence, like in a library or an exam room or a nice relaxing crypt.

This time, the man registered me. He glanced at the sticker, nodded and continued his conversation. I sank into my seat. I wasn't prepared to make a scene.

You've got to lighten up, Buckles, I told myself. There's more important stuff out there to go angry meerkat on.

But then another voice – one that sounded a lot like my dad – chimed in: 'Moments like these aren't merely some bourgeois pursuit of order. For those who aspire to a society in which we harmoniously coexist, the Quiet Carriage is a proving ground, and if you're too cowardly to challenge phone-call man then I hope you like chaos, because that's what you're going to get.'

RAMBLE

The thing is, I don't mind a bit of chaos, but Dad really hated the stuff. On *The Adam and Joe Show* in the late Nineties we asked him to review the techno track 'Higher State of Consciousness' by American DJ Josh Wink, and upon hearing its electronic shrieks and squeals, my dad seemed genuinely worried, likening the noises to dark wheeling systems in a universe coming apart. 'It's chaos!' he kept saying. 'Chaos.' But if you've liberated concentration camps and never tried ecstasy, techno is probably always going to be a tough sell.

Whatever my thoughts on chaos in the QC, I was too cowardly for a confrontation, so there was only one thing for it.

Whenever I took the train on weekends the conductor would regularly announce that passengers could upgrade from standard to first class for £7.50. I never took any notice of these announcements until one weekend when there was a big football match on in Norwich, and the train from London was rammed. Like many others I found myself without a seat, standing in the corridor outside the toilet, trying to digest a stomach full of impotent rage. The ticket collector pushed his way through, mumbling apology-style bollocks about the lack of seats, and when he came to me, I said it: 'Could I have an upgrade, please?'

A minute later the doors to first class slid open and I stumbled out of the corridor scrum into paradise. It was busy, but there were free seats, and it was cool and quiet, with a more relaxing colour scheme. I found a single seat by the window with my own power socket below the table. I opened my laptop and my little Wi-Fi radar locked in satisfyingly (that will be a useful line if I ever write robot porn).

The Wi-Fi was free.

My first-class upgrade also entitled me to free water, free tea or coffee, free crisps and free biscuits in the buffet car. I loaded up. The crunchy yet moist apple-flavoured biscuits were extraordinary and I returned for more, flashing my first-class upgrade like a detective flashing his badge at a DELI-CIOUS crime scene.

It was the greatest journey of my life.

The Rubicon had been crossed. As long as I could afford it, I would never return to standard class.

*   *   *

Nowadays I travel via Cambridge to King's Cross, which is closer to where I tend to record podcasts and do gigs for members of the liberal elite. The first-class situation on that route is not great, perhaps due to the relatively short journey times. The first-class compartment from Norwich to Cambridge currently sits just seven people and there are no free drinks – not even water – no snacks and certainly no fucking apple biscuits. But it's seldom busy and it's always quiet. Well, not quite always …

For the last year or so the train from King's Cross to Cambridge has run late more than half the time, which means I end up missing the connection to Norwich and have to wait around in Cambridge station for another hour. I like to use this time to have a run-in with a member of staff at WH Smith's before taking the next available, much busier train. This happened a few weeks ago and by the time I finally boarded the Norwich train I was desperate to sink into my favourite first-class seat (a single one at the back by the driver's door). To my dismay I found it was already occupied by a young person with a couple of non-first-class-looking plastic shopping bags. They were engaged in a loud mobile phone call and everyone else in the unusually busy carriage was obliged to listen.

'Yeah, I'm on the train. I'm in first class. I'm probably about to get moved cos I haven't got a first-class ticket. Well, they never really check. I did it the other day and I was just sat in first class all the way and they never checked! Yeah. I know. No, we're waiting for the train to leave. My battery's low. I don't have my charger. No, she said that was her charger. I found that one on the floor, but it wasn't my charger. I haven't got a charger now ...' This was followed by several more minutes of urgent charger chat, then finally: 'All right, bye, then.'

Ah, luxurious first-class peace. But no, moments later: 'Hi, yeah, it's me. No, I'm on the train, just waiting for it to go. No, my battery's low. I know, I don't have my charger. No, she said that was her charger. There was a charger on the floor, but it wasn't my charger. No, she said that was her charger. I haven't got a charger now ...' etc., etc., etc.

'This cannot stand,' I thought. I need to speak for the meerkats. Chaos cannot reign. This is not a class thing. This is not a privilege thing. This is not even a 'you're in my favourite seat' thing. This is a quiet thing. A consideration thing. I'm on the proving ground, and it's time to step up.

When the second call finally ended I found myself standing up and approaching the young person. Trying hard to eliminate any trace of irritation from my voice I said: 'Excuse me, just to say, I've got no problem with you being in first class with a standard-class ticket, seriously, go for your life, but part of the reason we're in first class is that we just want some quiet so we can work. So please – don't make any more phone calls.'

'Oh yeah, I wasn't going to make any more calls,' replied the young person airily.

'Oh, thanks very much,' I said and returned my seat. It was all very civil and straightforward. 'What a great result,' I thought.

I luxuriated in the gratitude and admiration I knew my fellow first-class meerkats must be feeling. 'Finally!' I imagined them thinking. 'Someone who isn't trying to humiliate another person on the basis of status but who has the guts to strike a blow for order and harmonious coexistence.' Then, before we'd even pulled out of the station, the young person got up and left the first-class carriage.

The doors slid shut and my triumphal bubble popped. I had a strong urge to call the young person back. 'Hey! Young Person, who I definitely would have challenged even if you'd been a giant angry-looking football supporter, I wasn't trying to get rid of you! I only wanted you to keep the noise down! Hey, look, if you want to sit in first class, that's cool with me! I like sticking it to The Man sometimes, too! Bloody Man! You should be aware, there is an on-the-spot fine for sitting in first class with a standard-class ticket on this route, but hey, if it comes to that, I'll pay! I'm one of the good guys! Young Person! Come back ...' but it was too late.

An oppressive silence engulfed our shabby cubicle of privilege. Order had been restored. First-class ticket holders only.

Another phone rang. The first-class ticket holder sat across the aisle from me scrambled to answer it, shooting me a nervous glance as they did so. They mumbled in hushed tones for a few seconds and concluded the call hastily. They had learned their lesson. The hot heat of shame burned my hairy cheeks and spread to my ears. When did I become such a cunt? Was it back in the Quiet Carriage, or was I always a first-class bastard?

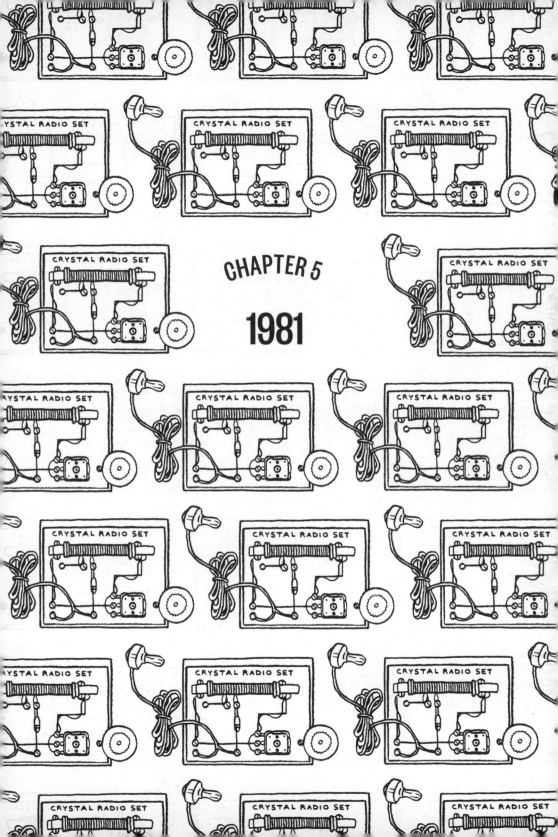

CHAPTER 5

1981

It was during my third year at boarding school that I discovered the power of drama. If I was in a class that I really struggled with – maths or French, for example – I would quietly hyperventilate until I started to feel faint, whereupon I would ask to be excused for a lie down in 'The San' (the sanatorium: a mini dormitory where the school nurse tended to ailing children). Later, when my friends saw me looking perky at lunch and accused me of being 'a skiver' I would tell them truthfully, 'I really *was* feeling faint.'

As for the school's 'legitimate' drama productions, I tried to get myself in as many as possible, as it seemed like the most magnificent scam. Of course, I cared deeply about the craft, but I also loved the fact that rehearsals often meant you got to miss lessons, avoid sport, go to bed later than everyone else and generally get away with murder.

Nineteen-eighty-one was the year I got the lead in the school play, *The Thwarting of Baron Bolligrew* by Robert Bolt. Throughout production on *Bolligrew* I received so much attention and praise, I started to believe that I might be one of the most special people that had ever lived, a suspicion that was borne out when I was awarded the Acting Prize (one of the school's most prestigious honours) for my explosively powerful portrayal of the Baron.

My parents came to see the play and afterwards Dad, worried that I was in the process of becoming a monster, gently urinated on my parade. 'You were good, old boy, but for God's sake, don't get any ideas about going into acting.'

'Why can't he?' said Mum.

'It's just a terribly hard life,' replied my pa, 'fraught with sadness and disappointment, even if you're good at it.' (Oddly enough, that was exactly what Mum said about being gay when the subject came up a few years later.)

Acting wasn't the only reason I was enjoying school more. By 1981 I had a best friend: a big, blond, charismatic boy called Tom. Tom was excellent at Latin, sometimes wore a spotty handkerchief like a cravat, claimed he had legally changed his middle name to 'Apollo', understood all the jokes in *Not the Nine O'Clock News* and showed me how to turn a can of Right Guard deodorant into a flame thrower.

Tom was also the first person I knew whose parents were divorced, which added greatly to his mystique. What was more, Tom's mum was cool and weird and hooked him up with non-regulation Day-Glo socks (extremely ace), a T-shirt with Mickey Mouse's head exploding (a bit much) and a load of Fat Freddy's Cat and Freak Brothers comics (totally mystifying). Tom also shared my growing enthusiasm for music.

Throughout the whole of 1981 I knew and liked nearly every song in the Top 40 and was always one of the people crowded round the school TV to watch *Top of the Pops* at 7.20 p.m. on a Thursday. Particular favourites included Adam and the Ants, Madness, Toyah, Kim Wilde, The Human League, Altered Images, Soft Cell, The Teardrop Explodes, The Specials, Ultravox, OMD and, yes, Joe Dolce.

RAMBLE

Joe Dolce's comedy song 'Shaddap You Face', about the things his Italian mother would say to him as a boy, was a worldwide hit in early 1981 and was Number One in the

UK charts for three weeks, famously preventing the epic 'Vienna' by Ultravox from reaching the top spot. I loved 'Vienna' and would play air syndrums whenever the mysterious video (imagine Fellini making a perfume commercial) was played on TV, but I didn't have a problem with 'Shaddap You Face' being Number One, because I like funny songs. It made me laugh when the mother in the song would say to her little boy, '*Why you look-a so sad? / It's-a not so bad!*' only to immediately become impatient and say, '*Ah shaddap-a you face!*' But laughter in music, as in so many other art forms, is dismissed as ephemeral and cheap, even when it comes with a very amusing Italian accent.

At home, my musical ally was my mum, then aged 42. She had been a Beatles fan as a young woman and as we drove back to boarding school on a Sunday night she was happy to make the transition from Disney cassettes to Radio 1's Top 40 countdown. Dad, meanwhile, was 58 and regarded pop music as proof that society was in a state of collapse and would soon be extinguished.

One Sunday, in an effort to indulge me and my sister before we were dropped back at The Reformatory, Dad reluctantly switched off Wagner and let us listen to the Top 40. One of the new entries that week was 'New Life' by Depeche Mode, and within a few bars it was speaking to me on a very clear line, the way that 'Cars' by Gary Numan had done a year or two previously when I'd heard it on a jukebox while on holiday in Greece. Songs like these used a language of cool sounds to tell me that instead of wrestling with difficult emotions the ideal thing would be to behave like a robot from the future.

As 'New Life' played on the car radio I leaned forward for a better dose of boingy, synthy Depeche Mode goodness and to my surprise Dad suddenly started singing along as he drove. Wobbling his head from side to side, he screwed up his face and whined derisively: 'Operay-ting, generay-ting, nyooo loyfe. Nyooo loyfe.' It took a few moments before I realised Dad was taking the piss out of Depeche Mode as if he were a child in a playground. He practically spat when he was finished.

Part of me was crushed that he didn't like it, but another part of me was impressed that he could come down to my level of juvenility. It didn't make me think any less of the song. When Dad unleashed his impression of whiny Dave Gahan (pronounced '*Garn*'), it was one of the first times I remember thinking, 'OK, I love you, but I think you're wrong about this.'

Yes, the vocals are weedy and the melody is basic, but 'New Life' is operating (and generating!) on its own terms and exceeding targets in all departments. The sounds are harsh and inorganic compared with the warm tones of classical instruments, and Dave Gahan cannot sing like Ella Fitzgerald or Kiri Te Kanawa (my dad's favourites, along with jolly old Wagner), but if he could sing like Ella he'd be doing different songs. For an oblique three-minute futuristic musical cyborg drama, you need reedy, emotionless Basildon vocals and bur-bling machine pulses delivered from a collection of circuits by a grumpy-looking midwife in a leather jacket – congratula-tions, Mr and Mrs Mode, it's a hit!

It's taken me 40 years to formulate that brilliant defence, and even if I'd been able to convey it to Dad back in 1981, I don't suppose it would have changed his opinion of 'New Life'. Instead, I just stared out of the car window and contin-ued to fantasise about being a robot.

Tom's Library

I could never get excited about superhero comics. I thought they tried too hard to be cool and funny and didn't do an especially good job at either. I preferred Asterix and Tintin, especially the intensely trippy Tintin adventure *The Shooting Star* with the giant spider, exploding mushrooms and the end of the world. Later I went through a phase of thinking Charlie Brown and Garfield were clever and hilarious, and I loved the film spoofs in *MAD* magazine, though I found the drawings much funnier than the dialogue. Then Tom turned up at school with some books that raised the bar considerably.

In addition to his impenetrable stoner comics and *Not the Nine O'Clock News* book, Tom allowed me and the other straights to pore over his big coffee-table tomes of sci-fi and fantasy art by airbrush wizards like Roger Dean and Chris Foss, as well as a collection of classic record-sleeve art called *The Album Cover Album*, which I studied for hours, admiring the surreal imagery, the cool typography and the see-through underwear of the women on the cover of *Country Life* by Roxy Music. But the most in-demand items in Tom's subversive library were *The Adventures of Phoebe Zeit-Geist* and *Alien (The Illustrated Story)*.

The Adventures of Phoebe Zeit-Geist (or 'Fo-eb Zeet-Geest' as Tom and I mispronounced it) is still one of the odder things I've ever stumbled across. Phoebe is a beautiful, posh young woman who, entirely nude throughout the book, is kidnapped and rescued by assorted monsters and weirdos including Nazis, Chinese foot fetishists and lesbian assassins. I've since read that the series was intended to satirise the way female characters were treated in certain erotic comics of the 1960s, but that sailed way over my top bunk aged 11. Mainly I just couldn't believe there was a comic in which the hero was a beautiful naked woman. Yes, she would occasionally kick ass, but I think if I told my daughter that Phoebe Zeit-Geist was a fable of female empowerment, she'd give me only the shortest bit of shrift.

Alien (The Illustrated Story) represented the only way 11-year-old Buckles was going to see any actual images relating to a film that loomed large in the dark, backlit corridors of my imagination. All I had seen of it was the creepy egg poster and a clip on *Film 80* one night, which my mum switched off when she saw me watching from the doorway in my PJs. It seemed clear to me that this was a film so appallingly terrifying that if I was to watch it before I was at least 30, I would instantly lose my mind and spend the rest of my life wearing a straitjacket and rocking back and forth in a padded room (which is what mental illness was like in the 1980s).

Someone in a senior dorm had a copy of Alan Dean Foster's novelisation of *Alien* and I had broken my 'No Reading for Fun' rule in order to verify the rumours that the film contained a scene in which a monster ripped its way out of a man's tummy. Once I'd located the relevant paragraph, I wandered from dorm to dorm before lights out, reading aloud the chest-bursting description to anyone who was interested, not so much to freak them out as to deal with my own fearful preoccupation by sharing it.

The arrival of *Alien (The Illustrated Story)* rendered my wandering audiobook minstrel skills instantly redundant, and little groups formed round Tom's bunk to gaze at the spectacular full-colour, double-page illustration of what appeared to be a big snake with incredible abs and two big sets of teeth erupting from a man's chest 'in a scarlet shower of flesh and blood'. Most of Tom's library was confiscated within in a few days, but by then it was too late; I had resolved that one day, though it would almost certainly undo me, I would see *Alien*.

OVERLEAF: *Alien* poster design from 12-year-old A. Buckles. *Not having seen the film at that point, I decided instead of a nobbly egg, what the poster needed was incredible 3D lettering, a spaceship that looks like a Yorkie bar and a big angry snake fish.*

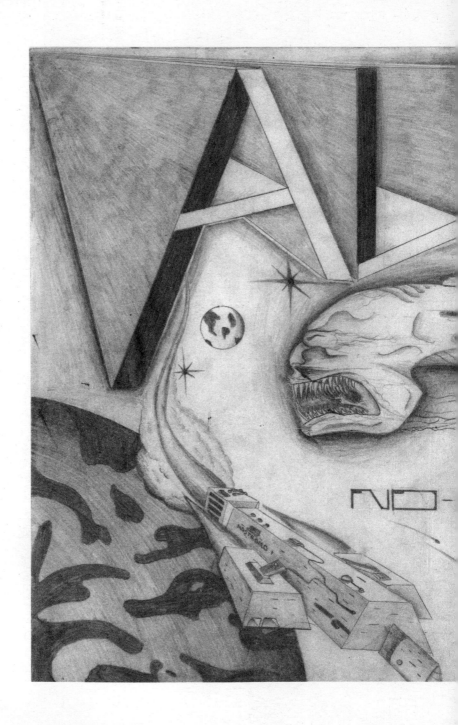

The Crystal Set

In 1981 the two things I wanted most in the world were an Atari 2600 video games console and a Walkman. My dad felt that buying me either of those things would have the same effect on my development as shooting me full of heroin. He still clung to the hope that his eldest son might be moulded into a person who appreciated books, the natural world and the company of other humans, rather than becoming just another dull-eyed consumer drone, obsessed with gadgets that would isolate him from anything real or important (he would have loved being a parent these days).

Dad's idea of a compromise was to give me a crystal radio set for my twelfth birthday. This was an inexpensive piece of kit consisting of a couple of bits of wire, three tiny electronic components, a little plastic dial and a single flesh-coloured earpiece that, when assembled, could pick up faint AM radio signals. It required no external power and no batteries, which made Dad happy, as he hated how much batteries cost and would become apoplectic if he ever came across a battery-operated gadget that had been left switched on. Not a problem with the crystal radio set.

I knew there was no way I was getting the Atari, but I was so disappointed that my parents hadn't got me a tape player or even a real radio that I just shoved the crystal set under my bed, unopened. Then one incredibly boring and depressing Sunday afternoon I got it out and put it together.

RAMBLE

It's hard to communicate to anyone born in the Internet Age just how dull, bordering on physically painful a Sunday in England could be at the end of the 1970s and early Eighties, even in central London. In deference to Jesus, anything that might provoke even the mildest excitement was off the menu.

Everything was closed – literally everything – and TV (by some way the most powerful domestic entertainment device in those days) was neutered by televised church services and current affairs programmes.

Sub-Ramble

I would sometimes watch the Sunday-afternoon political interview programme *Weekend World*, presented by Brian Walden, not because I relished Walden's crackling exchanges with the politicians of the day, but because I loved the theme tune – a short blast of supercharged rock that preoccupied me partly because I assumed I would never be able to identify it.

Thirty years later I googled '*Weekend World theme tune*' and that tantalising childhood mystery was gone in six seconds – it turned out to be a section from a song called 'Nantucket Sleighride', a long, otherwise tedious track by Mountain. Yay! The Internet!

Nowadays any hint of boredom can be treated instantly with a couple of clicks that will deliver punching, kicking, special powers and space lasers, but when I was little, the only time anything that exciting found its way into your home was Christmas, and in those days Christmas took an eternity to come round.

One Sunday afternoon, Dad found me with my face inches from the thick, curvy glass of the boob tube, trying to make out patterns in the static as if I were Carol Anne in *Poltergeist*. Remember static? The Digital Revolution got rid of that before the Internet, Wi-Fi and portable screens banished boredom forever.

Now, the dream I dreamt as a child of an entertainment ubiquity has come true, but I'm too old to celebrate it. I'm just some old fart who thinks we threw boredom out with the bathwater before realising how valuable it was, not just philosophically but physiologically. Did you know, for example, that when we become bored our brains release a protein-rich neuro-balm that not only mends broken synaptic pathways, it also forms new ones vital for creative thought? OK, so I made that up, but it sort of sounds right, doesn't it?

I assembled the components of my crystal radio set on the plastic base provided and after a few hours of fiddling I got a faint blast of white noise through the earpiece. Then, turning the dial in tiny increments, I started to hear voices and music. It was thrilling, as if I had made contact with aliens from a distant galaxy where they also had middle-of-the-road music and annoying radio adverts.

We weren't allowed electronics at boarding school; they were worried expensive gadgets might cause feelings of envy and resentment or get stolen. Nevertheless, some children lucky enough to own radios or tape players smuggled them into school where, sure enough, they caused envy and resentment and got stolen. I decided the chances of someone stealing my crystal radio set were very low, though, so the following term, having installed a false bottom in my tuck box, I sneaked it in.

For a while I got into a routine of lying in my bunk after lights out and surfing the airwaves, slowly and softly, finding the clearest signal coming from a station that identified itself as Radio Luxembourg – The Great 208. A DJ called Stuart Henry would play all my favourite songs from the Top 40 at the time: 'Bedsitter' by Soft Cell, 'Spirits in the Material World' by The Police, 'Joan of Arc' by OMD and, one night, a song I didn't know. A stripped-down electronic song that pulsed and twinkled urgently, stirring the emotions despite a vocal that sounded bored and detached. 'At last!' I thought. 'The apotheosis of all my romantic robot dreams!'

For the next few weeks I listened to Radio Luxembourg at the same time every night, hoping to hear the song again, until one night they played it, and rather than going immediately into another song, the DJ announced, 'The sound of Kraftwerk there. Their name is German for "power station" and that's a number from a few years ago called "The Model" that's been reissued on a double A-side with their song "Computer Love".'

I bought the single (my first) for 99p from WH Smith's on the Earl's Court Road, with a record token I got for Christmas that year. Most people's first singles are mildly embarrassing – something naff by a children's cartoon character or a DJ who turned out to be a sexual predator – but for once my taste was impeccable, and I suppose that's partly thanks to Dad and the crystal set.

Alison

There were certain weekends during term time when no one was allowed out of school, and activities were organised to prevent 350 students aged 9 to 13 going maximum *Lord of the Flies*. One summer weekend, Tom and I were the only boys to sign up for the senior disco-dancing class. Our plan was not to take the class seriously and to disrupt the efforts of the girls to learn dance routines for music we did not respect: 'Super Trouper' by ABBA (boring), 'This Ole House' by Shakin' Stevens (sad) or 'Making Your Mind Up' by Bucks Fizz (mega chronic).

The poster for the disco-dancing class said 'Dress cool', so Tom suggested we wear T-shirts underneath Sunday-best suit jackets that we turned inside out to reveal the shiny inner lining. A tie worn round the forehead like a bandana completed a look that was more than just cool, it said: 'Watch out, because these two 11-year-old guys don't give a solo fuck and are going to take the absolute piss out of your pathetic girly disco.' Then we arrived at the gym.

Groups of girls, mainly from our year, who previously we'd considered annoying if we'd considered them at all, were now ranged before us in silver leggings, hot pants, pedal pushers, leg warmers, tank tops, deely boppers, lipstick, eye shadow and glitter. (One of the advantages of boarding school, depending on your perspective, was that at moments like these there were no parents around to say, 'You are NOT going out dressed like that!') Tom and I, responding obediently to our monkey-boy/patriarchal programming, were instantly beguiled and decided to abort our piss-taking mission.

We were too young to be struggling with any desires more powerful than simply to flirt and make a few of the girls laugh, but to the extent we were able to do so, both of these produced an unfamiliar surge of excitement. My attention quickly focused on one girl I'd never spoken to before, though I'd seen her and her pals around and always found them vaguely irritating. In homage to the Pink Ladies from their favourite film *Grease*, they would often pretend to chew gum (real gum was contraband) and make belittling comments about passers-by in American accents. It was infuriating but also sort of funny.

To my mind the funniest, cheekiest and prettiest one of the Pink Ladies was called Alison, and unless I was greatly mistaken, as we struck heroic poses for our first dance routine – 'Prince Charming' by Adam and the Ants – Alison was smiling at me. Or possibly laughing at me. But even if she was, I felt for the first time that ridicule (or, as Adam Ant would have it, '*rid-di-kewl*') was nothing to be scared of.

RAMBLE

Before I was a full-time Bowie bore, I loved Adam and the Ants. Most of us did. Their album *Kings of the Wild Frontier* was always playing in the senior common room and every track was catchy and fun to sing along with despite being quite odd, like a lot of chart music in the early Eighties. When they played 'Antmusic' at a school disco, I pulled away from the wallflowers and danced along for the first time, thinking, 'So this is the point of discos!'

More importantly, Adam Ant was called Adam (which is also my name), and he was handsome and pretty at the same time (again, check!), but best of all, he was known to be short (5 foot 6 – the same height I am now). For some reason Dad's reassurances that I was 'taller than Napoleon and Genghis Khan' didn't stop me fretting about my height when I was young, and finding out that Adam Ant was a fellow short man provided genuine comfort. You can imagine how excited I was when I saw my first Danny DeVito film.

Everything at school was different after the disco-dancing class. Tom and I talked to the girls whenever we got the opportunity, and on a school trip to see a theatre production of *The Turn of the Screw* (or was it *The Taming of the Shrew*?) Tom sat next to one of the girls he fancied on the bus and I sat next to Alison.

The theatre trip was a fun break from the school schedule, seeing the outside world, being given a small tub of ice cream at the interval and sneakily buying my first bag of Toffee Eclairs when the teachers weren't looking. The play itself failed to make an impression – I recall it being dark and there was some scenery; all I could think about was how much I was looking forward to talking to Alison when it was over, to laughing at her rude jokes and having her laugh at mine.

In the bus on the way back we asked the driver to put on Radio 1 and 'Every Little Thing She Does Is Magic' by The Police started playing as Alison and I hid beneath my jacket, ate some Toffee Eclairs, put our heads together and kissed. I'd heard 'Every Little Thing She Does Is Magic' before and thought it was not as good as 'Message in a Bottle', but, kissing Alison, it suddenly sounded a lot better than 'Message in a Bottle'. In fact, it sounded better than anything I'd ever heard.

I don't remember if any kind of ceremony took place or if anything was written down to formalise the arrangement, but within a few days I realised that I had a girlfriend.

A local band came to play in the gym one weekend and part of their set was a cover of Supertramp's 'Breakfast in America'. Not having heard the song before, I was delighted by how apposite the lyrics were for my new romantic status. On hearing the line 'take a look at my girlfriend', I looked over at Alison and grinned, and she smiled back because she was my girlfriend and I was taking a look at her. At the line 'she's not much of a girlfriend', I looked over again and rolled my eyes, hoping Alison would realise this was visual banter rather than a genuine indictment of her girlfriend skills. Then

I did the same joke several more times and Alison started rolling her eyes, too. It was off-the-charts Eye-Bants.

That evening we went up to the overgrown maze on the hill above the football pitches, which was known as a hotbed of wayward behaviour. After some light snogging, Alison reached into her jeans' pocket and produced a small packet of powder, shaking it as she held my nervous gaze. It was Rise & Shine, crystalline orange juice concentrate, which the school had recently classified as contraband, and I was up for it.

We licked our fingers and dipped them into the packet, but rather than suck off the zesty powder immediately, we touched our fingers back to our tongues and dipped again until a damp, sugary orange mound containing enough concentrate for a full glass of fake orange juice had built up on our forefingers. Then we sucked it off. Tangy doesn't begin to cover it. Now and then I'd see other children round the school with orange forefingers and think, 'Hello, looks like you're in the tart but sweet club, too.'

On a handful of intensely exciting occasions, Tom set his Game & Watch to wake us at one or two in the morning, whereupon we put on our slippers and dressing gowns and crept out of our senior dormitory, down the stairs, through moonlit corridors and over to the girls' wing. If we'd been caught, it would almost certainly have meant suspension and to calm my nerves as we crept I listened in my mind to Madness's 'Night Boat to Cairo' and The Human League's 'The Things That Dreams Are Made Of'.

Once in the girls' dorm, we woke up our respective girlfriends, indulged in yet more snogging, then crept back to our beds feeling like sexy POWs. I loved kissing, though I always said 'snogging' so as not to come across as effete. Apart from the fact that Alison wore delicious peach lip balm, whenever we kissed it felt to me that we were defying the normal lonely order of things and forming a connection that went beyond the physical and into the telepathic, as if we were kids with psychic powers trying to evade shadowy government agents bent on exploiting our mind gifts for evil.

RAMBLE

I spent a lot of time wishing I had special mind powers as a child. During the Seventies films like *Escape to Witch Mountain* and TV shows like *The Tomorrow People* enthralled me with their depictions of telepathic and telekinetic children, and when left alone I would narrow my eyes, touch my fingers to my temples and concentrate hard on an object like a cup or a toy car, willing it to move with all my might because I knew that if it did, it would prove that I wasn't just an anxious thickie who couldn't do maths, I was in fact part of a new stage in human evolution. But all I managed to do was burst a few blood vessels in my cheeks from straining.

For snogging enthusiasts, the biggest event in the school calendar was the End of Term Film. This took place in the school gym the night before holidays began and was as significant for us as Prom Night is for American teens. Establishing who you were going to sit next to in the End of Term Film was a process of lengthy and fraught negotiation that began weeks in advance and could easily fall apart at the last minute if your date got a better offer.

The End of Term Film on Friday, 11 December 1981, was *Hawk the Slayer*, a low-budget British Sword-and-Sorcery adventure released the previous year. Alison and I found a space against one of the side walls of the gym where all the serious snoggers sat. Sitting against the back wall was no good because that's where the teachers sat and only 'Squits' and tragic losers sat in the middle of the gym, as I knew from bitter experience.

As the film started and the lights went off, Alison and I closed our eyes and began to snog (at least I did; Alison may well have surreptitiously watched *Hawk the Slayer*). Our mouths didn't part until the end credits had rolled and the lights in the school gym were back on; 90 minutes in total. If you can beat that, you've got problems. A year or so later they showed *Hawk the Slayer* on TV and I finally saw the images that went with the audio. It was better the first time around.

BOWIE ANNUAL

I'm sure there are French teachers who electrify their students with their passionate conjugations of irregular verbs, and physics teachers who state the principle of moments for a body in equilibrium so rivetingly that lives are changed forever, but you seldom hear about them. Meanwhile, all an English teacher has to do is tell the class to stand on their desks and read out some poetry and at least one or two of their students are guaranteed to crap on about how inspiring it was for the rest of their lives.

My first unconventional English lesson took place in a posh wood-panelled room in an old part of the school that I'd never set foot in before, though by that time I'd been there for three years. The classroom upgrade was one of the privileges that came with being a senior, along with suddenly being treated like an adult by some of the staff (after all, we were 12), and our new English teacher, Mr Davidson, was one of those who seemed especially excited at the prospect of laying some grown-up shit on our arses (that's not a good choice of phrase in this context, but you know what I mean).

Mr Davidson looked like Serge Gainsbourg with a hangover: unshaven, eyes heavy-lidded, hair messy and clothes rumpled – the kind of person my dad would have called 'a real creep'. (NOTE: My friend Patrick just sent me a picture he took of Mr Davidson back in those days and he doesn't look like Serge Gainsbourg with a hangover at all. He looks like a young, smart Serge Gainsbourg in a suit and a tie.)

As we filed into the posh room that day, an unsmiling Mr Davidson eyeballed us silently. There were a few nervous giggles after we'd taken our seats because Mr D still hadn't said a word. Instead, he went over to fiddle with a record player on his desk and suddenly the sound of a growling electric guitar rang out. Mr Davidson turned to the blackboard and began to scribble: 'Ziggy played guitar. Jamming good with Weird and Gilly ...'

This all seemed a bit daft to me and I looked over at Tom to see what he thought. He grinned and raised his eyebrows as if to say, 'Go with it!' Mr Davidson wrote out all the lyrics before the song had ended and when he was finished he turned and stared at us with crazed intensity.

For the rest of the lesson we analysed the lyrics to 'Ziggy Stardust'. Though I still struggled to take it all seriously – 'Why do you think the fly was trying to break his balls?' – I couldn't deny it was more fun than a 'normal' lesson. I was surprised when Mr Davidson told us the song was by David Bowie. I wasn't crazy about it. To me it sounded less interesting and inventive than 'Space Oddity' or 'Life on Mars', but later in the senior common room Bill Muggs put on a cassette of the whole *Ziggy* album and I heard 'Five Years' for the first time.

'Five Years' was like a whole film in a single song,

beginning with a silent, empty aerial shot that gradually zoomed to earth to the sound of a beguilingly odd drum pattern, before finding Bowie making his way through a busy market square as around him people struggled to take in the news that the world was ending, not that day or the next, but in five years. I didn't like to think about the end of the world, but because Bowie was there it felt OK somehow, and by the flashback to the ice-cream parlour and the '*milkshakes cold and long*', I was no longer on a beaten-up armchair in the senior common room with Bill Muggs, but smiling and waving from inside the song.

I bought *The Rise and Fall of Ziggy Stardust and the Spiders from Mars* on vinyl during the holidays (my first LP) and back home in the front room, studying the rear of the album sleeve, I saw the message: '*To be played at maximum volume.*' That wasn't going to happen because I didn't have headphones and I wasn't up for Dad interrupting to tell me to turn it down. Nor did I relish the prospect of either of my parents hearing the line about a cop kissing the feet of a priest and making a '*queer*' throw up.

Instead, I played the record at approximately one-third of the maximum volume but lay on the floor with my eyes closed and the shitty hi-fi speakers positioned right next to my ears. In that position I listened to 'Five Years' over and over, mishearing the line '*your face, your race, the way that you talk*' as '*your face, you' re ace, the way that you talk*', which made me think of Alison. By the time the song reached its emotional crescendo in the cold and the rain with Bowie feeling like an actor, my throat hurt and my heart ached, and it was tremendous to be alive.

CHAPTER 6

ARGUMENT
WITH WIFE LOG

SORRY SORRY SORRY SORRY SORRY SORRY RRY SORRY SORRY SORRY S SORRY SORRY SORRY SORRY Y SORRY SORRY SORRY SORRY SORRY ORRY SORRY SORRY SORRY SORR SORRY SORRY

hen two people live together for 25 years, from time to time there will be irritation. If those people share the money they earn, have brought one or more children into the world and continue to have (occasional) sexual relations, the potential for friction increases dramatically. If one of those people is in the habit of texting during movie night and thinks proper cutlery-drawer segregation 'feels racist', then it's argument time.

Underlying each argument are resentments and insecurities that haven't been satisfactorily dealt with. So a comment that was in no way passive-aggressive about always leaving the door of the dishwasher open (which is a tripping hazard) takes only a few minutes to spiral into a series of acrimonious accusations over class, money, parenting, education, climate change and the meaning of life.

In the heat of an argument the notion of admitting I might be wrong or attempting to unpack the disagreement is about as likely as being in the throes of sexual passion and suddenly deciding to make a start on those taxes. It's technically possible, but it's not top of the agenda.

Much more important is acting as though I'm innocent of all charges, turning my wife's every accusation back on her and, most crucially, having the last word. Sometimes we'll reach a point in the argument when we're just going round in an angry loop – in these situations I sometimes find it useful to deploy the Silent Walk-out in High Dudgeon. Medium or low dudgeon may also be effective.

Some might see the Silent Walk-out as a dick move. In the past my wife has called out, 'Go on then, off you go!' as I depart, but if I'm able to stop myself going back for more, the suspension of hostilities afforded by the Silent Walk-out is vitally important. Only when we're out of physical proximity is it possible to begin the Chill-out Section, and if all goes well, that's followed a while later by the shambling, shame-faced Apology Summit. The duration of the Chill-out Section needs to be right, though; turn up for the Apology Summit too early and you risk being served a giant helping of Argument Rehash.

When I argue with my wife it's one of the worst feelings in the world, because it brings into view, however distantly, the possibility that our differences are too great and it would be better for everyone if we were not together. Then I imagine the reality of splitting up. The pain and regret that I'd feel if I lost my closest and kindest ally. The sadness our children would endure. The admin. Oh God, imagine the admin! And, of course, one of my big podcast catchphrases would be fucked.

I'm happy to say that over the last few years my wife and I argue less. This is partly because we have both done our best to talk through some of the underlying causes of our trivial disagreements with an admirable degree of maturity, but I believe another important factor has been my determination to keep a log of our arguments, providing as it does an easily searchable database of grievances that reduces the chances of covering old ground during valuable argument time. For the record, my wife strongly disagrees.

Argument with Wife Log 1

SUBJECT OF ARGUMENT	FUNNY LOOK WHEN I WENT TO THE PUB WITH DAN
MAIN POINTS – WIFE	'I didn't give you a funny look. Maybe you feel guilty.'
MAIN POINTS – BUCKLES	'I don't feel guilty at all. And you DID give me a funny look.'
WINNER	BUCKLES

SUBJECT OF ARGUMENT	MONEY
MAIN POINTS – WIFE	'We need to save more and spend less on gadgets.'
MAIN POINTS – BUCKLES	'I need those so-called "gadgets" for my work.'
WINNER	BUCKLES

SUBJECT OF ARGUMENT	'RUDENESS' WHEN FRIENDS OF WIFE CAME TO STAY
MAIN POINTS – WIFE	'You immediately went to your shed when they arrived.'
MAIN POINTS – BUCKLES	'I needed to check on the rat traps, which, if you recall, you asked me to put there in the first place.'
WINNER	ONGOING

SUBJECT OF ARGUMENT	PAINTING A LARGE MURAL OF MY FACE ON THE SHED
MAIN POINTS – WIFE	'It's a waste of time and money and it's insane.'
MAIN POINTS – BUCKLES	'Remind me again who graduated with first class honours from art school?' (I did.)
WINNER	WIFE

SUBJECT OF ARGUMENT	WIFE NEVER BUYING MY FAVOURITE FLAVOUR OF JAM
MAIN POINTS – WIFE	'Everyone in the house likes raspberry.'
MAIN POINTS – BUCKLES	'I loathe raspberry. Do you even know my favourite jam flavour?'
WINNER	BUCKLES

SUBJECT OF ARGUMENT	TOILET-ROLL HOLDERS
MAIN POINTS – WIFE	'The vertical wooden pole is classy.'
MAIN POINTS – BUCKLES	'The wall-mounted holder is fine. The pole is bourgeois.'
WINNER	WIFE

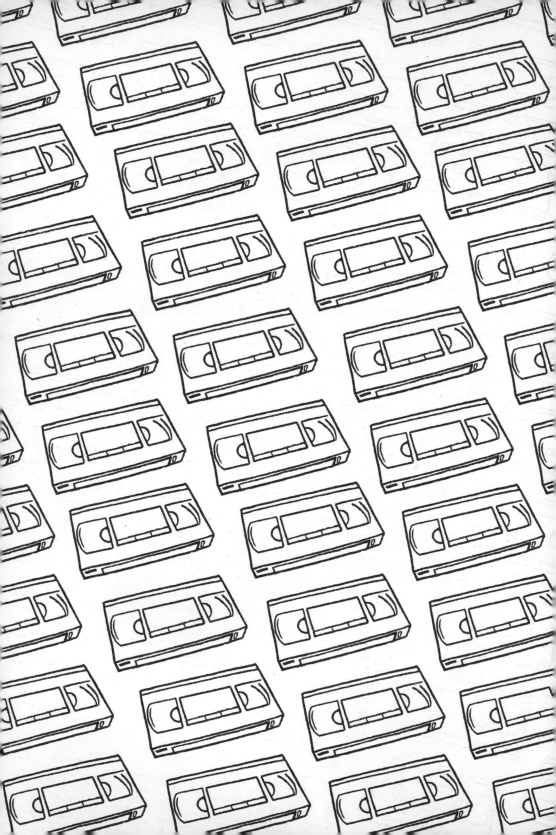

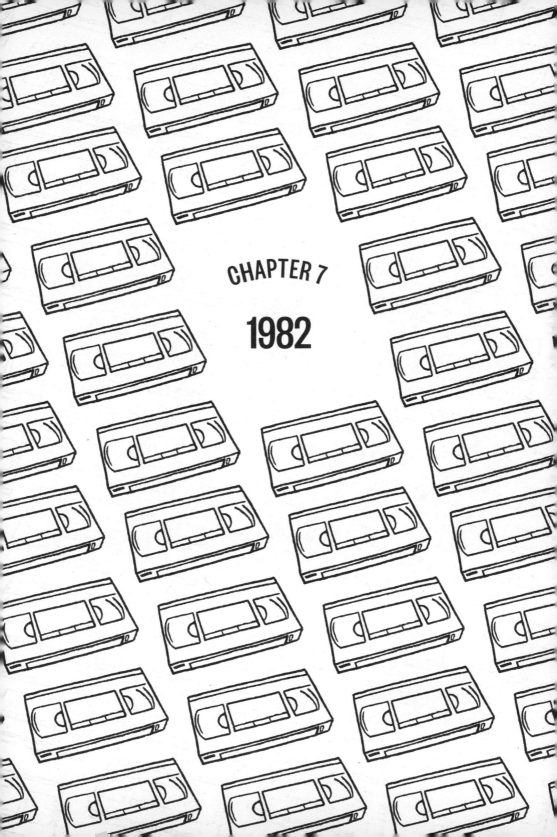

CHAPTER 7

1982

By the time I left my Sussex boarding school at the end of the summer term in 1982, a few weeks after my twelfth birthday, I preferred life at school to life at home, and though saying goodbye to my friends was painful I had every intention of staying in touch, especially with my girlfriend Alison, with whom I still held the snogging record, and my best friend Tom, who had promised me that somehow, someday we would see *Alien*.

Over the summer our family returned to the best place in the world: the USA. Whether we were staying in a smart resort or a shabby motel, every second out there was a vibrant and luxurious contrast to life in England in the early Eighties.

A fan of John Wayne and all things western, Dad adored places like Montana, Utah, Wyoming, Texas and Alaska, where he could indulge his cowboy fantasies of honest folk living decent lives in respectful harmony with magnificent nature, but I preferred it when we went to stay with Dad's older brother David and his wife Leslie in their hillside bungalow in Santa Barbara, California. As far as I was concerned, they lived in a paradise of permanent sunshine, palm trees, multi-coloured cereal that tasted of sweets, exotic household-product smells, giant air-conditioned shopping malls that looked like the lobbies of fancy hotels, friendly people who thought my British accent was 'cute', multi-channel 24-hour TV and, best of all, films that came out months before they did in the UK.

Virtually every aspect of Uncle David and Aunty Leslie's life in Santa Barbara made the materialistic monkey in me salivate. They had not one, but TWO big TV sets operated by remote-control devices like something out of *Blake's 7*. They had a fridge with a built-in ice machine that dispensed not boring cubes, but half-moons. They had two cars (one of them a sports car), which sat inside their own garage with an automatic door, and most extraordinarily of all, they had their own swimming pool. That's right, an actual pool with no one telling you not to run, dive bomb or engage in 'petting' (not that 'petting' was a priority with just my family using the pool, but still, nice to have the option).

I was also in awe of my cousin Leslie Anne, who had played in the garden with me during a Santa Barbara visit when I must have been about three and she was eleven, leaving me with an impression of a glamorous tower of legs, long brown hair and a big American smile. I've made it sound as though she was just a big pair of very hairy legs with a mouth, but actually she was a fairly standard beautiful cousin.

By 1982, however, things were different. Leslie Anne had just started college and this time when she came over she seemed irritable, rolling her eyes when her mother spoke and barely saying a word to her dad. 'How could she not get on with Uncle David and Aunty Leslie?' I thought. They're both so nice and they have such cool jobs. And look at that pool!

One afternoon Aunty Leslie came back from work at her real-estate firm with a briefcase that she set on the glass table in the living room. 'This isn't mine,' she said to me and my sister. 'It belongs to a client who's buying a house. Take a look inside.' We opened the briefcase and found it filled with wads of cash, like something from a TV cop show. Leslie let us take out the wads and throw them in the air as we cried, 'We're rich! We're rich!' Mum laughed. Dad smiled weakly. Leslie Anne passed the room and shook her head. Then we spent a while picking up the bank notes from the fluffy white rug and putting them back in the briefcase.

Uncle David was a sterner presence than Aunty Leslie, but he got more fun in the evenings when the adults started drinking. During the Second World War he'd been in the RAF, but now he worked at Vandenberg Air Force Base, testing some new rockets called M-X missiles. He knew people at NASA and brought me back a giant poster showing a detailed cross-section of the Space Shuttle that the previous summer we had watched making its first flight on TV. Uncle David could only have been cooler in my eyes if he'd turned out to be partly bionic.

The Summer of Spielberg

Before returning to the UK's entertainment Middle Ages, I tried to convince Mum to take us to the cinema as many times as possible. One of our first outings that summer in America was to see *Tron*, a film whose premise – bloke gets sucked into a video game – was so precisely what I wanted to see, it was hard to admit to myself that despite a few amazing moments, I had enjoyed my bag of candy corn more than the actual movie (though I was still delighted when Mum bought me the poster).

'You kids have to see *E. T.*,' said Aunty Leslie. 'It's about a little boy who finds an adorable alien in a shed and they go on bike rides. It's a really neat movie, you're going to love it.' My aunt's description did not supercharge me 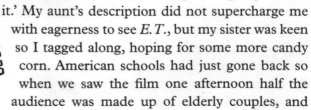 with eagerness to see *E. T.*, but my sister was keen so I tagged along, hoping for some more candy corn. American schools had just gone back so when we saw the film one afternoon half the audience was made up of elderly couples, and when the lights came up at the end, most of them were still seated, consoling one another as if at a funeral. 'Come on, let's go!' I said to Mum, but she too was still sitting and staring ahead, weeping quietly. Though I'd loved the film, seeing all the adults cry unsettled me. In those days you only really saw adults crying if something very bad was happening. Post *E.T.* it was a blub-o-rama.

The night before we had to fly home, cousin Leslie Anne took me and my sister for one last trip to the movies. The 1979 James Bond film *Moonraker* was playing in a double bill with a new movie that Leslie Anne said was 'kinda like *E.T.* but not so lame'.

Though *Moonraker* is not generally considered one of the great Bond films, that night in Santa Barbara I thought it was thrilling, scary and hilarious – I mean, come on! It's got punch-ups on top of swinging cable cars, a guy called Jaws who has metal teeth, rocket packs, space laser fights AND a pigeon double-taking at a hovercraft gondola driving through St Mark's Square in Venice! What more do you want?

However, I was confused by the bit at the end of *Moonraker* when the video screens at mission control suddenly flash up an image of Bond and Dr Goodhead ('A woman?') floating nude around a space capsule covered by a sheet. 'My God, what's Bond doing?' says an embarrassed official.

Without looking at the screen, Q replies, 'I think he's attempting re-entry.' The line got a big laugh from the Santa Barbara audience and I knew it must have something to do with sex but couldn't get my head round the specifics, especially as I'd misheard the line as 'I think he's attempting rear entry'. But that didn't make sense, surely? 'Ohmigod!' groaned Leslie Anne. 'I'm sorry you had to see that whole movie.'

My sister, who was just 12 at the time, was flagging after *Moonraker* and there was some debate about whether or not to stick around for the second film, but after a toilet break we rallied and headed back in … for *Poltergeist*. Leslie Anne shifted uncomfortably and looked over at us from time to time as it became apparent that *Poltergeist* was basically a full-on horror film with evil spirits that steal a little girl then terrorise her family with self-stacking chairs, violent trees, melting faces, a portal to hell and a clown toy that was disturbing even before it got possessed and started to strangle the little boy with the big teeth.

What prevented me from finding *Poltergeist* genuinely scary was the same tone of pleasant middle-class American suburbia that had pervaded *E.T.* Everything from the family dynamic at the centre of the film to the way it was lit and shot was so similar to *E.T.* that I assumed *Poltergeist* had also been made by the same guy.

RAMBLE

In fact, as I found out years later, Spielberg was going to direct *Poltergeist* while he was still working on *E.T.* but couldn't for contractual reasons, at which point he brought in Tobe Hooper. Hooper had been responsible for a film that Tom had told me about at school, a film that, even more than *Alien*, sounded likely to leave me permanently traumatised but in a less enjoyable way: *The Texas Chainsaw Massacre*. With Spielberg producing and Hooper directing (though to this day there is disagreement about exactly who did what), *Poltergeist* was initially given an R (or 18) certificate until Spielberg successfully argued it down to a PG. While it may not have deserved an R (a rating that probably would have sunk *Poltergeist* at the box office), it certainly didn't deserve a PG. Steven Spielberg cares more about money than traumatising children, that's the point I'm trying to make here, and no, I wouldn't be saying that if he'd got me involved in *Tintin* as well as Joe and Edgar Wright. I was born to play Captain Haddock.

By the time *Poltergeist* was finished my sister was in tears and Leslie Anne was terrified that my dad would freak out when we got back, but as far as I was concerned I'd just had one of the all-time great nights out.

On the flight home we experienced unusually heavy turbulence as we flew through a valley of storm cloud and my mother, an ex-BOAC flight attendant, wept in fear. Or maybe she and Dad had argued again. Either way, Dad didn't seem too sympathetic and I took my cue from him, thinking Mum was overreacting. I was yet to develop a fear of flying at that point, and listening to my Madness tape amid the violent lurching and the flashes of lightning was like being on a ride at Disneyland.

Westminster

Back in rainy England, Dad had managed to secure me a place at Westminster, a prestigious and expensive public school in central London, although, as he had got a last-minute cheap deal, unusual terms and conditions applied, one of which was that I couldn't start until January the following year.

So I spent the autumn term at Westminster Under School, no longer boarding and in uniform again for the first time since Cub Scouts. I was also joining a group of 13-year-old boys who had known each other for years, many of whom looked and sounded like Jacob Rees-Mogg. In fact, one of them was Jacob Rees-Mogg. Though far from being under-privileged myself, I was different enough for some of the more Lord Snooty-ish boys in my class to treat me like Julia Roberts in *Pretty Woman* when she visits the posh Rodeo Drive boutique to buy some non-sex-worker clothes.

At home I had my own room for the first time and decorated it with pictures of David Bowie, the *Tron* poster I'd brought back from California and arty full-page cigarette advertisements from Sunday magazines (then considered the acme of the ad man's craft). I sat at my desk listening to Radio 1 on the Sanyo radio cassette recorder I'd finally wangled for my thirteenth birthday (the lo-fi charms of my crystal set having faded by then) and wrote letters to my friends from boarding school, now scattered across the country at other private institutions.

Bad news came one day from Alison who told me she wouldn't be able to see me over the Christmas holidays because her family was moving abroad. It crossed my mind that she was making this up because she had a new boyfriend, but if that was the case it was a fiction she maintained for the next two and a half years, during which time we stayed in semi-regular contact without ever actually seeing each other.

When I wasn't writing letters, I was drawing pictures of robots, spaceships, imaginary album covers and film posters.

RAMBLE

I hadn't seen *Blade Runner* when I drew a poster for it that autumn, so my design was characteristically literal: a hand running a big machete blade through the words '*BLADE RUNNER*'. Though I was intrigued by the title, the official posters I'd seen in America during the summer made me think it looked like one of those dreary private-detective films with grumpy men in overcoats drinking whisky, chewing matchsticks and being disagreeable with unhappy women. In a way I was right, but I hadn't factored in the flying cars, gymnastic robot people and thrilling music. I went to see *Blade Runner* on my own towards the end of 1982 at the Fulham ABC and I emerged afterwards dazed and besotted, though more preoccupied than was necessary by Deckard's impossible precious photo-enhancing machine, which could look round the corners of a room inside a two-dimensional photograph. OK, it's science *fiction*, but there's no need to take the piss.

That autumn I spent many evenings at my desk with a blank tape loaded into the Sanyo, poised to hit record and play if a good song came on, whereupon I'd listen to it repeatedly, straining to make out the lyrics. Then, as if to satisfy some archival instinct, I'd write them down on sheets of Dad's *Sunday Telegraph* letterheaded paper. I was careful to keep the reams of scrawled transcriptions hidden away for fear that Pa would come across them. It wasn't that I imagined he would have beaten me with his belt while derisively reading out my misheard lyrics to 'The Message', 'Pass the Dutchie' and 'John Wayne Is Big Leggy', but I knew he would have been sad that instead of at least trying to write nineteenth-century naval adventure stories I was copying down the mouthings of creeps. And I didn't want Dad to be sad.

The problem was that, like most parents who love their children, Dad was unable to be consistent with the application of his values. When he was home he tried to steer us away from the most crass and deadening aspects of modern culture and technology, but when he was abroad all bets were off, as Mum lacked the time or the inclination to enforce his campaign of disapproval – a fact that probably drove him nuts and was no doubt the source of some of their rows.

But Mum couldn't be held solely responsible for allowing my pop-culture addiction to flourish. Now and then, perhaps feeling guilty for being away so much and keen just to see us all happy, Dad would capitulate big style.

The Best Day of My Life

Tom had an Atari 2600 games console and I thought he was the luckiest person I knew. If I wanted to play *Space Invaders*, and I wanted to all the time, I had to wait until we were on holiday somewhere with an arcade nearby, then plead with Mum and Dad to give me a few 10p pieces and let me loose for half an hour.

Essentially, Tom had a whole arcade in his front room. We had *Pong*. Don't get me wrong, *Pong* was great and I'll never forget the quasi-supernatural wonder of being able to control what was happening on our TV for the first time, even though it was just moving a white line up and down the side of the screen to the sound of '*bip*' and '*boop*', but the Atari was an entirely different species of amazing.

For a start it was called 'ATARI', a word that looked cool, sounded cool and was always accompanied by a logo that resembled three jet-plane vapour trails converging en route to space, which I think we can all agree is cool (when it popped up as a neon sign in *Blade Runner* I let out a little hoot of nerdy joy). Then there was the console, with its sports-car and bachelor-pad design aesthetic of futuristic black plastic ridges and fake wood veneer. The Atari console was also heavy and, unlike our Binatone *Pong* machine, it felt serious and powerful. All of this meant full arousal before even plugging in a game cartridge, an act that in itself made one feel like an employee on a starship (though admittedly, quite a low-level employee on quite a stupid and pointless starship).

Ever since playing *Space Invaders* on Tom's Atari the previous year, I seldom missed an opportunity to suggest to my parents that we should get one, too, though I knew it was one of the longest of long shots. Dad already thought we spent too much time in front of the TV, so why would he invest in a device that would keep us away from books and nature even longer?

One evening, when he was in a good mood, I told him that video games improved hand–eye coordination and were an important part of helping young people adjust to a machine-based future. He chuckled and put his hand on my shoulder. 'Well, I dare say you might be right, old boy.' 'Oh shit,' I thought, 'I think the motherfucker might be cracking.' (NOTE: That's a modern translation of my 13-year-old thoughts.)

Sure enough, that December Dad returned from another trip to America carrying a mysterious package, and on Christmas Day I found myself tearing away a corner of wrapping paper to reveal the Atari logo on the box of the 2600 with not only the *Combat* game cartridge included, but also my beloved *Space Invaders*. 'But it's not just for you, Adam. You make sure Clare and David get to play it, too,' commanded Dad.

'Of course, sure, whatever! Thanks, Dad! Thanks, Mum! This is the Best Day of My Life!'

Any anxieties Dad might have had about turning his children into dead-eyed video-game junkies were offset by the satisfaction he felt at having bought the console in the US, where it was about half the price it was in the UK. But the Best Day of My Life took a knock when I tried to plug it in.

In the days before travelling with a wide selection of electrical devices became commonplace, Dad had forgotten about the voltage difference between the US and the UK. The disappointment I felt was an entirely new kind of disappointment: a deep existential melancholy with some hopelessness mixed in. Dad got angry; partly with me for not dealing with the situation more stoically, but mainly with himself for going against his instincts and revealing himself as a voltage moron.

Much as he probably would have liked to have thrown the American Atari in a skip and have my memory wiped, Dad knew this was a genie that couldn't be squeezed back in the bottle. When the shops opened again on Boxing Day he went out first thing in the morning and spent all the money he'd saved with his transatlantic bargain on a power transformer the size of a shoebox, which would enable us to switch on the console. That's when we discovered that the American Atari wouldn't work on a British TV set. So much for the special relationship.

When I put in the *Space Invaders* cartridge and turned on the machine I could hear the sounds of the game, but the picture was just a scrolling Venetian blind of oranges and blacks. I sat there for hours vainly twiddling the TV's tuning knob, praying to God that the mess of lines would suddenly resolve into a coherent picture so I could start shooting down invaders, but apparently God did not consider this request a high priority.

Knowing that I would probably become a danger to myself and others if the situation was left unresolved, Dad eventually buried the pain of all the money he'd wasted and went down to WH Smith's at the end of the road where he bought a British Atari 2600 and the Best Day of My Life began again.

If anything the painful struggles I had bravely endured up to that point – the heartbreak of first the voltage problem, then the NTSC/PAL débâcle – just intensified the joy when our TV screen was finally filled with blocky yellow crab-like invaders and the harsh 8-bit sound of their inexorable marching reverberated around the room.

I suppose one obvious punchline to this particular story of parental love conflicted by technology would be for me to tell you that I got bored of the Atari after just a couple of weeks, but I didn't. Our relationship was deep, loving and lasted many, many months.

One of Dad's concerns was that video games would destroy our imaginations, but looking back, it's clear the opposite was true. Without a reasonably serviceable imagination, you wouldn't get more than a few minutes of gameplay out of the Atari before being driven mad by how basic the technology was.

The artwork on the Atari game packages resembled posters for blockbuster movies with lushly realistic paintings of men in action-packed situations (and the occasional woman running away from something), but the gulf between the artwork and the actual gameplay was comically vast. On the package for a game called *Outlaw*, for example, a couple of bearded cowboy desperados fired six-shooters in a rocky canyon at sundown as a covered wagon pulled by a team of stallions hurtled by. What you actually saw when you played the game, however, was a rectangle with some blocky shapes within it to represent two cowboys and a cactus. If your blocky bullet hit a blocky cowboy in the blocks, he would sit down suddenly with a disheartened electronic fart. It was basic but fun, and on a couple of memorably joyful occasions even Dad sat down to play a few games, claiming that it appealed to his love of all things Wild West.

No less primitive than *Outlaw*, at least graphically speaking, was a game called *Adventure*, in which the player was represented by a single square block that could be moved around the screen to explore a series of 'rooms', 'dungeons' and 'mazes' – in other words, rectangles of various colours, some containing more blocks than others. The object of *Adventure* was to locate a 'chalice' and bring it back to your 'castle'. Now and then blocky 'dragons' that looked like ducks would appear and move with alarming speed towards your block in order to eat you.

Most of the time the game was completely silent, with no

music and only minimal sound effects, contributing to a state of tense hypnotic absorption during gameplay. *Adventure* was my introduction to the experience of navigating a virtual space, only a small part of which was visible on the TV screen, and the slow process of mapping and mastering that phantom universe occupied my thoughts by day and my dreams by night.

RAMBLE

Last Christmas I bought a Nintendo Switch for my own children and gave them the same speech my dad gave me: 'This is for ALL of you to share!' Then I downloaded an Atari 2600 emulator, anticipating with relish the satisfying circularity of us all sat round playing *Outlaw* together. But the children found the sounds so maddeningly horrible that within a couple of minutes I was once again left blasting away on my own, while they went outside to dance, laugh and read to each other.

The Timeshifter

The other technological game-changer for me back in 1982 was also introduced by my dad and ended up playing a significant part in my friendship with Joe Cornish and our eventual entry into the world of DIY television in the Nineties.

One of the perks of Dad's job at the *Telegraph* was that from time to time he was sent free shit in the hope that he might mention the shit in one of his travel columns. One day he came back from the office with some state-of-the-art, solid-gold shit: the Sharp VC-2300H portable VHS video recorder plus XC-30 colour video camera.

Domestic video cassette recorders (or VCRs for younger readers) were only just beginning to become affordable at the time, with just a handful of video rental stores popping up in London's wealthier neighbourhoods before becoming commonplace towards the end of the Eighties. Video cameras were even more rare, and outside the TV and film industries the only places you might find them were educational and scientific establishments and the bat caves of techy millionaires.

The gear Dad had been lent comprised a VCR about the size and weight of a modern domestic printer and a camera unit that had to be attached to the recorder by a thick rubber cable. All this was 'portable' to the extent that it was physically possible to hold the camera and carry the recorder at the same time, but if you wanted to use the thing outside it meant attaching a heavy battery that would enable you to record for about 30 minutes, assuming your back hadn't given out by then.

Dad used the camera to film my last Sports Day at boarding school and I still have the desaturated VHS footage of me giving it one last spurt of effort at the end of the 800-metre race before coming in dead last. My mum can be heard chuckling off camera as Dad says sympathetically, 'Well, the idea was a good one.'

It wasn't until I started hanging out with Joe a couple of years later that I began to use the camera for anything more ambitious than the odd family home movie. Before then I was far more excited about using the VCR to tape programmes off the TV so I could watch them more than once – a concept that at the time was entirely novel, almost magical. I had to think carefully about what I would actually record, as we'd been supplied with only three 60-minute VHS tapes, and new ones were expensive and hard to come by.

The first programme I taped was *Top of the Pops* on 22 July 1982. The show included the video for 'Driving in My Car' by

Madness as well as The Stranglers miming to 'Strange Little Girl' and, most exciting in terms of rewatchability, the video for a song that ticked the same boxes that Kraftwerk's 'The Model' had a few months before: electronic; bored vocal; German. However, 'Da Da Da', a one-hit wonder by a band called Trio, made 'The Model' sound lush and overproduced by comparison.

'Da Da Da' was little more than a beat from a Casio VL-Tone pocket electronic keyboard on which the lead singer, a lugubrious skinhead in white T-shirt and suit jacket, played a five-note sequence during the chorus and sang in German: *'Da da da, Ich lieb' dich nicht, du liebst mich nicht'* or 'I don't love you, you don't love me'. While the football-chant choruses of 'Come On Eileen' were filling dance floors across the UK, it was Trio that set my pulse racing and afforded me that wonderful punk epiphany that making intriguing music might not be the sole preserve of trained or even talented musicians.

My next adventure with the VCR was figuring out how to use the timer record function and convincing Dad that if he got hold of some longer videotapes I could record some war documentaries and boring opera shite for him to watch of an evening. Thereafter the highlight of my week became the day that I'd get back from school to find Mum had bought the new *TV* and *Radio Times*. I'd sit at the kitchen table with a hefty slice of Battenberg and one of Dad's yellow highlighters (being careful to leave the top off and not put it back where I found it when I was finished) and scan the listings for anything interesting being shown past my bedtime that I could tape and watch at the weekend.

Most of what I taped was worthless crap that I'd fast-forward through on the lookout for gore, robots or boobs, but there were a few films that I ended up watching many times, even going so far as to break off the plastic tabs on the spine of the video cassette to prevent them being accidentally recorded over.

Rollercoaster was a thriller about a theme-park safety inspector on the trail of an extortionist blowing up rides with radio-controlled devices. It had everything: rollercoasters, which I adored and associated with our trips to America; radio-controlled devices and violent deaths, which all fine young men find exciting; George Segal, who seemed nice and funny; Timothy Bottoms, whose surname was 'Bottoms', and in one scene, which took place at the opening of a new theme park, a peculiar band playing two songs that I liked. Over a decade later I realised the band was Sparks and when I found the album that contained the songs they played in *Rollercoaster* (1976's *Big Beat*), the sense of closure and satisfaction was worryingly profound.

Another film that achieved protected VHS tape status that year also had a baldly descriptive title. *Alligator* was about an alligator that gets flushed down a toilet as a baby alligator, then starts munching sewage workers once it's grown into a giant alligator. Though entirely tame by modern standards, it was one of the gorier films I'd seen up to that point and, looking back, I can see it was a crucial part of my training for the day I would watch *Alien*. To that extent it was probably about as useful as jogging to a sweet shop to prepare for a marathon (though not, of course, for a Snickers – *pffrrrt*), but the fact that I wasn't scared by *Alligator* made me feel that I could probably deal with some pretty hardcore cinematic mayhem.

I experienced a subtler but far more enduring form of mind-mangling when I taped a film being shown late one night on BBC Two called *Dark Star*. It was a piece of low-budget sci-fi about a small group of hippy astronaut men touring the galaxy in a claustrophobic ship in order to blow up unstable planets. They did this using artificially intelligent bombs that chatted happily to the crew before being deployed.

I expected science-fiction films to feature clean-cut, straightforwardly heroic leading men, but *Dark Star* had five hairy weirdos (one in cryogenic stasis following a fatal seat malfunction), and none of them was especially heroic or even very likeable. The film also had an unusual sense of humour, and to the hypothetical question, 'What would it really be like to live and work on a spaceship?' *Dark Star*'s answer was, 'It would be boring and crap.' According to some people I showed it to over the years, the same could be said of the film itself – but I thought it was funny and full of moments that stuck with me for years.

One of the best things about *Dark Star* was John Carpenter's electronic score, which did a great job of transporting me beyond the cheap homemade sets to somewhere appropriately strange and science fiction-ish. There were also other bits of music in the film that were entertainingly inappropriate: easy listening, some surf rock and, best of all, the theme tune: a country song specially written for the film called 'Benson, Arizona', which is still in my list of Songs That Make Me Struggle Not to Cry.

RAMBLE

SONGS THAT MAKE ME STRUGGLE NOT TO CRY
These aren't sad songs so much as songs that have something in them that turns my sentimentality tap on full.

'S.O.S.'
– ABBA

Unrequited love is dreary and depressing for all concerned, but this makes it sound like standing on top of a mountain as fireworks go off while the meaning of life is revealed (and the meaning of life turns out not to be a disappointment).

'DANCE THE NIGHT AWAY'
– THE MAVERICKS

I think people assume I'm being ironic about this or suggesting it would make me cry because it's so crap, but no, it's the opposite. I think it's so good, so brilliantly produced and defiantly uplifting that it makes me weepy. No need to tweet how disappointed you are by my poor taste – it won't make me like it any less.

'I'M NOT THE MAN I USED TO BE'
– FINE YOUNG CANNIBALS

Funky drummer breakbeat + melancholy chords + sense of regret = Buckles struggling not to cry.

'LILAC WINE'
– NINA SIMONE or JEFF BUCKLEY

Both versions do the job.

'ONE DAY I'LL FLY AWAY'
– RANDY CRAWFORD

On occasions when I've made a mess of something in my life, I like songs that indulge my feelings of self-pity and promote the fantasy that I might just escape somehow, maybe by assuming a new identity and plying an honest trade in a small rural community in New Zealand or somewhere like that. By the end of the song I've usually thought through all the practical problems with the New Zealand plan and I try to start clearing up the mess.

'DISNEY GIRLS'
– THE BEACH BOYS

The Beach Boys are celebrated for their excellent goofy surf pop and their complex, hallucinatory evocations of mental turmoil, but they also had a good line in corny and sentimental stuff like 'Disney Girls'. It's a song about that feeling of being overwhelmed by modern life and yearning for a simpler, happier, more innocent time, while acknowledging that those good old days may never have existed. 'Reality, it's not for me,' admits the author.

'GRACELAND'
– PAUL SIMON

When the *Graceland* album came out in 1986, I thought it sounded like a boring old white bloke trying too hard to look more 'authentic' by hanging out with ethnic musicians. Then a few years later I went on a trip where for some reason it was the only tape I had with me and it got under my skin. Now the 'losing love is like a window in your heart' bit in the song 'Graceland' does me in every time.

'SUFFERING JUKEBOX'
– SILVER JEWS

Give it a listen and read about the man who made it and if you don't find it moving, well, then I guess you're just the most evil, cold-hearted person in the world.
Or maybe it's just not your sort of thing.

> ### 'BENSON, ARIZONA'
> #### – JOHN YAGER
> Missing people is easy. Connecting with them is harder, as anyone who has ever made an unsatisfactory call home from a business trip will attest. But if you were working in outer space, you wouldn't even be able to call home and missing them would be even sweeter and even sadder. Ah, the simplicity of outer space!

The character I liked best in *Dark Star* was the memorably named Sergeant Pinback, played by Dan O'Bannon (who also co-wrote the movie). Pinback's makes video diaries detailing his efforts to get along with the rest of the crew, decades before the concept of video diaries became familiar via TV reality shows and internet vlogs. Pinback's responsibilities include looking after an alien life form that he found on a foreign planet and brought aboard the ship as a pet. The alien is clearly an inflatable beach ball that's been painted red with black and yellow spots and has two clawed feet obviously being worn as gloves by one of the film crew, but with basic puppetry and some amusing burbly sound effects, it comes to life completely, especially in a confrontation between Pinback and the mischievous alien that plays out in a lift shaft, an idea O'Bannon hung on to for *Alien* years later, when he wrote the screenplay.

The climax of *Dark Star* is a philosophical debate between one of the artificially intelligent bombs and crew member Lieutenant Doolittle. After sustaining damage in a meteor shower, the bomb is unable to detach itself from the ship but is determined to detonate regardless as it received an order to do so. In an effort to convince it otherwise, Doolittle engages the bomb in a discussion about the difficulty of knowing for certain whether anything is real. Those kinds of ideas were new to me when I first saw *Dark Star*, so I felt I was watching something clever and deep rather than just eavesdropping on a couple of students who have recently discovered cannabis.

Later, when I learned about the concept of mutually assured destruction supposedly acting as a deterrent to nuclear war, it reminded me of Doolittle 'psyching out' the bomb and I couldn't quite believe that the safety of the world relied on a similarly dopey exercise in philosophical doublethink.

It Started with a Kiss

Somehow I made it through the first ten years of my life without absorbing any accurate information about sex whatsoever. Sure, I knew it was dirty, shameful and wrong, but beyond that, I was clueless.

I was first made aware of the concept of sexual intercourse when, for a short while aged around seven, I formed an odd friendship with a boy at school who, like me, was chubby, smutty and full of shame. I went round to his house one day and he revealed to me that his dad had stashed a variety of pornographic magazines under the carpet in the loft. We got some cakes and looked at the pictures. It wasn't long before our societal programming kicked in and we started to feel guilty, but rather than being put off, we doubled down. 'We like cakes and sex magazines!' we declared. 'We're SUPERPIGS!'

After a couple of these sessions, I decided I was no longer comfortable identifying as a Superpig and that was the last time I looked at pornography while eating cakes, at least with another person in the room.

Because my parents seemed too nice to ever do the kinds of things I'd seen in the carpet porn, I decided that sexual intercourse was not necessary for human reproduction. My theory was that women simply became pregnant from time to time, and if they wanted to have a baby, they just let it carry on growing until it popped out. If being pregnant wasn't convenient, they could take a pill and the foetus would evaporate, like a headache. As far as sex was concerned, that was something extra you could do if you were a pervert or a Superpig, but there was no way my mummy and daddy would ever do anything like that.

For a while my ground-breaking reproductive notions went unchallenged. Then one day, in one of my first proper biology lessons, the teacher asked if anyone knew which animals were able to reproduce asexually. Enjoying the unusual sensation of having the answer to a teacher's question, I stuck my hand up and began to outline my Spontaneous Pregnancy Theory. There was a strong ripple of laughter from my fellow students, but I didn't mind. In fact, I was looking forward to seeing the gigglers humiliated when they discovered that, actually, young Buckles was correct: of course humans don't need to have sex to reproduce; that would mean the willy of every single child's daddy had gone in and out of their mummy's fanny until seeds came out, which would be completely appalling. You can imagine my surprise and disappointment when it turned out the teacher was a Spontaneous Pregnancy Theory denier.

To his credit, he handled it nicely and didn't laugh in my face, but he made it clear that, contrary to my position, every human baby ever born had been the result of sexual intercourse. As one last desperate face-saving measure, I put up my hand again and said, 'Well, not EVERY baby ...'

'Yes,' said the teacher, 'every single baby.'

'Not Jesus,' I said as the bell went.

Once in a while my unfamiliarity with both birds and bees was mildly useful. Daniel Bradford, a boy from the year above who was always on the look-out for clever ways to humiliate people, approached me one day outside the dining room and showed me his hand, which he held in a claw shape as if it had been paralysed. He pointed to the clawed hand and said, 'Wanker's cramp. D'you get it?' The joke was that he was demonstrating how a hand might look after excessive mastur- bation, and I was supposed to say, 'Oh yeah, I get it,' to which he would then reply, 'Eurgh! You're sick! You get wanker's cramp!' Unfortunately for Daniel Bradford, I didn't under- stand a single word he was saying and he had to repeat the set-up three more times before I said, 'No, sorry, I don't get it,' at which point he huffed off in medium dudgeon.

More often, however, my lack of accurate sex info led to deep anxiety. One night as I lay asleep in my room I had a dream that featured June Whitfield from *Terry and June*, a British sitcom about suburban married life that I would some- times watch when I was out of options. In the dream, June (who must have been nearly 60 at the time) was straddling me as I lay in her garden. Terry was out or busy inside the house, I suppose. She raised her skirts as she lowered herself and the next thing I knew I was awake and ejaculating into the folds of my pyjama bottoms.

Completely freaked out, I cleaned up, stuffed the soiled PJ bottoms under the bed, put on a fresh pair and tried unsuc- cessfully to get back to sleep. No one had warned me about nocturnal emissions and I now believed I was an out-of- control little sex pervert with granny issues. The next morning at breakfast I prodded at the moat of Golden Syrup around my Ready Brek, nauseated with shame and anxiety. 'It Started with a Kiss' by Hot Chocolate was playing on the radio and every time I heard the song over the next few weeks it served as a powerful reminder that I was a sick freak.

Over the summer I had watched *Damien: Omen II* at Tom's house, in which the adolescent spawn of Satan finally comes to terms with his true identity when he checks his scalp in a bathroom mirror and finds 666: the tattoo of the beast. After another couple of night-time 'ejaculaccidents', I went into the bathroom, locked the door and conducted a thorough search of my scalp. I didn't find any beast tattoos, but that didn't stop the waves of guilt that would engulf me several times a day and the worry that I could never have a normal life, because I never knew when and where I might suddenly start exploding with jizz.

Science-fiction writer Arthur C. Clarke came to talk at Westminster Under School one afternoon. Someone asked if he believed in aliens and Clarke replied that there are many more stars in the sky than there are grains of sand on all the beaches of the world, so it's unlikely that we're alone in the universe, but I believed I was. You thought I was going to say that Arthur C. Clarke brought me to spontaneous orgasm, didn't you? I wasn't that far gone. Jean-Luc Picard? That's another story.

A few weeks later a boy in my class made a joke about 'wet dreams', which as usual I didn't understand. When he explained and I realised I wasn't the only little sex pervert in the world, it was the most wonderful and intense feeling of relief I had ever experienced. Apart from that time with June, of course.

Is Everything Going to Be All Right?

When it comes to existential threats these days, we're spoilt for choice, with everything from environmental catastrophe to sinister clown politicians encouraging us to compete for who can abandon most hope, but when I was 13 the prospects for our extinction seemed less varied and more imminent.

The characterisation of the Eighties as a gaudy pink neon festival of big-haired, good-time materialism was belied by a deeper truth, which was that many people of my generation were just waiting helplessly for a nuclear bomb to drop and for life to turn into the bleakest of horror films.

One drawing I did in 1983 that I was particularly pleased

with was of a nuclear mushroom cloud copied from an encyclopaedia. I smudged the pencil the make it look more realistic and at the base of the cloud I wrote the word 'NO'. Sure, it was angry, hard-hitting work, but I guess that's just the kind of artist I am. I just couldn't carry on drawing spaceships in the face of a possible nuclear war.

'There won't be a nuclear war,' counselled my mum, and though her confidence kept my fear at bay, the TV was full of programmes that brought it rushing back.

Nuclear war was such a realistic prospect that the British Government had hired the animation company responsible for a creepy children's show called *Crystal Tipps and Alistair* to create a series of EVEN CREEPIER public information films called *Protect and Survive*, designed to help people prepare if a nuclear attack was imminent. Extracts from the *Protect and Survive* films and booklets were leaked to the British media and turned up later in one of the TV shows I wish I'd never stumbled across.

A Guide to Armageddon, broadcast in July 1982 as part of the BBC's popular science 'strand' *Q.E.D.*, included hair-frazzling, meat-cooking, panic-inducing demonstrations of what would happen if a nuclear bomb fell on London. The programme featured a young couple doing their best to follow the handy hints in the *Protect and Survive* booklets but the implication (dramatised a few years later in Raymond Briggs's ultra-bleak animated film *When the Wind Blows*, complete with 'bombastic' Eighties Bowie soundtrack song) was that preparations such as painting windows white and making a shelter from a door and some mattresses were so pitifully ineffectual you'd be better off with instant vaporisation.

I got the impression from Mum's *Daily Mail* that worrying about this sort of stuff was the sole preserve of the lesbians and hippies protesting at RAF Greenham Common, but being confronted with it all on a BBC science programme suggested otherwise. And that was before *The Day After*.

A big-budget American TV movie, *The Day After* imagined what would happen in the event of a nuclear strike on the US. SPOILER ALERT: it would be bad. It focused on a group of people from Kansas (including Steve Guttenberg, later to star as Sergeant Mahoney in the more upbeat *Police Academy*), who, in the run-up to the strike, carry on with their lives hoping the worst won't happen. When the worst happens, loads of people die quickly, then the 'survivors' die slowly. Even Steve Guttenberg has the cheeky smile melted off his face.

I didn't plan to see *The Day After* when ITV showed it one Saturday night a few weeks before Christmas in 1983 (festive fun for all the family!), but I couldn't resist checking on it from time to time, looking at it for a few minutes before switching over again when my heart started pounding too hard (much the same way I check Twitter nowadays). By the time the BBC showed their own British nuclear disaster movie, *Threads*, in 1984, I'd learned my lesson and made sure I was nowhere near a television.

One of the things that made *The Day After* so chilling was that it was well made and didn't deliver the usual doses of Hollywood Stupidity Serum that would normally enable audiences to find horror and disaster highly entertaining. Instead, moments of special-FX-heavy destruction were juxtaposed with scenes that felt depressingly real: military men in bunkers, obediently following protocol.

Unlike a lot of children who saw *The Day After*, I never actually had bad dreams. Instead, the nightmare of nuclear Armageddon suffused my waking life, adding to each happy moment the addendum: 'but – we're all going to die horribly, probably quite soon'. My parents continued to brush off my concerns, but the banal fact of expensive nuclear weapons, buttons, bunkers and army men with laminated firing codes in ring binders ensured that I was never able to relax completely.

BOWIE ANNUAL

In my last term at boarding school I won the art prize, which was a book token. I used it to buy David Bowie: An Illustrated Record by Charles Shaar Murray and Roy Carr, and for the next few years this became the roadmap for my journey through Bowieopolis and its sprawling suburbs.

The book was the size of a vinyl LP and filled with critiques of all Bowie's musical output up to 1981 as well as great illustrations, photographs and full-sized colour reproductions of all Bowie's album sleeves up to *Scary Monsters*, but it was badly bound and fell apart after only a few months. That gave me the opportunity to stick my favourite record-cover images and other full-page Bowie pics on my wall at home, and then later in my study at school.

Bowie always looked so cool and strange that I thought having his face on my wall might confer those same qualities on me, but I probably fancied him, too, especially in pictures from the late Seventies, though I didn't yet appreciate that what I was attracted to was the look of someone who had made himself ill by taking more than the recommended daily amount of cocaine.

I was also unaware that Bowie had once been what certain newspapers liked to call 'a gender-bender', a phrase that was tossed about both willy and nilly after Boy George first appeared on *Top of the Pops* in September 1982. Between wet dreams of old ladies and not being sure if Boy George was a boy or a girl (or something else entirely), I had enough on my sexy plate without worrying about Bowie's 'zexuality'. To me, the man who made

Hunky Dory, *Ziggy Stardust* and *Scary Monsters* was straightforwardly wholesome, and maybe a psychoanalyst (albeit one who's only recently started in the profession) would suggest Bowie was a surrogate parent figure for me after all that boarding-school separation trauma. I just know that whenever I heard 'Kooks' or the vertiginous chord progressions of 'Life on Mars', it was more like being wrapped in a blanket than getting rogered by an alien.

Somehow I had convinced a friend at school not only to lend me their Walkman, but to make a copy of *Hunky Dory* on one side of a TDK D-C90 with *Scary Monsters* on the other (though it cut off the last few seconds of 'It's No Game (No.2)' – not a problem, as it's just wobbly clunking noises). Listening to *Hunky Dory* on stereo headphones for the first time was like suddenly being able to taste and smell again after a bad cold, especially a minute into the track 'Quicksand' when acoustic guitars began gently duelling from the left and right channels. I told my mum to listen and she, too, was impressed by this adventure across the stereo spectrum. 'But what's he singing about?' asked Mum.

I didn't know the lyrics of 'Quicksand' were derived from the 24-year-old Bowie's flirtations with the writings of occultist Aleister Crowley, nihilistic Nietzschean philosophy, and a load of other possibly unsavoury cobblers. I assumed that lines like '*Don't believe in yourself*' and '*Knowledge comes with death's release*' were just entertainingly odd Bowie bumper-sticker phrases that didn't detract from the overall loveliness and optimism of the music.

As for 'Ashes to Ashes' from *Scary Monsters*, I didn't have a clue what he was bollocking on about – '*Do you remember a gather spin, he search another zone?*' – and I couldn't even tell what instruments were being used to create the song's alien mood buffet. All I knew was that two minutes in, when it got to the '*I never done good things, / I never done bad things*' section, my emotional fuel rods would start to jump about uncontrollably and I felt transcendent.

An Illustrated Record also included overviews of music on which Bowie had collaborated, and I was particularly intrigued by the black-and-white image on the cover of an LP by someone called Lou Reed. I did a painting of it and wrote on the bottom '*Lou Reed Vicious*'. Dad came into my room and admired my work. 'It's a good picture,' said Dad, 'of a very creepy-looking man. What does "Lou Reed Vicious" mean?'

'He's called Lou Reed and one of his songs is called "Vicious",' I explained.

'Hmmm. All very sinister,' replied Pa as he walked out.

The next time I was at WH Smith's I flicked through the vinyl racks, found a copy of *Transformer* and studied the back cover for the first time. I liked the look of the fellow in the white T-shirt, tipping his leather cap to the long-legged lady on the left of the image, although it looked as if he had a baguette in his pocket, which I found confusing. Surely the baguette would get all linty and his pocket would be full of crumbs?

RAMBLE

I'm pretending to be naïve here, of course. I always supposed the man had an unusually large willy, but having just searched for more information about the *Transformer* back cover, I now know Big Willy Man was Lou Reed's former road manager and that the bulge in his jeans was actually a banana wrapped in a sock, making my linty baguette joke rather redundant.

The cassette of *Transformer* was only £1.99 so I decided to take a chance. I handed over a gift token and 10 minutes later I borrowed my dad's tape player, settled down at my desk with my drawing stuff in the room I shared with my sister and heard *Transformer* for the first time.

As far as I was concerned this was an album I had plucked from obscurity, generously taking time out from my busy TV, cake and biscuit schedule to give it a try. It's not a hard album to like, but I thought myself very sophisticated for instantly appreciating 'Walk on the Wild Side', despite a jazzy sound that I associated with old people's music and lyrics that hinted at something adult and transgressive, though I didn't really understand what. I assumed that '*giving head*' probably meant kissing with tongues, but just, like, really deep in someone's head.

It only took a few listens before I liked every song on *Transformer* and found them warm and comforting, especially 'Perfect Day' and, my favourite, 'Satellite of Love', on which I fancied I could hear Bowie's yelpy voice in the background, making me like it all the more. Even rockier tracks like 'I'm So Free' and 'Vicious' sounded to me like the rest of the album: bathed in golden light and love.

Twenty years later I would sing *Transformer*'s opening song 'Make Up' to get my baby son to sleep. I briefly considered changing some of the lyrics to suit his gender but decided that he probably wouldn't be too badly confused by being told he was '*a slick little girl*'. So far, he seems anxiety free in that particular department.

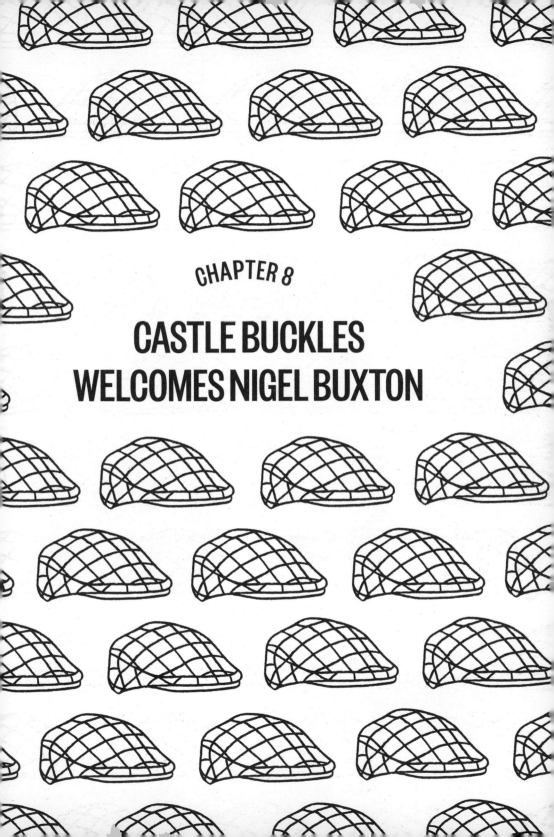

CHAPTER 8

CASTLE BUCKLES
WELCOMES NIGEL BUXTON

I n preparation for Dad's arrival at Castle Buckles, I moved all my stuff out of the flat where I had my studio and set up a new workspace in one of the adjoining barns. The physical effort this entailed was nothing compared to the mental trauma of sorting through a lifetime of accumulated crap. I started to make trips with carloads of crap to charity shops and the recycling dump, and each time I marvelled at how easy it was to part with that crap after so many years of careful hoarding. Then Dad's crap arrived.

It turned up in Norfolk a week before he did, and it filled one medium-sized farm shed. I knew he was planning to finish writing his autobiography while he was with us, so I made it my priority to turn the living-room space in the flat into a study where he could work. With his permission I sanded down and re-varnished the beaten-up writing desk he'd 'liberated' 30 years earlier from his office at the *Telegraph*, I put up shelves and filled them with his books and hung up his old pictures. 'I'm an amazing son,' I thought.

He's going to love this and we're going to have a moving and cathartic time together.

Once the flat was in order, I went back into the shed and continued searching through the rest of Dad's boxes, looking out for anything else he might need when he arrived. But unless he was planning on reading back letters from old girlfriends, checking menus from every restaurant he'd ever visited or taking one last look at his expenses claims, there was nothing there that anyone would ever be needing again.

It crossed my mind that in the course of looking through all this stuff I might come across evidence of outrageous secrets or scandals from Dad's life that would redefine our relationship, but no. The letters were polite, the people in the photographs were fully clothed and everything seemed boringly above board. Instead, it was the more mundane souvenirs of Dad's life that proved the most unsettling.

A couple of boxes contained bulging manilla envelopes into which Dad had begun to sort documents and souvenirs he considered particularly significant. I picked out one labelled 'FINANCIAL CRISIS' and found it stuffed with letters to bank managers, school bursars and friends. It told the story of Dad's struggles to stay afloat throughout the Eighties and on into the Nineties as school fees sank him deeper into debt. It was some dank *Death of a Salesman* shit.

I pulled out a letter from the end of the Eighties explaining that, due to modernisation at the *Sunday Telegraph*, my dad was to be let go. Looking at the date, I recalled that I'd been with Joe Cornish and Louis Theroux doing David Bowie impressions in New York at the time, having flown over on a ticket Dad wangled with his travel-editor connections. I'd phoned home one evening and he'd told me the news. 'I'm afraid it's the end of an era, old boy,' he'd said, 'so make the most of it out there.'

Then a letter from a few years later when I would have been at art school. Dad was still trying anything he could to keep my brother David at Haileybury, and he and Mum were sleeping in separate rooms, barely speaking to each other. The letter was from his former employers at the *Telegraph*, refusing to wipe out a debt from a previous loan. I think if I got a similar letter, I'd burn it, but Dad had kept it safe.

22nd February 1991

Dear Nigel,
I have read your fairly chilling letter of 20th February.

When I organised an ex gratia payment of £8,200 upon your retirement in May two years ago, there were those who counselled that this be used to diminish your debt to the company. I resisted them, and it would seem I was wrong to do so.

The arguments that you deploy about not being very well paid, etc., were the arguments that you put to the previous management in the letter you sent to [Mr Madeupname] seeking the loan. Since the loan was forthcoming, it could be said that it worked once; but I think it a bit optimistic to expect that it can be rehearsed again to wipe out the debt, most particularly in the light of the very considerable enhancements that were made to your salary in the years that you served the Sunday Telegraph under new management.

Looking at the figures you quote in your letter, I think a bank manager would say that you are seeking to achieve a lifestyle which is beyond your means. That you are paying for private education is laudable in so far as we all wish to do the best by our children, but frankly it would seem folly looking at your figures.

To that extent, you are asking the Daily Telegraph to expunge the debt currently standing at £14,500 in order to maintain a standard of living which you cannot afford.

I do believe that the company has behaved honourably and generously towards you since this loan was first advanced, and this was extended to what amounted as a gift upon your retirement.

While I sympathise greatly with your dire financial position, I cannot recommend to the Telegraph that they write off debt for a loan which was extended in good faith and on very favourable terms.

Yours sincerely,
Jimmy Namachangé, Executive Editor

Further down the stack of correspondence were copies of letters Dad had sent to wealthy friends and acquaintances asking if they might lend him some money and outlining elaborate schemes for repaying them. One of the people he had written to in 1991 was David Cornwell, a friend from his university days at Oxford, better known as the spy thriller author John le Carré.

Hardback copies of all Le Carré's novels had made the journey to Norfolk along with all of Dad's other books, and just the day before I had spent the afternoon arranging them on the shelves for him beside everything ever written by Winston Churchill, Patrick O'Brian and John Buchan. Apart from the odd Western, the only TV show I ever remember my dad liking when we were young was the 1982 adaptation of Le Carré's *Smiley's People*, starring old Ben Kenobi himself, Sir Alec Guinness. That Dad was able to call Le Carré a friend was a source of tremendous pride to him, and to unbalance that friendship with a request to borrow £40,000 surely scooped him out. The letter begins:

> *At the age of almost 67, I am ashamed to be writing to you like this. I know well enough that I have no right whatever to be asking for your help, but I have honestly, and lately desperately, tried every other conceivable way of raising the very large amount of money that I want, and so far none has worked. Now, I have run out of time and cannot think even of any other hope.*

It was a long letter, underneath which Dad had filed Le Carré's reply – a kind, well-worded refusal. I winced and stuffed the envelopes back in the box where I'd found them.

* * *

When I was little I thought Dad was just the absolute best guy around: clever, handsome, funny and successful. I loved travelling with him and seeing him charm hotel managers, flight attendants and heads of tourism who fell over themselves to do his bidding. In those days, no problem was too big for Dad to solve and no opportunity to make our lives more exciting was missed.

Sure, he could go too far sometimes. We once stayed at a resort in Barbados that Dad was writing about for his travel column, and one evening we were taken to an open-air reggae concert by a local PR person. I'm fairly certain it was Mum and Dad's first open-air reggae concert and it made a considerable impression on six-year-old Buckles. I wish I could report that it was the night my passion for music was awakened, but I was just confused by how different we looked to all the locals and how gut-quakingly loud the music was. Seeing the look of alarm on his young son's face, Dad leaned close to the PR person and asked in a loud, posh voice if the concert could be turned down. The PR person laughed before realising my dad was serious. Even at six, I had a sense that this was not cool. (I just emailed my mum to fact-check this recollection and she confirms, it was not cool.)

Once I was at boarding school, I started to get depressed whenever I knew Dad had to travel. I worried he might never come back. One of many low points during my first term as a boarder was when Mum and Dad came to pick me up for a 'leave out' (one of two weekends a term when you could stay out overnight), only for us to drive to Heathrow, where Dad had to catch a flight to New York.

'Arthur's Theme (Best That You Can Do)' by Christopher Cross was playing on the radio as we approached the terminal and the chorus '*When you get caught between the moon and New York City …*' – which may just have been a euphemism for severe delays – struck me instead as a sign that Dad's plane was going to crash. I knew it wasn't a rational thought so I stayed quiet, but I couldn't shake it. As I did my best not to cry, Dad reached back from the front passenger seat, found my hand and gave it a series of soft squeezes. Thereafter Dad used the language of squeezes whenever he had anything emotional to communicate. As we got older and the emotions got more complicated, the squeezes became more expressive.

*   *   *

When Dad looked round the flat in Norfolk and took in the preparations we'd made for his arrival, I got a shoulder squeeze that, even in his weakened state, bordered on painful.

My brother had driven him up that day, and while Dad pottered about his new digs, Uncle Dave and I went out to unload the last of his possessions from the car. There, on the top of the pile of bags, cooking implements and bedding, was the black briefcase, still tightly locked.

'Where do you want this, Daddy?' I asked back in the flat.

'Somewhere safe, old boy. Somewhere out of the way,' he replied, but before I had the chance to quiz him further our dog Rosie boinged into the room, followed closely by my daughter, then aged six, whereupon I was treated to a rare sight: an unforced beaming smile from Dad.

RAMBLE

Pa was never much of a smiler, especially in photos. Even when he was young and handsome he was more likely to smoulder than smile. Perhaps that had something to do with my determination to smile in press photographs as much as possible. Though it's an unreasonable prejudice, I can't help thinking that when comedians smoulder it's vain. If you want people to think you're mysterious and sexy, be a rock star. But some people just don't suit a smile. When Dad smiled in photographs he usually ended up looking as though he was trying not to cry.

For the next couple of months the black briefcase sat on top of a tall filing cabinet in the corner of my office, as it had in Dad's study back in Earl's Court when I first encountered it 35 years previously. I gave it a shake before I stuck it up there and heard something small and heavy bumping about. It didn't sound like porn, but the urge to establish the exact contents of the black briefcase was quickly superseded by more prosaic concerns.

✳　✳　✳

Dad had been given between three and twelve months to live and it was agreed that there was little to be gained from any aggressive treatment for his cancer. Soon after he arrived in Norfolk, we met with the local GP, who explained that if he took his various pills when he was supposed to, Dad was unlikely to be in any significant pain and the main challenge would be keeping his energy levels up. To that end, a nutritionist at the Norfolk and Norwich Hospital encouraged him to load up on noodles, butter, cheese and other foods that for most people might be considered naughty.

That was bad news for me. I'm not fond of dairy products, and cheese makes me especially sad. In the months that followed I found cleaning up after toilet accidents infinitely preferable to preparing cheesy noodles, cheesy scrambled eggs, cheesy liver and other cheese nightmares for Dad, which, more often than not, he didn't even eat.

The nutritionist also arranged for a regular supply of smoothie supplement drinks and stressed the importance of consuming at least one a day. They came in a wide range of foul flavours and only ever acted on Dad as a powerful emetic. Between the smoothies and the cheese, one of us was gagging most of the time.

We got to know our local district nurses, who came over every week to check on Dad and drain the fluid building up in his lung bags. They used a plastic beaker with a tube and a needle on the end, and on their first visit the younger and more nervous-looking of the nurses got to push the needle into Dad's chest. She was rewarded with a hair-raising yelp that left her ashen. 'Have you done this before?' spluttered Dad.

'I'm sure she knows what she's doing,' I offered, smiling at the pale nurse, who replied, 'Actually, this is my first time with the chest drain.'

'Jeeesus Christ!' was Dad's response. It was hard to know where best to direct my sympathy.

RAMBLE

Dad had a tendency to make loud noises long before he got ill. When he would come and stay with us, I often heard him cry out at night. I'd check on him and he seemed fine, but the noises would persist. Anguished cries that suggested he was either dreaming about the war or bank managers.

During his last year, his weakened lungs made his voice thin and high, but his arsenal of howls, moans and groans expanded and was no longer confined to the night.

Whenever a new nurse or carer attended to him, they'd leave looking shaken after enduring what sounded like the cries of a *Game of Thrones* torture victim. However, Dad himself confirmed that despite the yowling, he wasn't in much pain. From then on, the nurses would sometimes refer to him as 'The Prince of Wails'.

By the end of summer 2015 Dad was averaging two or three minutes to make the trip down the six-metre corridor between the living room and the dead room – I mean bedroom. His legs, which just a few years before had popped with hiking muscles, were now papery and wasted, and as he shuffled along with his bathrobe, cane and tufts of white hair sticking up from his skinny head, he looked like Yoda but pale pink and with all the Force used up.

For most of the time that Dad was living with us I was working on another failed pilot. It was one that got quite close to becoming an actual TV show, so the pressure was on to deliver several scripts. In practice, that meant I'd spend several hours a day staring at my computer, not writing scripts and feeling that I ought to be making the most of the time I had left with Dad.

Before he moved in, I'd imagined conversations filled with tender reminiscences, confessions and closure. 'Hey, Daddy, do you remember that holiday to Greece when I was 12 and Clare trod on a sea urchin and you told us we should pee in a bucket and pour it on her foot to make the spines come out?' We'd laugh with gratitude for all the good fortune we'd enjoyed over the years, then Dad would say, 'Come closer, Adam ...' I'd lean in and he'd say haltingly, 'I'm ... I'm sorry I didn't smile more,' or 'I wish we hadn't sent you away to boarding school. We did it for the best reasons, but I would have liked to have spent more time with you when you were still so young,' or 'I just wanted you to know that I thought the three-star review you got for *BUG* in Edinburgh that time was very unfair – they were reviewing it as if it were a one-man show when it was clearly a presentation of other people's work with some of your own very funny material mixed in, but people often find it hard to properly appreciate things that aren't easily categorised.'

Any version of that scenario, even one that wasn't entirely based on things I wanted to hear, was overwhelmed by the unsatisfactory routines and role reversals we'd unwittingly signed on for. Thing is, you're unlikely to strike up a heart-to-heart chat with your son for the first time while he's standing over you until you've finished your smoothie, getting annoyed when you don't take your pills or hoisting your nappy on before bed. Also you're more or less deaf. And you've got cancer. In the end we were just two uptight men who found it easier to be on our own.

One morning when script deadline stress levels were peaking, I went and looked in on Dad to ask what he wanted for breakfast. As soon as he mentioned eggs I made for the kitchen. I was keen to avoid the usual lengthy instructions about how best to prepare cheesy scrambled eggs so I could get the job done quickly and return to work on the failed pilot, but a second after I'd left the room he called after me, 'Wait! I haven't finished!'

There was no need to finish, I told him. I knew what he was after. 'Yes, but sometimes you say that and what you get me isn't quite right.'

'When have I got you something that wasn't quite right?' I asked, heart beginning to flutter with exasperation.

'Well, I don't keep a record. The other day, for example, you got me some scrambled eggs, but you put it on toast, which I didn't ask for.'

'I gave you toast because I thought you might like it, but I thought if you didn't like it you could just leave it, which you did. You know, Daddy, you asked me to tell you if there were ways to make things easier for me while you're here and this is one of them. I just need you to be concise, that's all.'

'You get very touchy,' he said.

It wasn't even 9 a.m. and already I was fizzing with nervous stress like Ray Liotta running errands at the end of *Goodfellas*, but with fewer amphetamines and more self-loathing.

I needed to calm down, so as soon as I'd delivered the eggs (without toast), I went out for a walk with Rosie and we had a therapeutic chat. 'I'm fucking this up, aren't I, Rosie?'

'Go on,' said Rosie.

'This is my last chance to spend some time with Daddy and get to know him a little better, and instead I'm just getting annoyed with him for not behaving exactly the way I want him to. And in the meantime I'm fucking up this pilot, too.'

'How does that make you feel?' said Rosie.

'Bad. I feel bad. I'm a bad person doing a bad job, but you know what? I'm going to try harder and make sure the time Dad has left is beautiful and cathartic and meaningful.'

'For him, or you?' said Rosie, a bit annoyingly.

My phone buzzed. An email from Dad. It said:

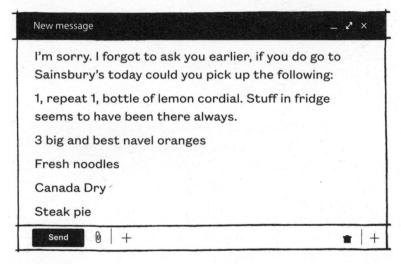

New message

I'm sorry. I forgot to ask you earlier, if you do go to Sainsbury's today could you pick up the following:

1, repeat 1, bottle of lemon cordial. Stuff in fridge seems to have been there always.

3 big and best navel oranges

Fresh noodles

Canada Dry

Steak pie

Send

Later that afternoon I presented Dad with a steak pie lunch and a new positive attitude. 'You got the wrong steak pie,' he said after the first bite.

'**Oh Five Two Six.**' (*Said when answering our phone in Earl's Court.*)

'**We're gone!**' (*Said when trying to get everyone out of the house and into car at the start of a family trip.*)

'**You can tell a lot about a person by looking at their shoes.**' (*Said when I would complain about how hard it was to polish my leather Clarks shoes using a brush – 'Why can't I just use the scuff coat?'*)

'**Life is a vale of tears.**' (*Dad was definitely a glass-half-empty guy. Prepare for the worst and hope for the best, was his philosophy.*)

'**The people who care don't matter and the people who matter don't care.**' (*We've covered this one.*)

'**Life itself is unfair.**' (*Said whenever any of us complained that something was unfair.*)

'**They should be put in a leaky boat and sent out to the middle of the North Atlantic.**' (*Said about people Dad didn't like on TV, including Noel Edmonds, Jan Leeming, Barbara Dickson, Bruce Forsyth, Petula Clark, Keith Chegwin, Esther Rantzen, Terry Wogan, Barbara Woodhouse (the Thatcher-style dog trainer) and Jimmy Savile.*)

'**You little basket!**' (*Said if I did something naughty when I was little.*)

'**It's all good copy.**' (*Said whenever something bad happened.*)

'**Almost certainly.**' (*Said whenever I asked if he could help me with something.*)

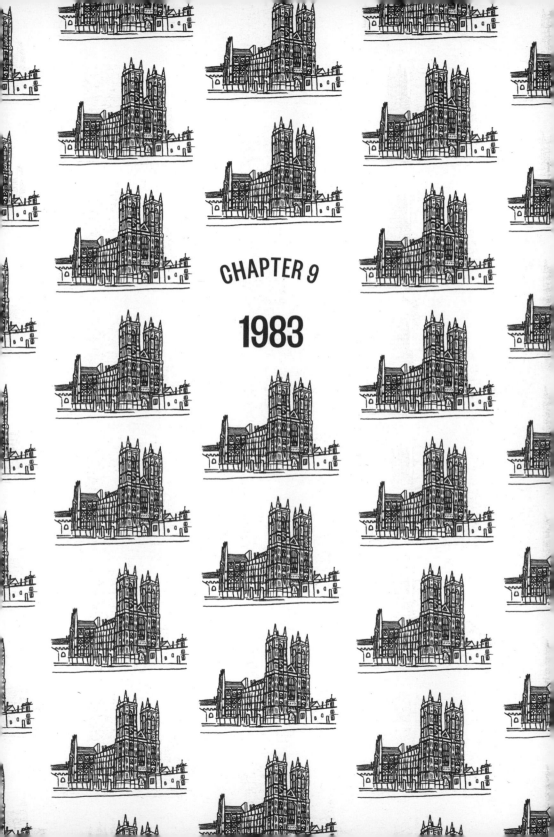

CHAPTER 9

1983

n January 1983, aged 13, I made the move from Westminster Under School to Westminster, the fee-paying school next to Westminster Abbey in central London where Dad had secured me a place. The student population was made up of day pupils and boarders. If you were a day pupil you went home at the end of the school day, and if you were a boarder you would sleep at school, in small dormitories at first, then single studies when you were more senior.

Overlooking a central courtyard, known imaginatively as 'Yard', were the various 'houses' into which every pupil was sorted when they arrived at the school (I have no idea by whom – may well have been a magic hat, or even a magic twat). As well as dormitories and studies, most houses contained an area where the juniors did their homework under the supervision of house prefects, a common room, which, depending on the house, might contain books, games, a TV or even a pool table, and a dining room where you ate lunch with your housemates. Breakfast and supper happened in the communal College Hall, one of the more ancient buildings next to the medieval cloisters that lead to Westminster Abbey. College Hall was like Hogwarts' dining room, but scruffier and without the nice food and the floating candles.

Some houses at Westminster were more desirable than others, with bigger studies, better facilities and nicer décor. The students that got into these houses tended to have fathers who were either Old Westminsters themselves, celebrated establishment figures, millionaires or all three. As my dad didn't tick any of those boxes, I ended up in one of the houses generally agreed to be 'bad'. Entering it for the first time, my impression was of prisons and mental institutions I'd seen on TV: cold, hard and shabby.

Even though my family still lived in Earl's Court, less than half an hour away by Tube, my parents decided that I should be a weekly boarder. After three years of boarding in Sussex, the idea of living at home seemed stranger than living at school, and for my parents having a quieter house was probably a bonus, too. So I slept at Westminster during the week and returned home on Saturdays after a morning of lessons (as long as I was at Westminster I never stopped resenting Saturday-morning school).

The other five boys in my junior dormitory were unimpressed by my tales of life at a mixed boarding school and clearly felt threatened when I told them about my 90-minute snogging record. One boy in particular never missed an opportunity to take the piss, and though we ended up being friendly once we were in the sixth form, his campaign of mental attrition contributed to my hatred of Westminster during my first few terms there. Years later my tormentor told me the reason he'd been so unpleasant in that junior dorm was that he found me intimidating, though he didn't mention the snogging record specifically. He went on to claim that some of the things I'd said in retaliation back then had wounded him badly, which only very fleetingly made me happy. Beware cornered boys with low self-esteem.

My only real friend during my first terms at Westminster was Patrick Dickie. We had been at boarding school together, though back then I had been wary of Patrick, as he was intensely passionate about things that seemed clever and grown up and which I knew nothing about, like CND, politics, football and the Beatles. We were in the same dormitory when we heard that John Lennon had been shot in December

1980 and Patrick, aged ten, was distraught. I felt he'd reacted in a way that might now be dismissed as 'performative' or some form of 'signalling' and ventured, 'What's the big deal about some old hippy dying? You didn't even know him.' Patrick had to be restrained.

Our English teacher at boarding school, Mr Davidson (who played 'Ziggy Stardust' in class that time), had invited a few of his more enthusiastic students, including me and Patrick, to a sort of cultural salon in his flat. We sat on cushions as Mr Davidson put on *Hunky Dory*, smoked cigarettes, drank something grown up and stinky (coffee, Scotch or possibly Coffee-scotch) and talked to us like adults. This worried the little conformist in me who suspected the natural order of things was being violated. Adults, especially teachers, were supposed to be the rulers and children their obedient subjects, so what was the deal with all this hanging out, listening to David Bowie and being allowed to say 'shit'? Patrick was into it and as he chatted away with Mr Davidson I envied his confidence.

The only thing I was confident about was that I really liked the song 'Ch-Ch-Ch-Changes'. Patrick agreed and that provided us with a basis for further dialogue.

At Westminster Patrick and I were in different houses and his housemates were in every way more colourful than mine. In Patrick's house they spent their evenings watching TV, playing pool and listening to The Sisters of Mercy, U2, Echo & the Bunnymen and, of course, Bowie. Most people's idea of a stimulating evening in our house was to sit on a more junior boy and fart on his head.

Cornballs

With the exception of Patrick and some of his friends, I hated more or less everyone at Westminster. I missed my co-ed prep school, and especially the company of girls, who had made it so much easier and more fun to talk about important things like the Top 40, feelings and myself.

Now I was surrounded by dreary, stuck-up boys in black uniforms who seemed to spend most of their time being casually loathsome to one another, but there was someone in my English class who was different. He was tall and haughty, but with a charm so many of the other boys lacked. I asked Patrick who he was. 'Oh, that's Joe Cornish,' he said. 'He's really good at English but he's a smart-arse. You'd get on.'

RAMBLE

I asked Joe if he was OK with what I'd written about him in this book and this was his only note:

'How many times can you and Louis describe me as "haughty" in books? Do you perhaps mean to say "tall"? Or maybe "generous" or "handsome" or "very imaginative"?'

Patrick was right, and as well as Joe's smart arse, I admired his sense of humour. Our first conversation happened after an English lesson one morning and took the form of a riff on a *Not the Nine O'Clock News* sketch about a spymaster who seems to be trying to recruit a secret agent but is in fact just looking for a boyfriend. We didn't do the boyfriend bit because I didn't understand that was the joke, and instead we just stood at the window and looked down over Yard as we exchanged enigmatic sentences for a while. It was one of the first times I'd enjoyed myself at Westminster.

With the formalities out of the way, Joe and I established

that we'd both recently discovered Monty Python after watching their sketch film *And Now for Something Completely Different* on TV. I had taped it and watched it over and over, though much of it went over my head entirely. What did 'Nudge, nudge, wink, wink' mean? What was funny about a group of men dressed as old women stealing a telephone box and riding around on motorbikes? What was an 'accountant' and who cared if he wanted to be a lion tamer?

I couldn't answer any of these questions, but it didn't matter. I liked the voices, the animations, lines like 'Miss Spume dreamed her dreamy dreams' and the general tone of authority being undermined by childishness. I liked quoting Graham Chapman's Colonel character and saying, 'Stop that, it's silly.'

One day in English class before the teacher arrived Joe reached into his bag and produced the lavishly illustrated book of Monty Python's new film *The Meaning of Life* and proceeded to show off the full-colour photographs of the more gory and graphic scenes. There was a man having his guts pulled out by surgeons, a large group of topless women on roller-skates and, most grimly fascinating of all, a hugely fat man emitting torrents of vomit in a smart restaurant before exploding. How could *Decline and Fall* or even *Catcher in the Rye* compete with that?

'I can get preview tickets for *The Meaning of Life* if you want to come and see it,' said Joe.

'Isn't it an 18?' I asked.

'Doesn't matter. I was on a film-review show for teenagers on Crapital Radio so I can get preview tickets for petty much any fillum.'

'Who is this guy?' I swooned. 'He's been on the radio! He changed the name of the station from Capital to "Crapital"! He says "fillum" instead of film! He's going to get me into an 18 with guts, topless women and an exploding vomit man in it! And he's drawn a Thompson Twins logo on his bag!'

The Meaning of Life was the first 18-rated film I saw at the cinema. I was 13 years old and it was every bit as confusing and disturbing as Joe's book had suggested. However, what impressed me most was the music.

'Galaxy Song', 'Penis Song (Not the Noël Coward Song)', 'Every Sperm Is Sacred' and 'Christmas in Heaven' were all funny, clever, catchy and I had to admit even better than 'Shaddap You Face' and one of my favourite songs from earlier in the year, Kenny Everett's 'Snot Rap'.

The Meaning of Life was also my first movie date with Joe and over the next few months we also went along to *Twilight Zone: The Movie*, *Bullshot*, *Psycho II* and another 18-rated film, *Videodrome*, which made me realise *The Meaning of Life* hadn't been that confusing and disturbing after all.

Missions to the Dark Side

Outside of Westminster, my other passport to everything my parents (especially Dad) would have disapproved of was my best friend from boarding school, Tom. On a couple of occasions we stayed at his cool divorced Mum's place in Clapham and, as she wasn't much in evidence on either occasion (probably hanging out with other cool divorced people), we were left to explore the many mystifyingly adult items strewn about her sitting room, the walls of which were painted a cool, divorced dark blue (the colour of naughtiness).

Tom pointed out comics that contained swearing on the coffee table (*The Fabulous Furry Freak Brothers*), drug paraphernalia on the mantelpiece (a pack of rolling papers) and at the front of a stack of LPs leaning against the wall, a record with three bare-breasted, mud-covered women on the cover. The '*Slits*'? What does *that* mean? I couldn't imagine what music made by The Slits would sound like, but I knew it would almost certainly be bad for me.

In the safety of Tom's bedroom, we played *Manic Miner* on the ZX Spectrum, and when we weren't listening to Tom's new discovery, Deep Purple, we listened to the Top 40. We liked Siouxsie and the Banshees' darkly psychedelic cover of the Beatles' 'Dear Prudence' (which would have made a good theme tune for Tom's mum's place), but I preferred 'All Night Long (All Night)' by Lionel Richie, which made me think of family holidays in America and transported me to a sunset party on a Hawaiian island where the Minute Maid fruit punch flowed, the young ladies found me irresistible and I had unlimited quarters for *Q*bert*, *Donkey Kong 3* and *Pengo* at the arcade.

However, our spiciest cultural explorations took place not in bohemian Clapham but in Barnes, leafy south-west London where Tom's dad and his second wife lived in an atmosphere far closer to the middle-class cosiness of our house in Earl's Court, i.e. no swearing, set bed times, pleases and thank-yous, Laura Ashley curtains and no illegal drug paraphernalia or albums by The Slits – at least not left out where impressionable children might find them.

Nevertheless, a portal to the dark side had opened up in Barnes in the form of a video rental shop on the Upper Richmond Road. During the Easter holidays we cycled down there and Tom, sporting his finest spotted hanky worn as a cravat and with his deepest voice, used his dad's membership card to rent anything that looked exciting and/or disturbing, preferably rated 18, though some boxes still had the old X certificates on the covers, making them even more alluring.

Tom was keen to explore titles like *Driller Killer*, *I Spit on Your Grave* and *Cannibal Holocaust*, films I'd seen mentioned in articles about 'Video Nasties' in my mum's *Daily Mail*. That was where I'd learned that some of these sicko horror directors had even filmed real acts of violence and murder and included them in what were known as 'snuff' films. Though I was certainly interested in blood and maybe a few guts, I definitely wasn't up for anything that might actually be real. As a result, our first few forays into more adult viewing (undertaken when Tom's father and stepmother were out) included less overtly horrific titles like the 1979 version of *Invasion of the Bodysnatchers*, *Soylent Green*, *Rollerball* and *Mad Max* before we took a deep breath and dived deeper into *Scanners*, *The Evil Dead*, *American Werewolf in London* and John Carpenter's *The Thing*.

American Werewolf and *The Thing* made an especially deep and long-lasting impression. *The Thing* was a brilliant counterpoint to *E.T.*'s alien cutesiness and tapped into four of my biggest fears: isolation, bodily mutation, stomachs that develop giant teeth then bite off people's hands and detached heads that sprout big spiders' legs and scuttle away.

American Werewolf in London, meanwhile, had not only spectacular gore and special effects, but proper humour and, most affectingly of all, Jenny Agutter, whose intelligent, unthreatening prettiness I associated with simpler times back before boarding school, when viewings of *The Railway Children* were a comforting Christmas staple. Now here she was, all grown up, shagging a werewolf in the shower to the sound of Van Morrison. It could only have been more confusing if Hayley Mills had appeared and started rogering John Noakes with a strap-on while Shep licked his nuts.

But the box that immediately caught our eye on our first visit to Tom's local video store was black and on the front, leaking green smoke, was a knobbly, cracked egg.

Alien Time

I had nearly seen *Alien* on a recent family trip to Florida where I found it listed on the hotel's free cable TV service. Waking up at 3 a.m. with jet lag, I checked that my brother and sister were still asleep, then crept into the dark lounge outside my parents' room and, ensuring the volume knob was all the way down and breathless with nervous excitement, I turned on the TV and navigated to the channel where the film was about to start.

My face was inches from the screen as across a shifting star field the vertical, horizontal and diagonal bars of the word 'ALIEN' appeared very slowly, one at a time, accompanied by eerie strings and cavernous groans barely audible from the mono speaker. 'This is silly,' I thought and switched off the TV before returning to bed, telling myself I was waiting for an opportunity to watch the film properly. The truth was that the title sequence alone, in all its dreadful, empty slowness, was the most chillingly adult thing I had seen up to that point and I knew I couldn't handle any more.

A year later, Tom reached up high and plucked the box for *Alien* from the video-store shelf, then waggled it at me with his raised-eyebrow grin. Then, setting it down on the counter, he drew himself up to the fullest extent of his 5 feet and 11 inches, presented his dad's membership card and half an hour later he was sliding the cassette into the VCR in his front room.

The mid-afternoon sun was streaming through the bay windows, so Tom went over to close the curtains. 'Don't make it too dark!' I said, trying my best to sound nonchalant, even though I was about as chalant as it's possible to be. It was finally happening. I was about to see *Alien*, albeit on a TV, in the middle of the day and with both of us fully intent on pausing it, replaying certain sections and generally not in any way experiencing the film as it was originally intended to be experienced.

To this day those first 45 minutes of *Alien* remain the most completely absorbing and frightening experience I have ever had watching a film. Every one of the first few shots in the quiet, gloomy interior of the *Nostromo* reminded me that I was a 13-year-old peering into a shadowy adult realm where events way beyond my emotional pay grade were about to unfold. This wasn't the *Millennium Falcon*. No lovable dog-men here, no wise-cracking rogues or avuncular laser-sword grandpas; just a little plastic drinking-bird toy to indicate that this wasn't going on in a galaxy far, far away. This was part of our universe – this was REAL.

RAMBLE

The plastic drinking-bird toy dipping its beak into a glass in perpetual motion was one of a number of things that encouraged me to think of the world as magical when I was little. Similarly marvellous and inexplicable to me were lava lamps, the glowing stars on the ceiling of my friend Lucy's bedroom, the brandy glasses that looked full but were actually empty and the waiter in a restaurant in Greece who appeared to be able to disconnect the end of his thumb and slide it along his forefinger with two fingers from his other hand.

'How do you do it?' I cried.

'It's magic,' explained the waiter with a smile.

'It's not magic,' said my dad when the waiter had left, but when he couldn't show me how the trick was done, I was forced to conclude that it absolutely was magic.

When it finally arrived, the Chestburster scene that for so long had squatted malevolently in my imagination was not the 'crimson shower of flesh and blood' promised by *Alien: The Illustrated Story*, but it was certainly shocking and more explicitly gory than anything I'd ever seen, so that was good.

And yet, as dead Kane's arms twitched hammily in the background and Alien Jr looked round the room, I was aware for the first time that I was watching something fake. I mean, I knew it was all fake, I wasn't fully moronic, but seeing that little yellow fellow with its tiny metal teeth, all I could think about was the person under the table, twisting it left and right.

Towards the end of the film I even found myself becoming mildly impatient, first at the number of steps required for Ripley to initiate the *Nostromo* self-destruct sequence, then with all the sirens, countdowns, strobe lighting and random blasts of smoke as she ran about trying to save the fucking cat. As for the moment when Ripley decides to cancel the self-destruct sequence only to be foiled by the infuriatingly slow action of those hydraulic cylinders, just thinking about it makes me itchy.

But we'd done it. We'd seen *Alien*, and before Tom had to return the cassette to the video shop we watched it twice more, freeze-framing the goriest scenes, saying 'H.R. Giger' a lot (we knew about the Swiss designer of the *Alien* creature from one of Tom's mum's nutty coffee-table books) and admiring Sigourney Weaver's very clean and extremely small underwear in slow-motion.

RAMBLE

God, I love *Alien*. I think I've watched it every year since that first viewing with Tom, on video, TV, DVD and Blu-ray, and waded through every second of related documentary material thereon, even those utterly pointless 'stills galleries'. My dad would have considered that a colossal waste of time. But what if I visited the same art gallery every month to admire a particular Velázquez painting and filled my shelves with books about him? Would that be better? Was it being infected by post-modernist theory at art school that makes me think *Alien* and Velázquez represent a comparable level of artistic achievement? Does anyone worry about this kind of thing any more? Should they?

BOWIE ANNUAL

My younger sister Clare got into Bowie around the same time I did, but her appreciation of his work was often less superficial than mine. As we weren't yet getting regular allowances, we relied on parents, relatives and Santa for our music purchases and for Christmas 1983 Clare had asked for *Aladdin Sane* and *Diamond Dogs*, albums that I'd avoided because I thought the red bouffant hairdo Bowie sported on both covers made him look like Cilla Black ('How nice does he look on the cover?' was the chief criterion for my Bowie album purchases for longer than it should have been – that's why the last of the Seventies albums I bought was *Lodger*).

I was also wary of *Aladdin Sane* because I'd been scandalised by the song 'Time' that I'd heard one evening at school as Patrick and his friends played pool in their house common room. At the line '*Time, he flexes like a whore / Falls wanking to the floor*', I'd leapt up from the tatty sofa and demanded to know what I'd just heard.

Patrick repeated the lyric, laughing at what he assumed was my parody of prudish conservatism, but, genuinely outraged, I huffed off to bed, announcing that if this was the kind of filthy nonsense Bowie had tucked away on the rest of his albums, I wasn't interested.

The next day, when I had calmed down a bit, one of Patrick's friends – Dan Jeffries – suggested I try some of Bowie's earlier stuff and, using Patrick's tape-to-tape boombox, I copied Dan's cassette of *Another Face*, a compilation featuring a wonky selection of novelty songs, rhythm and blues and Anthony Newley rip-offs that the young Bowie had hoped would make him famous.

Dan told me to listen to 'The London Boys', an atmospheric snapshot of the lows and highs of leaving home for the Big City and falling in with the wrong crowd. It's considered an early classic, with Bowie making his voice sound tired and feeble to evoke hangovers and bedsit squalor, but I just thought it was dreary and depressing. And as for 'Please Mr Gravedigger', a monologue about a child murderer plotting to eliminate a witness set to sound effects of church bells, rain and thunder, I soon became adept at hitting the fast-forward button before the first bell pealed, releasing it for the much more up-tempo and goofy 'Join the Gang', which takes the piss out of Swinging London winningly.

I couldn't decide if *Another Face* was the weirdest album I had heard up to that point or just the most rubbish. The songs on *Hunky Dory* and *Ziggy Stardust* were confident and perfectly formed, and compared with them everything on *Another Face* was like, well, a laughing gnome. But perhaps because it felt like a strange old boarded-up house in the scrubland of Bowie's career that only Dan Jeffries and I knew about, I kept returning to it, and soon I was fond of every crumbly corner (except the one with 'Please Mr Gravedigger' in it).

The experience of being initially indifferent to Bowie's records, then finding myself drawn in when I was more familiar with them, was one that repeated itself with each of his Seventies albums, though the transition always took me by surprise.

During the Easter holidays I managed to set aside my disappointment with Bowie's potty mouth and borrowed my sister's cassettes of *Aladdin Sane* and *Diamond Dogs*. It didn't take me long to realise I'd been wrong to be so uptight about 'Time'. Though the 'wanking/whore' line still rankled, I found myself caught up in the grandiose emotional sweep of the song and was similarly taken with the title track, 'Aladdin Sane', with its dreamlike verses paving the way for the maddest and best genre-melting piano freak-out I'd ever heard. I'd play the song to people and when the piano solo started I'd nod sagely and say, 'That's Roy Bittan. Bruce Springsteen's piano player. Pretty good, eh?' But it wasn't Roy Bittan. Mike Garson played piano on 'Aladdin Sane'. Roy Bittan played on 'Station to Station' – a piece of information I'd read in *David Bowie: An Illustrated Record* but hadn't properly processed because I was busy Bowie-ogling the pictures.

Diamond Dogs took longer to appreciate, but once I was in, I was in deep, especially during the 'Sweet Thing' section, which initially I had dismissed as 'pretentious', a word I'd recently learned and tended to use about anything I found too emotional or arty. Once I'd been swept away by 'Sweet Thing', rather than re-examine my definition of the word, I concluded that actually I rather liked things that were pretentious.

I wished *Let's Dance* had been a lot more pretentious. It was the first new music Bowie had released since I'd become a serious fan, and whereas listening to his older albums felt like being part of a pretentious underground club (i.e. excellent), seeing the videos for 'Let's Dance' and 'China Girl' on *Top of the Pops* left me feeling sort of betrayed. Though he looked lovely with his bleached hair and olive skin, maybe he was a bit too handsome now and a bit too ordinary, like the music, which sounded altogether too keen to be popular. If I was the kind of person that crapped on about people selling out, I would have said he'd sold out.

At least he looked cool in the 'Let's Dance' and 'China Girl' promos, but when I saw the deeply unpretentious performance video for 'Modern Love', filmed on the Serious Moonlight Tour, my heart sank. Seeing his yellow suit and bouffant hair, my first impression was of a big vanilla ice-cream cone from a van that did equally unpretentious hot dogs and burgers, both of which had probably sold out as well.

I didn't buy the album when it came out, but Mum got me the cassette for my fourteenth birthday and I discovered that the rest of the songs were as unappealing as I'd feared. There were the big slamming drums that I liked so much less than the robot percussion used by my favourite electronic bands, the squealing, honking horns that had none of the hazy warmth of 'Changes' or 'Fill Your Heart' and there was Stevie Ray Vaughan's big macho guitar, which just reminded me of boring old-man bands. And what the shit was Bowie doing with that Welsh accent on 'Ricochet', a song that appeared to be trying to deal with the subject of Britain's three million unemployed by having a groovy street party? Nope, I wasn't having any of it.

As usual, a few weeks later, I was having nearly all of it, and though *Let's Dance* occupied a space far less personal than those Seventies records, it made me happy every time I heard one of the singles blasting out in public that summer.

Towards the end of the year, Bowie's performance in *Merry Christmas, Mr Lawrence*, in which he played a Second World War POW at a Japanese internment camp in Java, fleetingly raised the prospect of bringing my dad into the Bowie fold. Laurens van der Post, who had written *The Seed and the Sower*, the book on which the film was based, was one of Dad's literary heroes and, he claimed, a friend. I suggested to Dad that he join me and my sister on a trip to see *Merry Christmas, Mr Lawrence* at the Fulham ABC, but he said he was too busy. It would have been fun to see what he made of peroxide-blond Bowie defiantly munching flowers, saying, 'What a funny face, beautiful eyes, though,' to Takeshi Kitano and, as punishment for kissing Ryuichi Sakamoto on both cheeks, getting buried up to his neck in the sand until his lips got badly chapped and he died.

I suppose there's a good chance Dad would not have enjoyed it, but my sister and I did and came out even more in love with Bowie than we had been before. Mum gave Clare the soundtrack for Christmas, unaware that it was by Ryuichi Sakamoto, not Bowie, and I got into that, too, finding it superbly pretentious and enjoying it almost as much as the albums Mum had given me: *Synchronicity* by The Police and *The Essential Jean-Michel Jarre*.

CHAPTER 10

BROMPTON, UNFOLDED

 have a folding bike. A pink Brompton. I'm aware that being a middle-aged man with a beard and a Brompton marks me out as a wanker for some people, but I don't care. If you think convenience, comfort and a commitment to reducing my carbon footprint to save this beautiful planet is wankerish, well, I guess I'm just a massive wanker.

One day I wheel my Brompton down to the end of Platform 9 at King's Cross and get on the front carriage of the 14.12 to Cambridge (if I'm in the front carriage, it'll be a shorter walk to Platform 5 at Cambridge to get the Norwich connection). The train isn't busy and it's direct, so after I've boarded I lean the Brompton, unfolded, against the doors on the opposite side. I always do this if I'm travelling at this time of day, knowing that when we're pulling into Cambridge I'll rejoin the bike and swiftly wheel it off the train when the doors open, rather than waste time folding and unfolding at either end.

Then I take a seat, put on my headphones and zone out for 45 minutes.

I look up when we're approaching Cambridge to see that on this occasion several people have walked through the train in order to exit from the front carriage, which doesn't usually happen at this time (it's only just gone 3 p.m.). Probably the knock-on effect of cancellations. Now there's four or five people all eager to be among the first to disembark at Cambridge and they're standing round my unfolded bike as it leans against the exit doors.

A couple of them exchange looks of contemptuous irritation when they see me stand up in my stylish high-vis jacket
and Day-Glo yellow helmet. To me, the neon yellows
and the bright pink of my bike frame say 'PUNK'.
At this moment, however, I suspect they suggest
another four-letter word to my fellow commuters.

I try to make my way over to the bike, but a large
man with raincoat and briefcase is unwilling to step
aside. He wants to teach me a lesson about selfishness. His hair is close-cropped and a fold of bristly skin
sits in a muffin top above the back of his collar. 'Excuse
me,' I say cheerily and edge past him to get to my Brompton.

The man closest to the door, standing directly over my
bike, is in his late thirties with backpack, jeans, chewing gum,
headphones, greying hair, and a somewhat ratty aspect. He
shoots me a disgusted look. I return his gaze with low-level
defiance. He holds it.

'Shame it doesn't fold up,' he says, looking down at my
bike.

'Oh, it does,' I reply.

'Why don't you fold it up then?'

'Because this train makes only one stop, so I knew it
wouldn't be blocking anyone's exit.'

'It's blocking mine.'

'When the doors open I'll get out and you'll be able to
disembark without delay.' Ratface rolls his eyes.

My heart is pounding. My breathing is no longer under
my control. The muscles in my face are betraying me. 'People
like Ratface,' I think, 'are not making the world better.'

He chews his gum. Exhales mintily. Taps his fingers on the
handrail to the music in his headphones.

Then, for my benefit, he shakes his head slightly. Before
I've thought better of it, I've said, 'Why do you need to make
this a problem?'

'Why do I?'

'Yeah. I'm interested. Why do you feel you need to make something like this into a problem?'

'I'm just making a point, that's all,' says RF.

'OK. And were you happy with my response to your point?' I ask.

'Yeah,' he drawls, in a way that might not be sarcastic, though we both know it is.

Tap, tap, tap, go his fingers to the almost certainly shitty music he's listening to. I will say this for Ratface: he's doing a much better job of pretending not to be flustered than I am.

I look around at the other commuters who have been watching this exchange with interest. Judging by the frostiness of their expressions, they're not on my side.

I consider their irritation. It's understandable. I get irritated by people dragging wheelie bags, especially on rough surfaces. I don't like the noise, but they also take up extra space and they're gradually destroying historical pavement surfaces in places like Venice.

The thing is, I've thought through my irritation with wheelie bags on several occasions and concluded that it's not actually reasonable. Wheelie bags may take up more space, but on the whole they allow people to move faster. And cobble erosion is the least of Venice's problems. So why can't other people realise that their irritation with me and my foldy bike is similarly unreasonable?

We pull into Cambridge and the train comes to a stop. Now I must disembark with 100 per cent efficiency to show my fellow passengers that my unfolded bike and I haven't slowed them down at all, and they're just miserable arseholes. My hand hovers over the button for the doors as I wait for it to become active.

It's a long moment, during which I make a decision.

I look over at Ratface and say, 'I'll make sure I fold it from now on.' He seems confused. I just handed him victory on a silver tray, and he doesn't know what to do with it. He goes for a look that says: 'Whatever, you're still a wanker with a Brompton.'

Maybe. But I'm the wanker who got off that train first.

RAMBLE

A NOTE ON THE MONIKER 'RATFACE'

I don't approve of commenting negatively about a person's physical appearance. In fact, I think making any comment about the way someone looks is unhelpful, unless you're describing them for storytelling purposes. I decided to call the man in this story 'Ratface' for a few reasons:

1. Giving him a nickname makes him more of a character.

2. Giving him a negative nickname conveys my dislike while giving the reader a humorous insight into my own petty defensiveness.

3. He was a rat-faced twat.

CHAPTER 11

1984

 think 1984 was the year I really fell in love with Joe. I was a boarder, as were most of the people I was friendly with, but Joe was a day boy, so for my first few terms at Westminster he seemed slightly spectral, drifting about sardonically during the day before vanishing at the end of school or earlier if he had any skippable lessons in his timetable.

By 1984 we were in the same classes for English and art, subjects we both enjoyed, and maths, which baffled us both. Rather than try seriously to understand whatever our maths teacher, Dr Barron (aka Dr Boring), was explaining, we sat at the back and drew comics. Joe's comic was about a flamboyantly camp James Bond-style hero called Hyde Pilchard. Mine was a Hyde Pilchard rip-off filled with tortured puns delivered by a smarmy, square-jawed superhero called Vernon Crazy.

Occasionally Dr Barron (imagine a less pointy Mr Burns from *The Simpsons*) would bust us doodling away and lose his shit, but on one occasion he just smiled and said, 'If only you two put as much effort into your studies as you do into those comics, you could achieve so much.'

At the end of another lesson Dr Boring called me and Joe over and we braced ourselves for a talking-to about our ongoing doodlism, but instead he presented us with photocopies of some of his own artwork – beautiful, robotically precise line drawings of various Christopher Wren-designed school buildings and Westminster Abbey's ancient cloisters, through which we trudged to Chapel every other morning. Looking at Dr Boring's drawings was one of the few times it properly sank in that we went to school in an extraordinary place.

I'd love to be able to report that from then on Joe and I knuckled down and fell in love with the beautiful magic of mathematics, but it didn't happen. Just now I had to use the calculator app on my computer to figure out how old my dad would have been in 1984, even though my dad was born in 1924. I'm sorry, Dr Boring.

As well as our struggles with maths, Joe and I bonded over an aversion to football. We liked to think we were above the 'beautiful game' and the grunting, angry monkey boys that got so emotional about it, but perhaps the truth was that, as with maths, we just couldn't be bothered to make the effort with something we knew we'd never be any good at. Friends of ours who adored football would say that Joe and I were better suited to standing on the sidelines and making snide comments than actually getting involved and being part of a team. Well, that may have been true or maybe we just preferred pastimes that didn't include incessant angry shouting, casual racism and violence. For any sensitive football fans reading, that last sentence was just a bit of light-hearted football-style banter, so please don't beat me up next time you're out yelling at people in a big threatening mob.

Joe told me that the best way to avoid football was to sign up for 'Leisure Swimming'. This entailed a walk to the Queen Mother Sports Centre in Pimlico followed by about 20 minutes of sploshing about in the pool along with the other football dodgers, misfits and oddbods. With our weekly dose of physical exercise taken care of, we'd wander over to a café just a few hundred metres from what, a decade later, would become the Channel 4 building on Horseferry Road, and there we each ordered a pack of Salt & Vinegar Chipsticks, a Pyramint and maybe a can of Quatro before sitting down to discuss a variety of important topics: was the new Thompson

Twins album *Into the Gap* even better than *Quick Step & Side Kick*? Who was the funniest guy in the *Police Academy* film – the one with the mad voice or the one who did impressions of electrical appliances? What was the secret of the insane creature transformations in *American Werewolf in London* and *The Thing*? (Running the film backwards, said Joe.)

Most of the time, however, the conversation came round to the same question: who in our year was a 'dude' and who was a 'goony bird'?

Tribes

By the end of 1984 several groups and wider social tribes had begun to emerge from the mulch of boys in our year, each with their own distinctive hairstyles, musical taste and dress codes. Joe and I formed the core of a little gang of friends who, depending on your perspective, were either cool, fun, creative guys or insufferably smug cunts.

There was Ben Walden, a horse-racing enthusiast and passionate fan of Billy Bragg whose father was the political TV interviewer Brian Walden, the man who proved to be one of Margaret Thatcher's most formidable media sparring partners. 'Your dad does *Weekend World*? Wow! Do you know who does the theme tune?' was one of my first questions for Ben.

Ben's parents split up when he was little, and Joe and I theorised that growing up in an atmosphere that was sometimes fraught had contributed to a brooding intensity he channelled into his main passion: acting. His George in *Who's Afraid of Virginia Woolf?* was a revelation, his Iago in *Othello* was a triumph and his annoying Italian guy in *A Servant of Two Masters* was much less annoying than it could have been, so for the next few years Ben – also known by the deliberately inappropriate luvvie nickname 'Bunny' (to be said in a gruff cockney accent) – was a crucial part of whatever creative scheme Joe was cooking up and I was tagging along with.

Mark Sainsbury was one of the Sainsbury's supermarket family, which initially I found hard to get my head round. 'So, could you could go into Sainsbury's and just take whatever you wanted without paying for it?'

'No,' said Mark.

'So, do you get in trouble if you shop in Tesco?'

'No,' said Mark.

'So, do you live in a massive house with servants?'

'Well …' said Mark.

Mark's house (not the London one, but the one in the Hampshire countryside) had columns out the front, so many floors that they had a lift and works of art on the walls that I recognised from books. On one visit when Mark's parents weren't there, Joe and I zipped about and, with the greatest care and respect, licked and kissed the surfaces of some of the most famous paintings by artists that included David Hockney and Claude Monet. For anyone interested, Hockney's paintings have a sweet, tangy taste, but Monet's too tart to mention.

Boundlessly gregarious and easy-going, Mark was determined neither to be defined by his family's wealth nor to pretend it didn't exist. He threw the best parties and Joe and I were often on hand to help with the party prep, making giant wall hangings by spraying Terry Gilliam-style cartoon faces on old sheets and draping fairy lights as we listened to tape compilations and discussed the guest list. I came to learn that the party prep was often more fun than the party itself.

Zac Sandler's superpowers were art, music and comedy. It was he who introduced us to the explosive, deconstructionist strangeness of early *Viz* comics and constantly made up funny songs that he would serenade us with in Yard between lessons. Wearing an earnest expression, Zac sang peculiar lyrics that would occasionally give way to invented scat phrases, often delivered in a high-pitched yelp: '*Rooty-shpooty*', '*Neesa-hooteh*', '*Tit-a-hooteh*', etc. Zac was also the first of us to draw his own comics, in which he combined his own entertainingly odd outlook with elements of *Viz* and the sci-fi magazine *2000 AD*, which published some of his work a few years later. If our little gang was like Pink Floyd (which, other than the fruity accents, it wasn't), Zac was our Syd Barrett.

It wasn't until our final year at Westminster that Zac became a regular at our social gatherings. Around 1984 he would have been hanging out a lot with Louis.

Joe told me Louis's father was a famous travel writer. 'That's something we have in common then,' I thought. Next time I saw Dad I told him I was friends with Paul Theroux's son, but rather than express delight that I was associating with the progeny of another travel-writing superstar, Dad was a little dismissive, mumbling something about him being 'awfully trendy' and 'overrated'.

'Louis?' I said. 'I wouldn't say he was *that* trendy'.

Louis was more intelligent than most people in our year, despite having been 'accelerated' from the year below, a fact that sometimes made me a little wary of him. Louis and Zac would occasionally embark on impenetrable comedy riffs that once or twice included friendly but quite pointed piss-takes of me and Joe and our creative schemes. We'd get back at Louis by teasing him about his unbroken voice and his emotional immaturity, though in truth he was no more immature than the rest of us, and usually a lot nicer and funnier with it.

Louis shared our enthusiasm for pop culture in all its forms, which offset his more intimidating intellectual tendencies. As well as comedy, music was always an important touchstone for me and Louis, and over the years he introduced me to some of my favourite stuff, such as The Doors, Van Morrison and Bob Dylan, and after we'd left school, Howard Devoto, Can, Pulp and Radiohead.

Anyway, look, I've listed the main social tribes in our year

Dad giving it maximum smoulder aged 18 as a newly commissioned subaltern in the Royal Artillery, 1942.

Dad took this picture of me, aged two, standing on a wall overlooking the Grand Canyon in 1971. Mum still can't look at it.

The Buxton family c. 1981. Left to right: David, Nigel (worried that the photographer is aiming too low), Adam, Valerie and Clare.

Dad took this one of me walking into Yard at Westminster in 1984. I was too embarrassed to stop and pose so I'm a bit blurry, and then the picture was accidentally double-exposed with a sunset. Sorry.

Joe, A. Buckles and Mark Sainsbury (in the background), catching up on *Cahiers du Cinéma* in a Paris photo booth, 1988.

'Yup, we're holding one of the most important films of the twentieth century.' Adam and Joe with *Twitch*, 1986.

Halloween party at Joe's house, 1986. Left to right: Louis Theroux as Hat Ghost; Joe Cornish as Count Gas Mask; Mark Sainsbury as Video Nasty (with VHS tape and bandages); Ben Walden said he was Freddy Krueger, and we never got to the bottom of what Guy Gadney was supposed to be. I was taking the picture dressed as a cool vampire, I think. There were no other guests.

A page from my 1987 diary, featuring a newspaper picture from one of the 'Toff Balls' fashionable at the time, a drawing of my history teacher warning me that I was going to screw up my exams (which I did) and me and Joe posing in the photo booth at St James's Park Tube station.

Me and school friend
Zac Sandler buried
beneath some of his
favourite records and
comics. Taken by Joe
after seeing *Do the
Right Thing* in 1989.

Behind the bar,
London, 1989. If only
I still had that shirt.

Aged 25 in my Clapham bedroom/second-hand tech dungeon after leaving art school in 1994. I'm saying, 'Mum! Can you not take pictures of me while I'm making experimental video pieces for *Takeover TV*?'

Me, Joe and Louis in 1995, aged around 26, enjoying our traditional Christmas Eve get-together at my parents' place in Clapham.

Me and Cornballs in 1999 (aged 30) doing press for
the third series of *The Adam and Joe Show*.

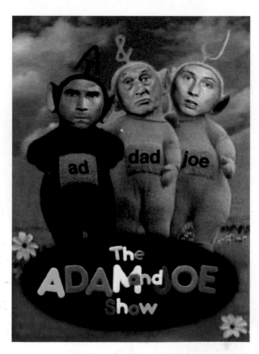

My *Teletubbies*-themed TX card for series two of
The Adam and Joe Show in 1997.

Me and Dad in the front room in Clapham doing a photoshoot for *The Times* newspaper's Relative Values feature in 1998. Dad was always a good sport in these situations.

'You're very beautiful.' BaaadDad at Tribal Gathering festival in 1997.

Louis Theroux and BaaadDad in the moshpit for a Foo Fighters show at V97.

Me and Rosie. Speaking in tongues. Norfolk, 2017.

for you below. If you were at school with us, you'll know there was a lot of crossover and you might take issue with some or all of these categories, but tough luck, this is my book and this is what it looked like to me.

THE BRAT PACK

Our gang, which at various times included me, Joe, Ben, Mark and Louis (though Louis was one of those people who could float from group to group and was hard to pin down). Back then I thought of our gang as rather cultured and sensitive, and we certainly could be, when we weren't being snooty and obnoxious, that is.

> **DRESS CODE** – Being fans of all things American, many of us went through phases that incorporated baseball jackets, Levi 501 jeans and Converse high-top shoes. There were a lot of checked shirts in my wardrobe for a while. I started to develop a slightly more eccentric fashion sense when we got to the sixth form and girls came into the picture. One weekend I went through Dad's old wardrobe and discovered a shiny black suit jacket that was far too large for me. I put it on and decided it made me look like David Byrne in the Talking Heads concert film *Stop Making Sense*, albeit in the wrong aspect ratio. Sometimes I would wear this jacket at school but was frequently told to take it off by teachers who were probably less worried about the jacket being non-regulation, and more worried that I just looked ridiculous. I would also wear my dad's old collarless dress shirts with the top button always done up.

> **HAIR** – None of our gang ever went for particularly trendy hairdos. That would have meant standing out too much, and standing out would have meant piss-taking, a little of which Joe experienced when he came back after one

summer holiday with a blond streak at the front of his floppy fringe. He got a lot of comments, most of which were some version of: 'Ha-ha! You got a blond streak! Blond-streak ponce!' Joe insisted that the blond streak was due to the brand of spot cream he used on his forehead accidentally getting into his hair. Though I'm not sure I said so at the time, I thought Joe's blond streak looked good, and the next time I was home I cautiously combed in some of the hydrogen peroxide my sister used to lighten the hair on her upper lip. The result was a curious orange fringe that I thought made me look a bit like Bowie on the cover of *Low*. Not everyone agreed. 'Ha-ha! Orange-fringe ponce!' was the consensus. I explained that it was the result of some lemon juice that I had accidentally wiped into my hair during a sunny holiday.

MUSIC – David Bowie, Thompson Twins, Thomas Dolby, then later on Prefab Sprout, Orange Juice, The Doors, Roxy Music, Joe Jackson, The Cure, Talking Heads, The Blues Brothers, Aretha Franklin, Otis Redding, James Brown, Prince, etc.

THE HARD LADS

The Hard Lads (or just the Lads) were embarrassed to be at a posh school and would behave like punky, ruffian ne'er-do-wells being forced to do a strange kind of community service that involved studying Latin and attending prayers in Westminster Abbey. It was easy to spot one of the Lads during prayers because they refused to bow their heads and would sit up and look around defiantly, hoping a teacher would force them to pray so they could make a scene. The rest of us were happy to bow our heads and enjoy a nice little nap. I liked many of the Lads individually, but as a group we didn't get on. They thought we were annoying drama pricks and we thought they were yobs who were too desperate to be cool.

DRESS CODE – This depended on whether you were more a Goth Lad or a Rockabilly Lad. The Goth Lads tended to favour winkle-pickers with long tapered tips, buckles and straps. Rockabilly Lads preferred suede brothel-creepers with rubber soles so thick they were basically platforms. Drainpipe trousers, taken in neatly by their mums or badly by themselves, were mandatory for all Lads, as were skinny ties, shirts untucked and long overcoats purchased at Kensington or Camden Market. Their book bags were covered with the logos of favourite bands, carefully painted on with white Tipp-Ex correcting fluid (OK, maybe it was just one guy who did this, but he did it really well and the other Lads should have copied him).

HAIR – Crew cut or flat top for the Rockabilly Lads, Jesus and Mary Chain/John Cooper Clarke birds' nest for the Goth Lads. One of the more non-conformist Lads shaved his head at the sides and left his hair long and floppy on the top and at the back, like an off-duty Mohawk.

MUSIC – The Lads all listened to John Peel's Radio 1 show and loved all the pasty-faced indie bands Peel championed (many of whom I ended up liking a lot, too): The Psychedelic Furs, The Smiths, The Gun Club, The Pogues, The Cramps, Xmal Deutschland, The Sisters of Mercy, Bauhaus, Alien Sex Fiend, The Birthday Party, Echo & the Bunnymen, etc. I also remember a few Lads joining an expedition to see U2 on their Unforgettable Fire tour, though they may have been excommunicated afterwards.

SPORTS GUYS

Westminster wasn't a very sporty school (one of the reasons my parents thought it might suit me), but there were a few impressive physical specimens who regularly represented the school in Sports of Privilege: Rowing, Rugby, Fives, Golden Pog, Sprinto, Yippee Hoops and Super Larkabout (I made some of those up).

DRESS CODE – Sports Guys tended to stick to the regular school uniform, but it just seemed to fit them better than the rest of us.

HAIR – Short, practical. Some of them even knew about conditioner.

MUSIC – AC/DC, Bon Jovi, U2. Big, fun, uncomplicated songs for big, fun, uncomplicated boys.

SCHOLARS

Scholars were students who had done so well in their entrance exam that their fees were reduced by as much as 50 per cent. For that reason, Scholars often came from less wealthy backgrounds than some of the other students, and that probably contributed to them seeming unusual and interesting. The Pogues' lead singer Shane MacGowan got a literature scholarship to Westminster in 1971 but was expelled after a couple of years for drug possession. Sixteen years later, when I was in the sixth form, MacGowan was the hero of every Hard Lad in the school.

DRESS CODE – I recall the Scholars wearing ill-fitting suits, but that might have been just one guy. Let's call him Mungo.

HAIR – Dandruff. Again, might have just been Mungo. I'm sure there were many Scholars at Westminster who knew about Timotei.

MUSIC – Queen, Genesis, avant-garde jazz, Gregorian chanting, Steve Reich, The Flying Pickets. I'm guessing here, to be honest, though I'd say Queen is a good bet.

HIPPIES

Louis would often hang around with the Hippies. Despite an affected flaky demcanour and a fondness for referring to everyone as 'man' (which rubbed off on Louis, then me and Joe, and afflicts us to this day), the Hippies were usually sharp and could be withering if crossed.

DRESS CODE – Hippies wore their uniforms loose, jackets open, shirts untucked, ties askew or round the head like bandanas when hanging around Yard at the end of the day.

HAIR – Loads. But not lank and greasy like Neil the Hippy from *The Young Ones*. The hair of Westminster Hippies was luxuriant and lovely. Think young Kate Bush.

MUSIC – As with the Lads, music was important to the Hippies and they liked a lot of classic stuff: Leonard Cohen, Neil Young, Van Morrison, Woody Guthrie, Janis Joplin, Lonnie Donegan, Joni Mitchel, etc. Not Queen.

Balls to the Wall

Some people in our year didn't really fit into any group except maybe the 'Rich' group. Joe introduced me to a friend of his called Omar who, with his well-cut black suit, immaculate black hair, black briefcase and aviator sunglasses, resembled a member of the secret service transporting classified documents, but was actually the son of a rich Middle Eastern family. He thought the music Joe and I liked was lame. Omar preferred heavy metal and claimed to have attended a gig by a German band called Accept at which he stood so close to a speaker that his ears began to bleed. He said he loved it. It was hard to tell if he was bullshitting with those aviator shades on.

Omar saw me admiring an ad for some Sony B-10s – desktop speakers that could plug into a tape player – and said he would buy me a pair for my birthday. It was strange, because we weren't really best buddies and the speakers were expensive – a more lavish gift than I could expect from my parents – but I coveted those B-10s and decided to accept Omar's kind offer. It took longer than it should have done for me to realise that this effectively turned our friendship into a weird contract under which it was in my interest to remain in Omar's good graces.

Over the following weeks, if I did something to annoy Omar or disagreed with him in any way, he would shake his head and say, 'Shame about those B-10s,' whereupon I would capitulate. I began to suspect the price I was paying for this free gift was too high and that the deal didn't reflect well on either me or Omar. The next time he threatened to withdraw his offer, I told him I didn't care, and that even if he had bought me the B-10s I would have just stuck them up his arse, which would have been difficult and painful, but better than turning our relationship into a tawdry financial arrangement (at least, that's what I was thinking – in reality I probably just mumbled something inaudible).

We didn't hang out so much after that. Then, on my birthday, Omar handed me a card. Inside it said, '*Hope your B-10s make your ears bleed.*' When I went back to my study, the speakers were sat on my desk. They seemed incredibly powerful (though a small Bluetooth speaker would outperform them today). The first thing I played on them was Omar's cassette of *Balls to the Wall* by Accept, a jolly, Spinal Tap-like fusion of hard rock and some Gregorian chanting. I turned it up very loud until the house master stuck his head round the door and asked what the hell was going on. I said I was learning a confusing lesson about greed, friendship and power dynamics (again, paraphrasing).

Machine Gun Etiquette

I looked forward to English lessons because there was always a chance that the teacher would announce that we were taking a break from *King Lear* or *To the Lighthouse* or Philip Larkin and instead were going to spend the lesson drinking Earl Grey tea and talking about our worst fears, or lying in the sun on College Green and reading poems to each other or making up advertising slogans that could be used if fellow class members were being sold as products.

One day Mr Field (who along with Mr Stewart was one of the English teachers I liked best) announced that in the next lesson we would be required to deliver a talk about music. Rather than talk about music I was genuinely passionate about, I decided it would be more fun to take the piss, so at the next lesson I turned up 'in character' as one of the Hard Lads, reasoning that the Lads regularly made hurtful comments about Thomas Dolby and the Thompson Twins, so now they would feel the sting of my satire sword.

I messed up my hair to make it as birds' nesty as possible, used safety pins to turn my school trousers into drainpipes and, in order to approximate the pointy winkle-picker style of footwear that many of the Hard Lads favoured, I taped long black paper cones to both of my shoes.

Then I set my Sanyo tape player on the teacher's desk and pressed play. I had borrowed my friend Patrick's cassette of *Machine Gun Etiquette* by The Damned, and as 'Love Song' played I delivered my talk about how the length of my winkle-pickers was making it hard to manoeuvre in tight spaces, how a family of mice were living in my hair and how I liked whatever music John Peel told me to like.

In stand-up gig terms, I CRUSHED, but with no high-ranking members of the Lads in the room, the stakes were low. Also, *Machine Gun Etiquette* was probably the kind of album the Lads had grown out of, but I had recently fallen in love with it and just wanted people to hear how good 'Love Song' was, or 'I Just Can't Be Happy Today', or the tumbling, disintegrating, reintegrating and exploding 'Anti-Pope', a song that has supercharged many happy moments since I stood there with my paper winkle-pickers, taking the piss out of a gang that part of me wished I could join.

Dune

The 20th of December 1984 was Joe's sixteenth birthday and we celebrated in style, taking the Northern Line up to the Empire Leicester Square to see David Lynch's adaptation of Frank Herbert's 1965 sci-fi novel *Dune*.

On the Tube Joe filled me in on the industry gossip about the film, gleaned from his many movie mags. In those days most ordinary people didn't know all that much about films, other than who was in them and maybe who had directed them, but as we discovered in the Nineties when Quentin Tarantino became a household name, the previous decade had incubated a new breed of film nerd, able to get enthused as much by mainstream shlock as by foreign classics and extreme left-field weirdness.

Joe's shoulder bag might contain not only the latest issue of Hollywood industry mag *Variety*, but also the horror-and-splatter magazine *Fangoria*, as well as high-brow French film digest *Cahiers du Cinéma*, which J-Corn would refer to now and then in a comedy French accent intended to cover up the fact that he actually did consider himself a deep-level cineaste.

Joe's pre-screening briefings were often better than the film itself, and *Dune* was no exception.

The scuttlebutt was bad. Clashes over editing. Confusing story. Shit special effects. Sting. Lynch was so unhappy with the studio's interference that some versions of the film (there were several floating around) were credited to Alan Smithee, which Joe explained was the name they use 'for films that are so shit, no one wants the director credit'. But it's David Lynch, we reasoned. How bad could it really be?

It turned out the answer was: quite bad. Scene after scene featured a succession of queasy-looking actors reciting daft names in big rooms, interspersed with blue-screen effects that looked as if someone had put them together on a phone app in 2007 and faxed them back to 1984.

Nevertheless, there were a handful of Lynchy moments that managed to break through the cobblers and linger disturbingly in the memory, especially the scenes featuring the grotesque Baron Harkonnen. Apart from the Baron's own antics, which included floating over to a young man, removing a plug from his heart and drinking him like a strawberry milkshake, there were the Baron's cronies: the superbly crazy, giant-eyebrowed Piter De Vries, and the Baron's doctor, syringing his master's pustules and reciting, 'Put the pick in there, Pete. Turn it round real neat.'

After about an hour I looked over at Joe to make an amusing comment about Sting's pants, only to find Corn-balls fast asleep. I reached back into my box of Fruit Pastilles and thought about Christmas, which was only four days away. Exactly one year later, on Joe's seventeenth birthday, his parents let him have a party at their house in Stockwell, and I spent most of the evening throwing up, having drunk too many vodka and oranges. On balance, I think I preferred the trip to see *Dune*.

RAMBLE

In 2013 I watched *Jodorowsky's Dune*, a documentary about the efforts of Chilean-French director Alejandro Jodorowsky to bring *Dune* to the screen nearly a decade before David Lynch did. It's a great doc about bad timing and missed opportunities that suggests Jodorowsky's version of *Dune* might have been visually extraordinary, but probably not much more coherent than Lynch's effort.

Towards the end of the documentary Jodorowsky talks candidly about the envy he felt on discovering that Lynch, whom he greatly admired, was to be the director that would finally bring *Dune* to the screen. Jodorowsky then describes seeing Lynch's version after being dragged to the cinema by his son in an effort to force his father to confront his toxic regret.

The director spent the first few minutes doubled up in his seat with self-reproach, only to find with each passing minute of Lynch's version that he was feeling lighter and happier, because it was so totally rubbish. By the end of the film Jodorowsky was euphoric, drunk on schadenfreude, which I believe tells you much of what needs to be known about most artists.

BOWIE ANNUAL

I'd always avoided Bowie's 1977 album *Low* because I wasn't familiar with any of the song titles, but I liked the orange floppy hairdo he had on the cover so I decided to give it a go.

I hated it.

I found the first side harsh and ugly, especially the drums, which sounded like bricks being lobbed into a metal bin. Some songs, like 'Breaking Glass', appeared to have been designed to repel the listener by interrupting the boring melody with loud, atonal electronic alert sounds.

Side two of *Low* didn't even have proper songs, just long, slow instrumentals, some with faux-operatic warbling in a made-up language. These, I decided, were not just bad, but so rotten and pompous they were quite funny. And yet in those days the mood-altering experience of exploring a new album, even a rotten and pompous one, was enough to keep me coming back.

Then over the next few nights the thing happened again, and *Low* started slipping its hand into mine. A pleasing change of key in 'Speed of Life' distracted from the ugly drums. The mess of 'What in the World' became an amiable clown car bouncing along with its intoxicated occupants singing winsomely in the back. 'Always Crashing in the Same Car', which initially seemed such an unappealing mix of plodding greyness and hysterical warbling, suddenly located a nascent seam of teenage melancholy and mined the self-pitying shit out of it.

Meanwhile the turgid instrumentals on side two

transformed into the soundtrack to my own sci-fi epic. Lying in bed with my headphones on, I imagined flying over the surface of a hostile planet at multiple sunrise during 'Warszawa', exploring twinkling underground cities to the sound of 'Art Decade' and getting tipsy in the sun-lit cloud palace of a saucy alien as we listened to 'Subterraneans'.

Low was also my introduction to Brian Eno, whose name I took to be an invented juxtaposition of the mundane and the exotic, like Mike Fooza, Ron Swoosh or Gary Voobelix. I didn't really understand what Eno did on *Low*, but given his name I thought there was a good chance he was responsible for a lot of the electronic sci-fi stuff, and I was up for more of that.

When Mum asked me and my sister for Christmas-present ideas that year, I mentioned Eno, and in my stocking, along with a cassette of the music from *Ghostbusters* (one of the year's movie highlights), I found *Apollo: Atmospheres and Soundtracks*. Credited to Eno with Daniel Lanois and Roger Eno (ooh! More Enos?), *Apollo* contained electronic instrumental pieces embellished with pedal steel (or 'country guitar', as I thought of it) that had been created for the soundtrack to a documentary about the 1969 moon landings called *For All Mankind*.

RAMBLE

Mum had picked out *Apollo* from the wide and weird array of other possible Eno options because she knew I liked space and she had a sentimental attachment to the moon landings. Very early one July morning in 1969, she had sat in front of the TV in Earl's Court and watched Neil Armstrong step onto the moon with me, just six weeks old, sat on her lap. As she tells it, Dad came in at one point and said, 'What on earth are you doing?'

'Look! They're on the moon!' exclaimed Mum.

'Why would you want to watch that in the middle of the night? You must be dotty,' said Dad and returned to bed.

The second side of *Low* had shown me how pleasurable it was to be immersed in a largely instrumental moodscape rather than the three-minute pop songs that made up most of my musical diet, but on first listen *Apollo* was as cold and forbidding as the lunar surface itself. Most tracks sounded like distant industrial machinery with some whale noises on top ('Matta', 'The Secret'), and the more overtly melodious, country guitar sections ('Silver Morning' and 'Deep Blue Day') struck me as the kind of inoffensive sludge that might be played in a care home to keep the geriatrics passive.

I discovered the trick with *Apollo* was to have it playing in the background while I was drawing and not listen to it so much as let it become part of the room (the way my wife sometimes does with me). Once I'd forgotten it was supposed to be music, I became aware that *Apollo* created a mood of calm strangeness, and as my familiarity with the individual tracks grew, so, too, did my appreciation for the industrial machinery, the whale noises and the care-home muzak, all of which, as ever, I had massively underestimated.

Modern Bowie, meanwhile, was still dutifully plopping out the product.

At the end of the summer holidays in 1984, Bowie

released 'Blue Jean', the first single from his new album *Tonight*. The song was amiable but daft, like one of the characters Bowie played in *Jazzin' for Blue Jean*, the extended pop promo directed by Julien Temple that accompanied the single's release. Joe and I went to see the bizarre British horror fantasy *The Company of Wolves*, and *Jazzin' for Blue Jean* was shown before the main film as a short support feature (a practice once common in British cinemas that was becoming increasingly rare by 1984).

I had assumed that Bowie's best years were behind him and that he was now a rather wearisome old rocker more interested in selling a lot of records than doing anything as interesting as *Low*, but *Jazzin' for Blue Jean* suggested the coma patient might at least be twitching.

The two characters Bowie plays in the 20-minute film are Screaming Lord Byron and Vic. Byron is a ludicrous rock star who veers between the arrogant self-assurance of Bowie in Ziggy mode and the whimpering paranoia of mid-Seventies cocaine Bowie. In one scene Byron sits in his dressing room before a show looking glum, munching pills and applying his make-up while listening to 'Warszawa' from *Low*, a reference I was convinced that only I could possibly have appreciated.

Bowie's other character Vic is a geezerish chancer who ends up stalking Lord Byron in the hope of impressing a girl he fancies. With hindsight, the Vic character, as well as eerily prefiguring many of Ricky Gervais's comic ticks and mannerisms, was far more like the public persona Bowie adopted in the late Eighties when he was hanging out with the lads in Tin Machine.

In an age before celebrities taking the piss out of themselves became mandatory, the self-deprecating in-jokes and meta-textual references in *Jazzin' for*

Blue Jean were, for the 15-year-old Buckles at least, thrillingly fresh and clever.

At the end of the video the girl cops off not with cheeky Vic but with ludicrous Lord Byron, and as his car pulls away Vic calls after him, 'You conniving, randy, bogus-Oriental old queen! Your record sleeves are better than your songs.' 'Marvellous stuff,' thought Buckles, but there was more! As the camera pulls back and the credits roll, Bowie breaks character and, playing himself, starts complaining to the director that the ending was not what they'd agreed. Take that, Fourth Wall!

My renewed enthusiasm for modern Bowie took a kicking when I listened to the whole of the *Tonight* album. Though I agreed with Mum that 'Loving the Alien' was rather great, and I was fond of the cod-reggae swagger of 'Don't Look Down', which had featured throughout *Jazzin' for Blue Jean*, the rest of the album sounded as though Bowie had sat at the mixing desk and demanded: 'More massive drums! More backing vocals! More cheesy synth! More zaxophone! MORE Eighties!' Like so much mainstream culture around at that time, *Tonight* was one big messy Moregasm.

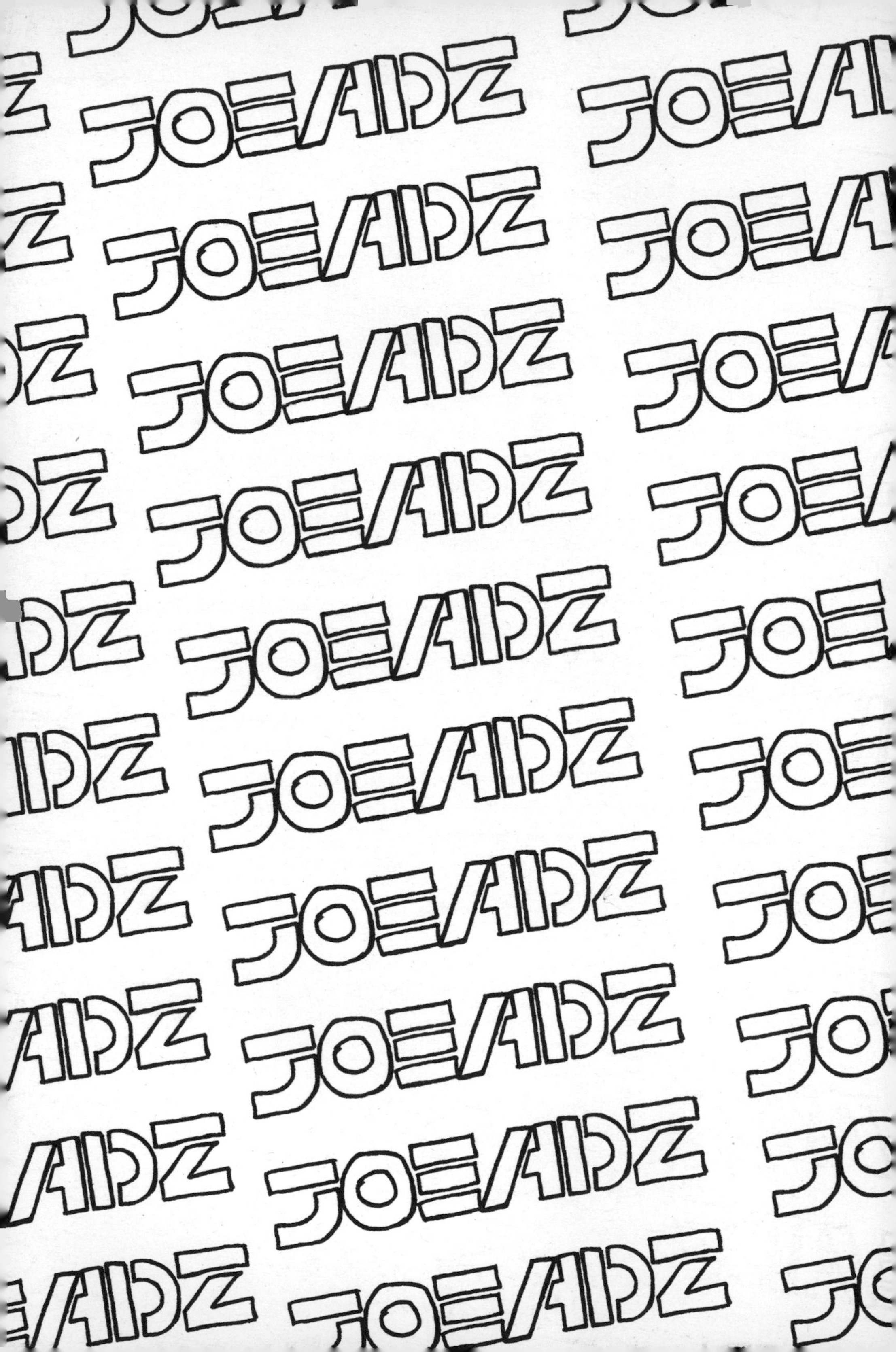
JOE ADZ

CHAPTER 12

ADAM AND JOE'S
SCHOOL PROJECTS

Look, I wish I could tell you that when we were at school Joe and I were dreaming up ways to save the planet and cure society's ills, but the truth is we were fantasising about running a giant media company called The JOEADZ Corporate.

I honestly can't recall if it started ironically or not, but within a few months of becoming friends Joe and I had designed a corporate emblem in the style of the Thompson Twins logo that we agreed was futuristic and cool, and I'd drawn a picture showing us standing on top of our corporate headquarters: a giant industrial communications tower from which we could survey our vast media empire. It was a different time.

But let me tell you about the JOEADZ creative vision, and how Joe and I synergised within it.

'*Life is serious, but art is fun!*' Joe had scrawled on his school bag. I assumed Joe had coined the phrase himself and I was impressed, not realising it was a reference to the motto of a suicidal street clown in John Irving's book *The Hotel New Hampshire*. I don't know if Joe thought of himself as a suicidal street clown or not, but it occurs to me now that all our creative schemes were informed by that philosophy and what we convinced ourselves was a noble desire to escape serious things and have fun.

Joe was older than me by six months (in fact, he still is), and that age difference along with his confidence and

My drawing of the JOEADZ Corporate telecommunications tower from 1984.
That platform Joe and I are standing on doesn't seem safe at all.

imagination conferred on him a seniority that meant he was the one who decided what projects we should pursue, and whether we were making a video or a short film or putting on a play, Joe directed and I helped out. What I brought to the table, apart from contributing very good ideas and being great fun to have around, was an awesome versatility as a performer and a unique vision as a designer/producer of artwork and publicity material when it was time to unveil a new JOEADZ joint.

You'd think this level of drive and self-belief would be met with nothing but respect and admiration from our fellow students, but surprisingly that wasn't always the case. One day in the school yard, Louis, smirking, said that he and Zac were also forming a media company. 'It's going to be called "LOUZAC",' said Louis. 'What do you think?'

'It sounds like toilet cleaner,' said Joe defensively, 'so, yeah, probably about right.' Ooh! Time to quit smirking, Theroux!

Before we started to collaborate on more ambitious projects, the first things Joe and I made together were sketches and parodies (which we shot on the big, clunky video camera my dad had been given) of the Gold Blend coffee adverts, the science and technology magazine show *Tomorrow's World* and the children's current affairs programme *John Craven's Newsround*. We also re-enacted half-remembered bits of Monty Python sketches and regurgitated jokes we'd heard on topical satire shows such as *Spitting Image* and *Week Ending*. Then we'd play the tape back and chuckle away, just excited to see ourselves on a TV.

Friends for Dinner

We used the Sharp video camera to film behind-the-scenes footage for our first official JOEADZ production towards the beginning of 1985: a short film called *A Few Friends for Dinner*. The film itself was shot on a Super 8 cine camera that Joe had bought with money he'd managed to wangle out of some sympathetic teachers when they agreed to revive the school's defunct film club.

The story concerned a group of obnoxious toffs whose dinner party is interrupted by a hooded homeless man seeking shelter – a premise that perhaps owed a debt to Monty Python's *Meaning of Life* when the Grim Reaper shows up at a dinner party at the end. In *A Few Friends for Dinner* the toffs rudely rebuff the visitor and pay a terrible price when (SPOILER ALERT!) a monster emerges from the homeless man's robes and slaughters and consumes the toffs one by one (so you see the monster is 'having a few friends for dinner', i.e. eating them, whereas that phrase would normally indicate that you've invited some acquaintances to join you for a meal. The title works in more than one way).

Joe made the monster by customising a ventriloquist's dummy, ending up with something that looked like an angry teddy bear with a row of nails for teeth held in place with Sellotape, like a kind of cuddly Alien. As we were too timid to ask any of the sixth-form girls to help us, Patrick and I played the female dinner-party guests and we very much enjoyed putting on dresses and make-up in order to look as pretty as possible.

We had permission to film in a smart section of the school library and were given access to lights, sound equipment and a small budget that we spent on cine film and After Eights for the posh dinner party, most of which I consumed before the camera had even started turning, to the irritation of J-Corn.

RAMBLE

After Eight mints are thin, roughly textured chocolate squares with a layer of fondant minty brilliance at their centre. Each one comes in its own little black paper envelope and they sit together, like a tiny chocolate record collection in a tasteful green box, from which they may be individually plucked by wealthy-looking people in evening dress shooting each other saucy looks as their candle-lit dinner party draws to a close. At least, that was the image that After Eight portrayed in their TV ads during the Seventies and on into the Eighties, and in purely aspirational terms it worked well.

I can recall my parents throwing a dinner party in Earl's Court that looked exactly like an After Eight ad, with the men in dinner jackets and the women in nice dresses and sparkly jewellery, everyone smoking and laughing a lot, and at the end, out came the After Eights. I was supposed to be asleep, but the laughter woke me up and my mum, smelling sweetly of smoke and perfume, let me have one of the wafer-thin mints if I promised to go back to bed.

Whether that dinner-party memory is real or not, I grew up thinking After Eights were the most delicious and sophisticated thing you could possibly eat. Then, on my first trip abroad without my parents, I bought a box of them in duty free and a few minutes later I had munched every one and was vainly riffling through the empty paper sleeves hoping to discover one more that still contained its minty chocolate treasure. After Eights never seemed quite so alluring again.

Making *A Few Friends for Dinner* was the most fun I'd had since starting at Westminster, and though I had been the Andrew Ridgley to Joe's George Michael, it felt as though we made a good team. As far as the finished film was concerned, I don't recall anyone being particularly whelmed. Dad was worried that with only a few months to go before my O-level exams, I had been spending too much time 'fooling about' at the expense of my studies, though he did concede that Patrick and I made quite attractive young women.

Pvt Wars

The next JOEADZ production took place during our first term as sixth-formers. It was a three-man play called *Pvt Wars* (pronounced 'Private Wars') by American playwright James McLure, about three emotionally damaged Vietnam veterans who banter and bicker with one another while recuperating in an army hospital – perfect subject matter for three 16-year-old public-school boys of varying acting ability.

Joe played Natwick, a supercilious upper-class type from Long Island, Ben Walden was Silvio, a loudmouthed Italian-American given to exposing himself to the nurses despite having been rendered impotent by a war injury, and I played Gately, a hillbilly obsessed with fixing a broken radio. I didn't know what a Southern accent sounded like, so I ended up doing a sort of generic East Coast drawl while Joe kept his accent clipped, rolling his 'r's now and then. Ben, a *Rocky* fan, went full Italian Stallion as Silvio.

One autumn weekend during a rare family supper, Dad asked what had been taking up so much of my time and I showed him my copy of *Pvt Wars*. After studying it for a few minutes he declared, 'I would strongly advise you not to do this.'

'Why?' I laughed, not even considering taking him seriously.

'I think the subject matter, the bad language and the accents are likely to make you all look very foolish.'

'Screw you, old man!' I shouted as I overturned the kitchen table and stormed out of the room. Or maybe I just said, 'Oh, OK,' and continued making gravy channels in my instant mash.

RAMBLE

Dad must have known that I'm the kind of person who finds it almost impossible to take advice – it's a trait I probably got from him – and yet he felt compelled to dispense it. As I got older the advice transformed into critiques that were sometimes barbed.

In 2007 I phoned Dad to tell him I had been asked to appear on the topical TV panel show *Have I Got News for You*, thinking he'd be impressed. He responded, without a trace of malice, by saying, 'I would have thought *Have I Got News for You* is exactly the kind of programme on which you are thoroughly ill suited to appear. It's full of people being witty and telling jokes and that's not at all what you're good at.'

Now that I'm a parent I know it's very hard to stand by and watch your children making choices they'll probably regret. The instinct is to pull back the people most important to you from the cliff edge, but usually, as long as you think they'll survive the fall, it's best just to let them go over and to shout 'Good luck! I love you!' as they drop.

Dad was completely right about *Have I Got News for You*, though. It was a slow car crash and I wasn't invited back.

Pvt Wars went ahead, announced weeks before the first performance by a giant poster that I made and hung on the main school noticeboard, a hand-painted logo at the bottom proclaiming that this was '*A JOEADZ production*'. At the top of the poster was the movie-style tagline we'd come up with: '*Once they went over the top to kill people. Now they're going over the top to kill time*'. Some people missed the clever double meaning of 'over the top' and I had to explain on several occasions that the tagline referred to soldiers going 'over the top' of trenches into battle, as well as going 'over the top' in terms of the behaviour they displayed in the army hospital. I mean, who wouldn't immediately get that?

RAMBLE

In the weeks running up to the UK release of the first *Ghostbusters* film just before Christmas 1984, posters appeared all over London that bore the now-iconic *Ghostbusters* logo, a date and nothing else. Being good film nerds, Joe and I knew what the posters were about, but we didn't think of them as advertisements. To us, they seemed like the essence of something amazing punching through the dreary wall of phoney commercial imagery that characterises so much of the modern world. It was the first time we'd seen a 'teaser campaign'. If *Ghostbusters* had been shit, we'd immediately have become cynical about such tactics, but *Ghostbusters* wasn't shit.

Sub Ramble

Ghostbusters was one of a tiny handful of films (including *Flash Gordon*, *The Killing Fields* and *Dances with Wolves*) that I went to see with my whole family, even Dad. When we came out of the cinema after *Ghostbusters* I wanted to know if Dad had liked it as much as I had. He said he liked the bit with the smarmy, troublesome health-inspector character Walter Peck, who in one scene gets referred to as 'Dickless' by Ray Stantz. 'One comes across that type so often. He played it perfectly,' said Dad afterwards.

'Didn't you think Dr Venkman was funny, though?' I asked Dad, smiling to myself as I recalled Bill Murray's line: 'It's true – this man has no dick' – a type of humour that was new to me.

'He seemed rather too pleased with himself' was Dad's verdict on the comedy genius.

After the *Ghostbusters* teaser campaign, we were determined that when it came to JOEADZ productions we, too, would indulge in similar acts of poster foreplay, and a lot of time was spent inventing mysterious logos and taglines for our photocopied flyers.

In 1989 the teaser campaign for Tim Burton's *Batman* attempted to reprise the glorious build-up to *Ghostbusters* by covering every inch of public space with shiny Bat-logos, but by that time the word 'hype' had entered the public's consciousness and, as it turned out, *Batman* was no *Ghostbusters*.

The JOEADZ production of *Pvt Wars* turned out to be … A SENSATION. We received a rave review in the school magazine from a girl in the year above who didn't even know us, and there was even some grudging praise from a few of the Lads, all of which immediately went to my head and I started believing I was Robert De Niro.

Bugsy Malone

One morning towards the beginning of 1986, Joe, Ben and I sneaked out of school during a private study period and over Cokes and crisps in our favourite café Cornballs suggested our next project should be a stage production of *Bugsy Malone*.

Alan Parker's 1976 film musical in which children play Prohibition-era gangsters, drive pedal-powered sedan cars and battle each other with machine guns that shoot whipped cream was a thrilling, dreamlike experience when I saw it first

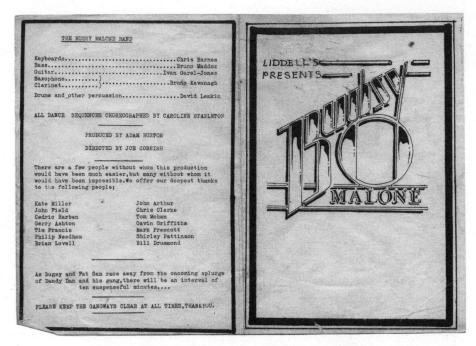

The play programme from the 1986 JOEADZ production of *Bugsy Malone* with design and layout by A. Buckles and passive-aggressive thanks by J. Cornballs.

aged nine. *Star Wars* was all well and good, but *Bugsy Malone* was the realisation of just about every childhood fantasy I'd ever had, so I was wary of taking a big 16-year-old crap on it.

How could we get anywhere close to the film's production values, I asked Joe? How would we do the sedan-car chases, the splurge-gun battles and, most important of all, how could we do justice to those amazing Paul Williams songs? I could see my dad shaking his head and saying (with lots of reverb), 'You'll make fools of yourselves …' But J-Corn reasoned that there were workarounds for all these problems, some even outlined at the back of the playscript specifically for amateur productions, and as far as the songs went, we knew lots of school musicians and we liked singing, 'So it'll be good, man, fuck it!'

My next issue with the production was casting. Joe decided Ben should play Bugsy, as he was more of a leading man, and I would be perfect as the rotund mob boss Fat Sam. This was a blow.

After the success of *Pvt Wars* I was still pretty sure I was Robert De Niro, and suddenly I was being told I was actually the overweight sidekick. Apart from the insult to my performing skills that this represented, I'd been self-conscious about my body ever since a girl I fancied at boarding school had told me: 'You'd be quite handsome if you lost some weight,' and now here I was being Fat Sam-shamed. 'Man, it's the funniest part,' said Joe when I failed to hide my disappointment. As soon as we began rehearsals I realised Joe was right, and once I'd relaxed, Big Boned Sam (as my character preferred to identify) gave me licence to go BIG in every way.

We wanted Louis to be involved with *Bugsy Malone* and cast him in one of the main parts as rival mob boss Dandy Dan. A few weeks into rehearsals, however, Louis baulked, claiming the size of the role was making him anxious. Joe gave Louis four small walk-on parts instead, but it was a drag having to recast at a time when we were scrambling to resolve problems with nearly every aspect of the overambitious production. In our paranoid moments we suspected that Louis was reluctant to be such a prominent part of a show he feared might be a spectacular turkey, though Louis has assured me over 46 times since then that this wasn't the case. I *think* I believe him.

In the end *Bugsy Malone*, which we performed over three nights in early June 1986, was another SPECTACULAR SUCCESS. In fact, I hope you won't mind if I just take this opportunity to say a few overdue thank-yous.

First of all, to our amazing cast – guys, you were great, and it was such a privilege to work with so many talented people who normally we would have completely ignored in

Yard because you were in different years or social groups. It was so cool for us, and probably even more so for you, to get to come together and create such a special JOEADZ event. To our musical director and the wonderful *Bugsy Malone* band, I just want to say – wow. The music in this production could so easily have been a messy cacophony, and there were times when it looked as though it definitely would be, but when it came down to it you guys pulled it all the way out of the bag. Even the horn parts on 'My Name Is Tallulah' only made the audience wince a couple of times. As for our amazing production crew, and all the people – including the cool teachers – who worked so hard to help us bring this show together at a time when some uncool teachers and uptight parents were giving us a lot of shit about not revising for our exams, all I can say is: you were incredible and I hope you didn't get too hung up on those occasions when Joe and I acted like appalling, spoiled arseholes. At least we didn't sexually harass any of you. Finally, to the school, thank you for believing in us enough to let us use the special ancient hall where you would normally have been putting on earnest productions of Pinter, Beckett, Stoppard and all that other predictable shit so we could do our ground-breaking production of a children's film from ten years previously. Sorry about the whipped cream messing up those seventeenth-century wooden carvings, but I think you'll agree that the amount of fun Joe, Ben and I were clearly having during 'You Give a Little Love' more than made up for it. THANKS!

The first of our sixth-form exams happened just a few days after the final performance of *Bugsy Malone*, so our euphoria and the sense that we were more than just a little bit brilliant was short-lived. It took a further bashing when my parents received that term's exam results and report cards, which predicted A-level catastrophe. 'No more plays,' announced Dad at another tense family supper.

Now that I know the extent of his financial difficulties at

the time, I can understand why Dad wanted me to focus on getting the results that he believed would eventually insulate me from a life of similar financial worries. Even if he hadn't had money problems, I dare say it was reasonable for Dad to be keen that I didn't screw up my education, but at the time I felt like Billy Elliot, being forced to deny my true fabulousness because it didn't fit in with my uptight dad's boring view of the world.

Twitch

To get around the parental play embargo, Joe decided we should make another film. Over a series of damp weekends during winter term 1986 we filmed *Twitch*, a version of the Sweeny Todd story that Cornish had adapted himself. (The title was a nod to *Twitch of the Death Nerve*, a 1971 film by Italian slasher pioneer Mario Bava. No, I haven't seen it either.)

Ben Walden starred once again, this time as psychotic café owner Maxwell Hitch, who along with his murdery wife (played by Susanna Kleeman, transcendent as Tallulah in *Bugsy Malone*) made meat pies out of their victims and enjoyed a huge upsurge in business subsequently.

My character was Donovan Spanner, a bad-tempered, no-nonsense cop on the trail of Maxwell Hitch. My work in *Wars* and *Malone* had showcased my mugging talents, but *Twitch* was a serious, gritty film drama, and if I was to do justice to the complexities of the part, I needed to step out of my comfort zone as an actor. I decided the best way to do this was to deliver all my lines as if I was absolutely furious, often emphasising the words by pointing aggressively. If even more depth was required, I would sigh, close my eyes and run a hand through my spiky hair.

To play the part of Detective Spanner's assistant Harvey, a

dim-witted and thuggish young policeman, we decided to give a still barely pubescent Louis Theroux one more try. Louis, pleased that the *Bugsy Malone* incident had been forgotten, was happy to be involved and insisted he was doing his best to be menacing, though Joe and I were concerned he was just playing his part for laughs and compromising the seriousness of the project. Perhaps the material was just beyond his grasp at that stage of his emotional development.

There are some clips of *Twitch* (as well some of that behind-the-scenes footage from *A Few Friends for Dinner*) on *The Story of Adam and Joe*, which can be found on the extras of *The Adam and Joe DVD*, which can be found in selected charity shops and extinct format museums. Joe's also been posting a few of those clips on his Instagram page recently. Powerful as they are, I think I prefer Cornish's more recent films.

*　*　*

At the end of our first sixth-form year our little gang was being compared by some people in school to the Hollywood 'Brat Pack', the posse of actors that appeared in films like *Weird Science*, *Pretty in Pink*, *The Outsiders* and *The Breakfast Club*, all of which we loved.

Unfortunately, the comparisons were heavily sarcastic, and one day I was handed an anonymously written, photocopied 'Gossip Sheet' that included a paragraph referring to us as 'The Prat Pack'. '*How much longer are they going to subject us to their tedious amateur theatrics?*' asked the author, before complaining that '*they seem to believe Steven Spielberg will turn up at any moment and whisk them off to Hollywood on his magic carpet*'.

Years later, Steven Spielberg did exactly that. At least, he whisked Joe off to Hollywood, along with Edgar Wright, to work with him on *Tintin*, but apparently there wasn't enough room on the fucking magic carpet for the most talented, funny and handsome member of The Prat Pack (which was

Buckles, in case that wasn't clear). And by the way, if I had been invited, I wouldn't have gone on my friend's podcast and made an anecdote about Tom Cruise doodling on a notepad last over half a decade.

Argument with Wife Log 2

SUBJECT OF ARGUMENT	WHETHER TO SAY 'LEASH' OR 'LEAD'
MAIN POINTS – WIFE	'A leash is used to tether an animal. A lead is used to walk it.'
MAIN POINTS – BUCKLES	'Jesus Christ!'
WINNER	WIFE

SUBJECT OF ARGUMENT	CHILDREN'S SCREEN TIME
MAIN POINTS – WIFE	'They have no more screen time than their friends.'
MAIN POINTS – BUCKLES	'Fuck their friends! We're talking about OUR children! To be clear, I'm not literally suggesting we fuck their friends.'
WINNER	ONGOING AT TIME OF WRITING

SUBJECT OF ARGUMENT	WAS HELENA CHRISTENSEN'S SON 'MINGUS' NAMED AFTER CHARLIE MINGUS?
MAIN POINTS – WIFE	'No. Mingus is a common Danish name.'
MAIN POINTS – BUCKLES	'Of course she named him after Charlie Mingus! Unless she thought it was funny to make a baby name out of the words "minge" and "dingus".'
WINNER	BUCKLES

SUBJECT OF ARGUMENT	CUTLERY DRAWER
MAIN POINTS – WIFE	'Does it really matter where the spoons go?'
MAIN POINTS – BUCKLES	'Does anything really matter?'
WINNER	BUCKLES

SUBJECT OF ARGUMENT	FAILURE TO TAKE REUSABLE SHOPPING BAGS TO SUPERMARKET
MAIN POINTS – WIFE	'I hadn't planned to do a shop so I didn't have the bags.'
MAIN POINTS – BUCKLES	'Had you planned to KILL THE PLANET?'
WINNER	BUCKLES

SUBJECT OF ARGUMENT	TEXTING WHILE WE WATCH TV
MAIN POINTS – WIFE	'I'm organising the entire running of this household.'
MAIN POINTS – BUCKLES	'You're missing the nuances of Ant and Dec's I'm a Celebrity ... links, which is rude and annoying.'
WINNER	WIFE

SUBJECT OF ARGUMENT	REFERRING TO A GROUP OF MEN AND WOMEN AS 'GUYS'
MAIN POINTS – WIFE	'Women find it offensive to be called "guys". It's a gender-specific term.'
MAIN POINTS – BUCKLES	'Not the way I use it.'
WINNER	BUCKLES

CHAPTER 13

1985

read somewhere (probably the *Guardian*) that people who went to boarding school often try to compensate for the trauma of being separated from their parents at a young age by developing unhealthily intense attitudes to love, sex and intimacy. Whatever – 1985 was the year of my sixteenth birthday and whether it was boarding-school trauma, teen-age hormones or just being self-absorbed and oversensitive, my attitude to love, sex and intimacy was beginning to get unhealthily intense.

I was still pining for my prep-school love, Alison. She was now at school out in the country and lived abroad the rest of the time (or she at least said she did), so we hadn't seen each other for nearly three years, but we still maintained a fitful correspondence by mail. I would tell her how much I loved her and how much I hated Westminster, and she would reply with long, stream-of-consciousness rambles in bubbled cursive that seldom attempted to match my level of romantic intensity. Instead, she would inform me that Anne-Marie was making blow-job faces at her, that Zoe had just farted on her favourite bubble-gum-scented rubber and that Tanya fancied a boy who had ginger pubic hair and was known as 'Rouge Pube'. I responded by insinuating that I had considered over-dosing on aspirin. That refocused her for a week or two, but by the end of the spring term 1985 it was clear that Alison and I were all washed up.

We had agreed that if either of us ever felt the relationship had run its course, that person would send the other a symbolic empty envelope. That way, we could bypass the inevitable break-up platitudes. Not for us the whole 'it's not you, it's me' routine – that bullshit was for 13-year-olds. We were 15.

One cold, grey afternoon I wrote Alison's address on an empty envelope, sealed it, then walked around St James's Park for a while thinking deep thoughts. I found a post box but hesitated. The point of the empty envelope was to save the recipient a load of self-involved moaning, but when it came to the crunch I was determined that, somehow, Alison must be made aware of my pain.

Leaning on the post box I scrawled on the back of the envelope: '*Love dares you to change our way of caring about ourselves. This is our last dance.*' I stopped short of writing '*... this is ourselves – Under Pressure*' because I worried that might destroy Alison completely.

A period of emotional convalescence followed. On weekends when I was home from school this took the form of a routine that began with McDonald's takeout in front of *The New Adventures of Wonder Woman*. If Dad was home he'd appear at the door of the front room, watch Linda Carter in action for a little while, then say something cryptically sleazy like, 'She's got nice eyes.' That was at least preferable to the usual rows we'd have about how I needed to take O-level revision more seriously.

I started to look forward to Dad being away so I could enjoy a lecture-free Saturday night of television-watching that concluded with episodes of *Auf Wiedersehen, Pet* and *Magnum P.I.*, often accompanied by a box of French Fancies – little square sponge cakes with vanilla-flavoured fondant topping, all encased in either pink, yellow or brown icing, eight to a pack. Though I always intended to limit myself to two French Fancies, one pink and one yellow, most weekends I was down to the browns by the end of *Auf Wiedersehen, Pet*, and they, too, were usually snaffled by the end of *Magnum*.

Preparing for O levels meant that for much of the first half of 1985 we had fewer regular classes and were expected to use the additional free time for revision, either at school or at home. I went home but decided that instead of revising I would use the time to watch more TV. On the rare occasions Dad was also in residence he would ask why I was slumped in front of Max Headroom with a pack of chocolate digestives when he was paying for me to go to an expensive school and it was term time. Rather than entertain that entirely reasonable question, I'd stomp out and go to the cinema with Joe.

Joe and I stood in a lot of West End movie queues that year, making stupid comments about whatever film we were about to see, hatching plans for our own brilliant projects and trying to stay out of range of the big homeless man who looked like Chief Bromden from *One Flew Over the Cuckoo's Nest* and stood motionless by the Empire cinema in Leicester Square for hours at a time, hawking up big gobs of spit that described his pavement patch in a semi-circle of flob. And of course there was Protein Man, an old guy with a Donovan cap and a big sign proclaiming that we were all at risk from dangerous levels of lust if we continued with lives that included 'fish, bird, meat, cheese, egg, beans, peas, nuts and sitting'.

RAMBLE

A lot of films made an impression on us in 1985 – some great, some not so great. We saw *Terminator* in January and emerged from the Odeon South Kensington so delighted that we ended up seeing every film Schwarzenegger starred in for the next decade, albeit with increasingly generous squirtings of irony sauce.

Despite our fondness for all things American, *Back to the Future* rubbed us up the wrong way for feeling too cheesily Yankocentric; all cars and high schools and proms, as epitomised by the enervatingly energetic Huey Lewis and the News on the soundtrack – 'FUCK Huey Lewis and the News,' I thought then (though now I'm old, I don't mind the odd slice).

Terry Gilliam's *Brazil* was a genuine mind-blower that colonised my thoughts for years and gave shape to a nebulous suspicion that the adult world was a meaningless nightmare of fear and conformity. We were particularly excited when Robert De Niro popped up as a heroic anti-establishment plumber whose parting words – 'We're all in it together' – struck me as especially ace.

We saw the sci-fi vampire/London zombie film *Lifeforce* in a busy Leicester Square cinema one Saturday night and had a hoot enjoying the badness of the dialogue, the over-the-top horror and the frequent full-frontal nudity. Fun though the evening was, I'm happy to say it didn't turn me into an adherent of the 'so-bad-it's-good' aesthetic.

Sub Ramble

Another of our favourite films in 1985 was *Beverly Hills Cop*. We already rated Eddie Murphy from *Trading Places*, but *BHC*, along with Harold Faltermeyer's brilliant synth-pop theme, sealed the deal and thereafter our interactions were peppered with quotes, especially (in Eddie voice) 'Get the fuck outta here!' (as said frequently by Eddie) and 'It's not sexy, it's animal' (as said by Bronson Pinchot as the camp art dealer). Later we would watch Murphy's concert film *Delirious* and a new set of words and noises entered our lexicon. Especially fun was pretending to be Eddie pretending to be James Brown, and 'SERIOOOOU!' became our rallying cry.

I recently found *Delirious* on Netflix and started watching it again for the first time in 35 years. Oh shit. I'd forgotten how extreme those first 10 minutes are. We're not dealing with a few jokes that would raise the eyebrows of the odd 'woke' teenager in 2020; it's full-on, aggressive homophobia. I have a feeling we used to fast-forward a lot of that stuff to get to the more fun bits, but even that seems strange by today's standards, when often it feels too difficult to enjoy some aspects of an artist's work if other parts of that work are indefensible shit. Did we have more sophisticated critical faculties back in 1985? Or were we just more comfortable with indefensible shit?

The film that left the biggest emotional crater on Planet Buckles that year was *The Breakfast Club*. It was released in the UK on my sixteenth birthday (7 June 1985), and like many teens at the time I felt the film spoke to me directly about the intolerable pressure being exerted by the adult world.

Though I wasn't directly affected by any of the issues that had been piled onto Claire, Allison, Brian, Andrew and Bender, the central message resonated loudly: us kids are important and sensitive and special, and adults like my dad don't get it because 'when you grow up, your heart dies'.

I made at least four trips to see *The Breakfast Club* at the cinema that summer and every time John Bender punched the air and 'Don't You (Forget About Me)' kicked in, my heart lifted off. I spotted a bad review of the film in *Time Out* (written by a fucking adult, of course) and I cut it out, stuck it in my diary and scrawled my review of their review over the top of it: *'THIS REVIEW IS CRAP. NOT TRUE!'*

The other night, after my wife had gone to bed, I stayed up flicking through TV channels and there was *The Breakfast Club*. I watched it for the first time in about 30 years, and though a few moments still raised a tingle – 'So, Ahab, can I have all my doobage?', 'The chicks cannot hold the smoke! That's whut it eees!' – I had to watch a lot of it through my fingers.

Times have changed and *The Breakfast Club*'s jarring moments include some casual homophobia, sexual harassment and a makeover that 'fixes' Ally Sheedy's alluringly odd character Allison by turning her into a pink-bloused girly girl (though I recall those moments feeling strange at the time). The thing I found most difficult about watching the film in middle age was remembering how much I once identified with those whiney, self-absorbed bellends. Then I wondered if I'm really all that different now.

Poster Boys

Joe's parents let him to draw a mural with felt pens on the walls of his bedroom at the top of their house in Stockwell. He tried to reproduce the cover of the Thompson Twins' 'We Are Detective' and Keith Haring's artwork from Malcom McLaren's album *Duck Rock* before losing confidence and covering every inch of his bedroom walls with posters.

These were not the Athena posters that hung in every other study at school – airbrushed sports cars and heavily made-up women with giant punky hairdos, pouting and 'being sexy' – Joe went for film posters.

Some of them were for classics from the Sixties and Seventies that he'd bought from shops in Soho frequented by film geeks (in those days they would have been called 'anoraks' or 'saddos'), others were for films that had only just been released.

'Where do you get these?' I asked him.

'I'll show you,' he said, and one Saturday afternoon we got the Tube from Stockwell to Tottenham Court Road. Upon arrival, rather than ride the many escalators up and out into the West End as we would normally have done, we hung around on the Northern Line platform and started inspecting the film posters.

Joe stopped at one for *A Nightmare on Elm Street*, a film we'd loved when we saw it at a preview screening at the Scala in King's Cross earlier that year. One of the top corners had come unglued and Cornballs flashed me a grin as he started tugging at the corner with little teasing gestures. Sure enough, the poster began to peel away easily, and after a quick look round the empty platform, Joe whipped it away from the wall with a flourish, before rolling it hastily and tucking it under his arm. 'There we go,' he said. 'It was coming off anyway.'

It took me a while to get up the courage to have a go myself.

I knew this was theft and vandalism, but I clung to the fact that, as Joe said, some of the posters were already hanging half off the station walls, either because they'd been put up badly or because the paste had been watered down too much, so actually we were sort of tidying up, which was public spirited of us. Also, we weren't stealing from an individual, just some rich film company who would never know or care that one of the thousands of posters they'd put up had made its way to a teenager's bedroom, where at least it could be seen by other cinema-goers, though admittedly in slightly smaller numbers.

With these bullshit justifications sloshing round my head and my heart thumping, I found a poster for the new Bond film, *A View to a Kill*, the corner of which was already flapping in the warm wind whistling down the Northern Line tunnel. The following Monday it was Blu-Tacked to my study wall at school where I could admire the artwork featuring Grace Jones and Roger Moore's ludicrously extended legs at my leisure.

Over the next few weeks we became expert at finding the least busy station platforms and the most peely-looking walls, and before long my study was completely covered with posters for *Terminator, Beverly Hills Cop, Brazil, 2010, Into the Night, Starman* and *Cocoon*. Sometimes we'd find that several posters had been stuck on top of one another in a big wad, so we'd dislodge the whole stack, roll it as much as possible and, once home, soak the posters in a warm bath until they slid apart, revealing the partial history of a year's worth of film releases.

One sunny Saturday afternoon during the summer holidays in 1985, Joe and I were deep in the tunnels of Leicester Square Tube and enjoying a particularly bountiful haul. We'd been down there a couple of hours, waiting for the platforms to empty after each train departure, then hopping and skipping with criminal glee as we harvested posters, when out of nowhere a policewoman and her male colleague suddenly appeared. In that special patronising voice the police are so good at, the policewoman called out, 'Hello! Do you two want to come over here?'

Joe, who was taller than both the cops, didn't seem worried by this development, but as we made our way over to the patronising police, I was struggling not to cry. 'We've been watching you two upstairs on the telly,' said the man cop, pointing up at the CCTV cameras that we'd never even registered before. 'Dancing around like a pair of berks.'

'That's nice,' said Joe. 'I'm glad we've been entertaining you.'

The man cop didn't like that. 'That's criminal damage,' he said, gesturing to the rolls of posters we'd abandoned further down the platform. 'You could go to prison for that. Is that what you want?'

I decided the time had come for something a bit more conciliatory and with my voice wavering I replied, 'No. We don't want to go to prison. We are really, really sorry.'

The woman cop smiled faintly. 'I think your mummies and daddies would be very disappointed by this, wouldn't they?' she said, and before Joe could make his contemptuous pony sound, I looked imploringly at both cops and in my poshest, wettest voice said, 'Yes, they really would be disappointed. We're never going to do this again, I promise.'

The cops exchanged a look and the man said, 'Well, you'd better make sure you don't then. Consider this a warning. Go on.'

Out in Leicester Square I savoured the sweet taste of liberty, but it was tainted by an uncomfortable feeling. Not for the criminal damage (the posters were coming off anyway), but for how quickly I'd tried to ingratiate myself to the cops and how being middle class and polite (and probably white) had got us off the hook. Or maybe they were just nice cops who correctly identified us as the kind of youths who would benefit from a patronising cop scare. Either way, from that day on we were much more careful when stealing film posters.

Holiday Time

Later that summer I went on two foreign holidays in the same month, something that must have pleased Dad as they were down to his wangling powers at the *Sunday Telegraph* and the privileges that came from sending me to Westminster.

First, Patrick and I got invited to stay at a hotel in Crete that was partly owned by the Greek Cypriot parents of Stelios, one of Patrick's housemates at Westminster. We spent two delirious weeks out there largely left to our own devices and discovering the joy of alcoholic cocktails, water-skiing and holiday discos.

A few days after I'd returned from Greece, I travelled with my family to China, a trip that was bookended by a couple of nights staying at the Mandarin Oriental hotel in Hong Kong, where each of us had our own room with personalised writing paper on the desk. 'Not too bad, eh?' said Dad. 'We're getting the red-carpet treatment!'

'Why though, Dad?' we asked.

'Why? Because I'm a very important journalist, that's why.'

RAMBLE

More exciting than the rooms, the writing paper and the red-carpet treatment at the Mandarin was the little menu on top of the TV detailing the six films available on the hotel's movie channel: *Thunderbolt and Lightfoot, Logan's Run, Victor Victoria, Bustin' Loose, Marathon Man* and *The Jerk*. Over the next few nights

I watched all of them but started with *The Jerk*, despite never having heard of Steve Martin or even knowing what a 'jerk' was.

My favourite moment was a scene in which Steve Martin's character, Navin R. Johnson, is working as a petrol-pump attendant. The new phone book is delivered and Navin explodes with excitement when he finds his name is listed in there. 'This is the kind of spontaneous publicity, your name in print, that makes people!' he cries. 'Things are going to start happening to me now!'

Cut to a deranged gunman (played by M. Emmet Walsh from *Blade Runner*) randomly selecting Navin's name from the phonebook, then turning up at the gas station to shoot him. Something about the way Walsh says, 'Die, gas pumper!' made me laugh a lot, and for the rest of the summer it was my favourite thing to say, along with, 'Things are going to start happening to me now!' – a phrase that still pops into my head whenever a particularly underwhelming offer comes in from my agent.

On several occasions during our stay in Hong Kong, Mum and Dad went off with boring public relations people and I was allowed to wander alone through the humid maze of markets in the Kowloon district. I had been given my first allowance – a very generous £40 a month – and I used it to buy my first Walkman from a tiny strip-lit Kowloon electronics shop.

Minutes later, as I drifted between the covered stalls wearing my new headphones and listening to *Autobahn* by Kraftwerk, I wondered how life could get any cooler.

Girlfriend Is Better

I came back down to earth when we got back to England to find my O-level results had arrived. Thought I feared the worst, I had done well enough in a handful of subjects to return to Westminster as a sixth-former in September, sporting a pair of brothel-creepers, trousers with legs taken in by Mum and a new spiky haircut that made me look like an affable lavatory brush. With exams out of the way and new looks on display, there was an atmosphere of excitement and possibility, intensified by the new intake of sixth-form girls.

One of them, Lottie, looked to me like the John Everett Millais painting of Ophelia, except with a bob and not drowned in a river. She was tall and stylish, gliding through the gaggles of awkward boys in Yard like a swan. That's how I remember it. Probably she just walked around normally.

Like all the girls that got into the sixth form at Westminster, Lottie was also extremely intelligent, though evidently not so intelligent that she knew to resist the charms of the French Fancy-snaffling emotional maelstrom that was the 16-year-old Buckles. Maybe it was the Eddie Murphy impressions that got her or maybe it was the bog-brush hairdo, but after only five weeks in the sixth form I was 'going out' with Lottie and I was in love again.

For a fortnight or so Lottie and I were blissfully happy. We wrote soppy notes in class, grinned at each other as our friends made puking gestures, and took every available opportunity to just kiss and kiss and kiss. Kissing Lottie's lovely Pre-Raphaelite face was so electrifyingly wonderful that for weeks I didn't seriously consider anything more advanced until we went on a date to the Fulham ABC to see *Prizzi's Honor*.

Though my eyes were aimed at the screen, my brain was in my left hand, which was undertaking an agonisingly slow trek from base camp at the hem of Lottie's skirt, up previously uncharted bare thigh to the cotton-covered summit, at which point Lottie made it clear the mission was over and I was embarrassed that I'd revealed myself as the dirty monkey boy I really was. Perhaps that was the moment the spell was broken, because despite a few more weekends of bedroom kissathons to the sound of *Swoon* and *Steve McQueen* by Prefab Sprout playing repeatedly on her new auto-reverse boombox, by Christmas it was becoming obvious that Lottie needed something more than non-stop snogging in her life, and my disastrous performance at a couple of parties that December sealed my fate.

Party Number One was for Joe's seventeenth birthday on 20 December and it took place at his parents' house in Stockwell. Ben and I got there a few hours early and started to indulge in our favourite recent discovery – no, not mutual masturbation, but alcoholic spirits. By the time Lottie arrived, I had turned myself into a tottering cocktail of overexcitement, anxiety, lust, vodka and orange juice. She'd barely had much of a chance to say hello to anyone or, God forbid, have fun hanging out with people other than Buckles, when I led Lottie away from the ground-floor partygoers to a spare room upstairs. There, my best groping efforts were frustrated by a serious case of the spins and after a few close calls I reluctantly retired to the toilet to spend the rest of the evening poised for puking action while the muffled sounds of the Pet Shop Boys, Level 42 and Nik Kershaw drifted up through the floor. When I eventually emerged, 'Boys Don't Cry' by The Cure was playing and Lottie, along with most of the other guests, had left.

Party Number Two was at Lottie's house on New Year's Eve and this time, instead of getting hammered, I sulked most of the night because I thought Lottie was flirting with Joe and Louis. 'Fucking tall people,' I thought, fully insane with covetous insecurity, 'of course they stick together!' With 1986 minutes away, I was still moping about asking Lottie's friends if they thought she still loved me. 'Still?' said her friend Julia, before telling me I should lighten up and have a good time – a piece of advice that for the chronic overthinker is up there with 'Just be yourself' for total redundancy. 'Oh! Have a good time! Yes, of course. I was so busy being turned inside out with jealousy I forgot about that option. Thanks so much for reminding me!'

At home the next morning I lay in bed sighing, replaying the previous evening's events. I was about to call Lottie when I heard the phone ring and Dad shouted from downstairs, 'Adam! Lottie for you!' We arranged to meet in Blushes Café on the King's Road and I walked there with *Strange Days* by The Doors on my Walkman, rehearsing an apology for my recent run of low-quality behaviour. Lottie was grateful for the apology but dumped me anyway. Very nicely, though. She really was a lovely person – tall-boy flirting aside. She went to catch the 137 bus back to Clapham and I trudged home in the rain listening to 'People Are Strange', sobbing my 16-year-old tits off.

BOWIE ANNUAL

My mother is Chilean and when I was a toddler I spoke Spanish. Then someone told my mum she was confusing her young son by talking to him in two languages, and from then on she spoke to me only in English, thereby robbing me of a superpower, which I think may be a form of abuse. Nevertheless, I did O- and A-level Spanish because I hoped an innate familiarity with the language would be an advantage and I imagined I could get my mum to do my homework.

It turned out Mum wasn't all that keen on doing my homework, although she did translate the *Hunky Dory* track 'Quicksand' into Spanish so I could sing it at my O-level oral exam, which I thought might impress the examiner. On the day, I was too embarrassed to sing and just recited, '*Estoy más cerca de la puerta de oro ...*' barely making it to the end of the first verse. The examiner turned out to be a Bowie fan and thought it was funny, but said, 'It's a shame you didn't sing it.' I learnt a valuable lesson that day: if you're going to get your mum to translate David Bowie songs into Spanish, you need to fully commit to the idea and sing them.

That summer holiday, in the sweaty gusset between the twin bummers of exams and results, my enthusiasm for Bowie received a boost. It came at the right time because though I'd enjoyed his appearances in *Merry Christmas, Mr Lawrence* and the *Jazzin' for Blue Jean* video, both *Let's Dance* and *Tonight* suggested he was no longer the cool and captivating musician I'd originally fallen in love with. Nevertheless, I was still intrigued when I read that he was to be one of the performers at Bob Geldof's charity concert in aid of African famine relief, Live Aid.

To the cynical 16-year-old Buckles, Live Aid seemed, at least from an 'artistic' point of view, like a bloated nightmare that needed to be avoided at all costs, and Bowie's involvement was the only thing that was at all interesting about it. That Saturday afternoon Mum and Dad took us to visit some friends of theirs in West London, and while the adults sat in the sunny garden and drank Pimm's, my sister and I joined the teenagers watching the coverage of Live Aid inside. Bob Geldof shouted at us, there was some famine footage, then Status Quo played 'Rockin' All Over the World', at which point I decided I'd be better off going outside to steal a glass of Pimm's or two.

But when we got back to Earl's Court I went to my room, turned on the new Sony Trinitron TV that to my brother's and sister's annoyance I'd somehow wangled for my birthday, and at 7.20 p.m. that warm evening, there was David, stepping onto the stage at Wembley wearing a grin that made me grin. His boring feathery haircut and powder-blue suit made him look like an estate agent from *Miami*  *Vice*, but when he introduced his band I perked up, as it included half of Prefab Sprout and Thomas Dolby on keyboards.

RAMBLE

Thomas Dolby's 1982 single 'Windpower' was robot music with a heart, i.e. the best kind of music. Sure, I liked 'She Blinded Me with Science' and it was fun seeing eccentric TV scientist Magnus Pyke in the video, back when cross-genre migration was still a novelty, but it was hearing 'One of Our Submarines' and 'Europa and the Pirate Twins' being played in the evenings on Radio 1 that deepened my curiosity.

When I became friends with Joe it turned out he liked Dolby, too, and asked me if I'd heard his second album, *The Flat Earth*. Cornballs made me a copy, and despite parts of it sounding dangerously close to lounge

music, it wasn't long before I was under its spell.
For a while it was a ritual to listen to the dreamy,
hypnotic title track and think emotional thoughts last
thing before I went to sleep in my study at school.
I played it to Mum one day, expecting her to love it, too,
but she shook her head. 'It's a bit soppy, isn't it, Adam?
I prefer Space Odyssey.'

Soppy or not, I went out and bought *The Flat Earth* and
Dolby's first album, *The Golden Age of Wireless*, and for
the next few years I played them nearly as often as
my Bowie cassettes.

And then there was Prefab Sprout. Their album
Steve McQueen came out a couple of weeks after
The Breakfast Club was released in 1985 and Joe and
I were delighted to find that it had been produced by
Thomas Dolby.

There was nothing robotic about the Sprouts, however
– it was all pure emotion, but with so many surprising
structural elements and lyrical ideas, it never felt gloopy.

A couple of years later I went with Joe to see Prefab
Sprout live at the Hammersmith Palais. My first gig.
I couldn't see much because I was too short and I was
disappointed it didn't sound more like the record.
Afterwards my ears rang for an hour. I used the cashpoint
round the corner from the venue and turned round
to find a jittery man showing me a knife and saying,
'All right, Star, give me your wallet.' My first mugging.
I walked home feeling sorry for myself but faintly cool
after being called 'Star'.

With Dolby and assorted Sprouts on stage alongside Bowie at Live Aid, it was as if he was sending me a message and saying, 'You know that music that your mum thinks is a bit soppy? Well, guess what, you and Cornballs aren't the only ones who like it. I like it, too, because, as you correctly guessed, we're kindred spirits who'd probably get on really well if we ever met.'

As if to further emphasise our psychic link, Bowie's Live Aid set began with 'TVC 15', my favourite song from *Station to Station*, an album I'd only recently got into, which had kept me going through O levels.
I'd never heard 'TVC 15' playing anywhere except on my headphones, so it was a thrill to see him do it with Dolby (filling in for Roy Bittan on keyboards, of course).

After just four songs Bowie introduced a video of starving African children set to the music of 'Drive' by The Cars. Presumably the organisers thought that the sight of children starving was not in itself sufficiently poignant to engage the emotions of potential benefactors and that what was needed was some syrupy synth-driven rock balladry. I resisted the urge to switch over in protest at such manipulative tactics, and while the sound of men in sunglasses holding down synthesiser chords oozed out of the TV, I watched as one starving child after another failed to brush away the flies landing on their faces.

By the time the video concluded I was crying, unable to tell for certain what had got to me more: those children, or a song I didn't even like. I rang the number on the screen and got out my bank card. I wasn't sure that £15 would make me feel better, so I went for £20, and with my new bank account depleted by 50 per cent, the sobbing subsided.

CHAPTER 14

FUN DAD

lthough I'm perfect now, I was a selfish baby man well into my twenties, and never seriously considered having children for a second. After all, I'd read the Philip Larkin poem and I'd seen what having children did to my mum and dad. They just argued all the time and never seemed to have any fun at all. No thanks.

One sunny Britpop day towards the end of the Nineties, I bumped into my old girlfriend Lottie in South London. I hadn't seen her since we were teenagers and I was surprised when she told me she was married with two young kids. My friends hadn't started doing that kind of thing yet. 'You should come round and meet them,' said Lottie.

'Sure, I'd love to spend a boring, noisy afternoon seeing how you've succumbed to your societal programming and thrown your life away,' I thought. But I didn't want to be rude, so I said, 'Yes, that would be lovely! I'll pop by tomorrow, if I'm not too busy.'

The next day I took a break from playing *Super Aleste* on the SNES (Super Nintendo Entertainment System) and cycled over to the small terraced house in Tooting where Lottie lived, arriving just as her husband Gavin was giving the two toddlers their lunch.

The first thing that hit me on entering the house was the overpowering funk of cheese with notes of vomit and poo, none of which I have ever enjoyed. Gavin (who seemed nice but a bit sensible) was feeding cheesy ravioli to the toddlers, and though they were certainly sweet, they had yet to embrace the concept of table manners. It didn't help that Gavin would occasionally scoop up a handful of ravioli and dump it on the Formica tabletop in front of the younger child, whereupon she would spank the gooey pasta delightedly, then smear it on her face. I tried to laugh, but I'd begun to feel queasy and had to stop breathing through my nose.

I asked if I could use the toilet, and when the door was safely closed behind me I took a deep breath, then immediately regretted it. Over in the corner in an uncovered basket was a pile of dirty clothes topped by a pair of children's shorts that had been dramatically soiled (at least, I assumed they belonged to one of the children). 'OK,' I thought, 'so Gavin and Lottie are anti nappies, but are they also anti basket lids, clean air and civilised table behaviour?' I said my goodbyes and cycled away, breathing fresh air luxuriously, resolving as I did so never to have children as it was just far too smelly.

A few years later I got married, and in all the excitement I forgot I was still selfish, immature and ignorant. When the subject of children came up I thought, 'Sure, why not? It'll be fun! My wife can teach them the important stuff and deal with the stinks (though cheesy ravioli will never be on the menu, the tabletop, the faces or anywhere else in the house), and I'll get them into music and films and be their best friend. Easy.'

Being pregnant for nine months forced my wife to make the transition from a life of staying up late, boozing and doing whatever else she wanted with her free time to an altogether more sober routine. I knew it would probably be good if I made that transition along with her, but I decided against it. I thought it was important that at least one of us should carry on having a good time. As a result, during our first few years of parenthood, we ended up leading lives that sometimes felt quite separate, and when we were together, much as I loved the additional company of our little sons and their sweet-smelling soft heads, I couldn't help missing the days when hanging out with my wife would involve friends, alcohol and laughter, with shitting, puking and screaming reserved for special occasions.

Time with my wife in those toddler days often meant a trip to a large indoor space that smelt of feet where we took it in turns to ensure that our children didn't eat too much of the faeces in the ball pit. Back home, our reward would be an episode of a box set after the angels had been successfully neutralised, but we'd be doing well if we got through 20 minutes before the ever-present baby monitor exploded into life, green lights flashing, as harshly distorted wails drowned out the screams of whoever Jack Bauer happened to be torturing.

And that was on the good days, when no one was ill, I didn't have a tax bill I couldn't pay and I wasn't depressed after another brilliant Adam-and-Joe TV pitch had been rejected by some barely sentient TV executive because it wasn't enough like *Banzai*.

RAMBLE

I thought I should check my recollection of these toddler times with my wife. She says: 'Maybe I've forgotten about the bad bits in the rosy haze of middle age, but I don't remember the early years being as crap as you do. I loved the early bit when they were tiny. The mundane routine was preferable to the office, any day. If I could have had ten more babies, I would. I probably still could. I also don't remember you not liking it as much as I did, or going to nearly as many children's play areas with stinky ball pits as you are making out – although I suppose you're hamming it up in order to make this part of the book more entertaining.'

Of course, there *was* more to those early days of parent-hood than bad smells, screaming and a vague worry that I'd made a terrible mistake. From time to time I got to be a FUN DAD. I would announce to my wife that I needed a break from mining nuggets of timeless comedy and was going to do the supermarket shop with the boys while she enjoyed a couple of hours of alone time. Choking back tears of gratitude at my thoughtfulness, my wife would hand me a hastily scribbled list and off we'd go to the Clapham branch of Sainsbury's, FUN DAD and sons on a shopping adventure.

Within minutes of our arrival at the supermarket, the boys would be clapping their hands with delight as their FUN DAD spun them around in the trolley. When they'd start to lose consciousness, I'd lean on the handle and we'd chat as we cruised down the aisles, them being sweet and naïve, me funny and wise, ensuring that the humour and the wisdom were delivered loud enough for passing shoppers to hear and be delighted by. I imagined them thinking, 'Wow, I wish my dad had been as fun as him. If only there were more parents like that, the world would be a better place.'

Back in the car, I'd reach back and give the boys' hands a squeeze the way my dad used to when we were little. Then, unlike my dad, I'd connect my first-generation iPod to the stereo and play a superb selection of left-field music sprinkled with some mainstream classics as part of the boys' cultural education. Sometimes, if a song came on that contained particularly strong language, I'd ride the volume knob and replace the expletives with something child-friendly.

The first time I did this was during the track 'Range Life' by Pavement, which contains a well-enunciated '*FUCK*' towards the end of an otherwise very pretty song. This live censorship technique was the inspiration for a sketch I did in 2006 on a BBC Three show called *Rush Hour*, in which I played a dad on the school run singing along with N.W.A.'s

'Fuck tha Police' but replacing the most explicit and angrily racial lines with blandly pro-establishment, kiddie-friendly lyrics.

RAMBLE

This sketch might now be considered an act of gross cultural appropriation (or 'hip-hopriation'? *Pffft*), but in a way, that's what it was about. A white, middle-class parent excited by music that has no relevance to his own life but wanting to pass on his enthusiasm to his son. Meanwhile, Mum (played in the sketch by actor and comedian Kerry Godliman) looks on disapprovingly.

After the sketch went out in 2007, someone uploaded it to YouTube where it found an audience among the N.W.A. fan community, many of whom, unsurprisingly, had never heard of me and were unsure how to feel about the sketch, as some of the comments made clear:

THENOTORIOUSKRP
hahahaah very funny. I have the urge to slap the guy for taking the song and its message and changing it...But still, its funny

It hadn't crossed my mind that people might be offended by the 'Help the Police' sketch. I thought it was clear the laughs were at the expense of the middle-class wannabe gangster dad. For some people, however,

'Fuck tha Police' is a protest song that articulates decades of fury and frustration with institutional racism and is too important to be bowdlerised (that's right, I said 'bowdlerised'), even for a solid-gold comedy classic.

13STYLEZ
gay. the men gay the boy gay the women ähh bitch coz NWA NOT Firndly to police

HALFLIFEGTA
FUCK THE POLICE not help em. This is gay as hell.

Comedy can be maddeningly confusing. Do I think people should help a racist cop? No. What about fucking a nice cop? I wouldn't advocate that either. Either way, when it comes to deciding whether to help or fuck the police, I don't think this sketch should be used to formulate policy.

Sub-Ramble

Back in the late 2000s a lot of people were still using the word 'gay' to mean 'not very good'. Many of them would argue that they were not homophobic and that the word had simply acquired two distinct meanings. I was one of those people, until one day I described something a bit crap as 'gay' while talking to a friend of mine who is himself a homosexualist. He looked crestfallen and I squirmed. I like the guy a lot and the last thing I want to do is make his crests fall. To my shame, I was too embarrassed to apologise at that moment, but I've never used the word that way again. Disappointingly, I still haven't received any kind of prize.

Meanwhile a professional football joins the YouTube discussion about my 'Help the Police' sketch:

PROFESSIONALFOOTBALL
the original is better

Hard to argue with that. In my defence, though, 'Help the Police' has not replaced the original version, which is still widely available.

GRE0006
if I was in nwa I wold kill him

Shit. gre0006 wants to 'wold kill' me. This is how gangs used to get rid of their enemies in the 'wolden days', i.e. take them out to a range of hills consisting of open country overlying a base of limestone or chalk and shoot them in the hillocks.

At this point, dookiefinder187 (the 187th of the proud dookiefinder clan) enters the discussion:

DOOKIEFINDER187
fuckin white fag, your not from the CPT, if eazy e was alive he come burn down your house with you in it and you be saying 'i'm a pussy, police please help me'

Setting aside the casual homophobia and minor grammar issues, I understand dookiefinder187's frustration. Compared to the average resident of Compton (the CPT), my life has been one of unearned comfort and opportunity and, yes, I would certainly call the emergency services if Eazy-E came back to life, got the train out to Norwich, found our house and set fire to it while my wife, my children, Rosie and I were still inside, but I don't think I'd start the call by saying, 'Hello! I'm a pussy, police please help me.' I'm not sure how it works in the CPT, but in south Norfolk the emergency services will usually respond even if you don't humiliate yourself on the phone first. Luckily 2pac2590 comes to my defence:

2PAC2590 @ DOOKIEFINDER187
wow your so fucking smart dis is a fuckin' joke. eazy e would probobly laugh.

Despite this reassurance from one of the extended 2pac family, dookiefinder187 is still worried:

DOOKIEFINDER187 @ 2PAC2590
I hope your fucking right cus this white fag could be making fun of this song

fender3924 also attempts to mollify dookiefinder187:

FENDER3924 @ DOOKIEFINDER187
Wow broham, shut the fuck up, its supposed to be funny, not serious... Chill out.

Thanks for the support, fender3924. And good to be reminded that if you want someone to chill out, the best way is just to tell them to 'shut the fuck up'. At this point dookiefinder187 has had enough and signs off with:

DOOKIEFINDER187
man fuck you asswipes its no joke if a white guy is rapping.

One day I was on a solo supermarket mission and in the car park I bumped into Matt, an older friend of mine who also has a couple of children. Matt asked after my boys, then aged two and four. 'Oh, you know,' I replied, 'they're exhausting, but wonderful! How about your two?'

'The youngest one's still pretty sweet,' said Matt, 'but the 15-year-old is a real prick most of the time now.'

I laughed, but I thought that was a harsh thing to say, even as a joke. I couldn't conceive of saying something similar about my wonderful fellows. 'As long as they always know how much I love them,' I told myself, 'I'll never need to joke about them being pricks, because they never will be.'

Fast-forward ten years. My eldest son is now 16. I wouldn't call him a real prick, but he does a very good impression of one from time to time. Though a 16-year-old boy treating his parents as if they were the world's biggest shit bags is far from uncommon, for a FUN DAD like me, it was still a nasty shock when it began. I spun this guy around in a supermarket trolley, for crying out loud! I provided a PG introduction to the music of Pavement and other seminal indie bands and I told him his drawings and *Minecraft* constructions were incredible, even though many of them were offensively inept and totally impractical. What more was I supposed to do?

The other day I asked him to sweep up the kitchen and he stared at me as if I'd just proposed selling him to sex traffickers. Looking in to see how he was doing after a few minutes, I found him long-faced, nearly crying, as he moved the broom over random sections of the floor with one hand, the other hand in his pocket (in the sweeping style of Alanis Morissette). I waited as long as I was able, then, helplessly channelling a million dead dads, I actually said the words: 'Come on, put your back into it!'

In moments like these I have to stop myself reminding Grumpy Longface of all those times he promised me he'd never be like this. He was the nine-year-old who thrust his hand into mine and squeezed it gently as we queued for a scary theme-park ride, and when I said, 'Promise me you'll never get too cool to hold my hand,' he promised before adding, 'I wish I could never grow up.' I mean, this guy is a total liar.

The bad sweeper's brother is now 14. His default household demeanour is such a cliché of teenage truculence that one day I showed him one of Harry Enfield's 'Kevin the Teenager' sketches on YouTube, thinking that seeing his shtick so precisely reproduced might give him a new perspective on it. 'Ha-ha! Omigod, you're right, Dad! The way he flies into a sullen rage if he isn't allowed to do exactly what he wants! The expression of utter boredom and contempt! The pathological selfishness! Yeah, fair play, I am exactly like that sometimes, but you know that basically I love you and Mum and I'm grateful for everything you do for me, don't you?'

That I genuinely imagined my 14-year-old son might react that way to a 'Kevin the Teenager' sketch is one of the many indications I've had over the years that a FUN DAD is not necessarily the same thing as a GOOD DAD. The older the children get, the more I feel like neither.

My son watched the 'Kevin the Teenager' sketch with no readable expression whatsoever. I may as well have been showing him a video about how to file a tax return. When it was over he nodded, then asked if he could leave. 'Sure,' I said, feeling bad. 'Hey, look, I'm sorry I showed you that sketch. I thought it would be funny, but actually it was like I was using YouTube to take the piss out of you, which isn't what I wanted to do. It's just that, to me, it doesn't seem long ago that you enjoyed being with us, and I would make you laugh, and you thought I was great, and then gradually all that went away and now what's left is me telling you to take out your AirPods when I'm talking to you and that cereal doesn't count as a healthy meal and that if you create a moat of urine around the base of the toilet, it's reasonable to expect you to clean it up. Meanwhile, you've acquired the ability to see all my shortcomings, and they must be as unattractive to you as the weird pet-shop smell in your room is to me. And before too long you'll leave home, and though you'll come round when you need to do some washing or re-up from the cereal stash, after a while you'll get bored of us nagging you for not looking after yourself properly, especially as me and Mum don't really look after ourselves properly either, and then you'll only come round at Christmas and then not even Christmas. I should know, because that's what I did. Anyway, I thought showing you the "Kevin the Teenager" sketch might give a glimpse of all that for some reason.'

I didn't say any of that, obviously. What do you think I am, some kind of self-absorbed, hyper-sensitive child man who worries he's making all the same mistakes as his own dad except in a more low-brow way?

RAMBLE

One of the many worries I have about being a parent is that the life of privilege my children enjoy will make them spoilt and obnoxiously entitled. A friend of mine told me about a time he was at a busy play area in London, talking with his young son about the family's plans for the holidays, only to have the boy shout loudly, 'Oh, we're not going to bloody Antigua *again*, are we?'

Back when Joe and I were on the radio in 2011, another friend forwarded me an email they'd received from their 13-year-old daughter whose birthday was coming up and who wanted to ensure she got what she wanted. I asked if I could read it out on air and my friend agreed as long as I was careful to keep their daughter anonymous.

The email read:

New message   — ↗ ×

If you want to spend your money wisely I suggest you stick to this list and do NOT buy anything other than the items on it, unless you see something which I may like, in which case, ask me first, otherwise don't get it at all …

RIHANNA TICKETS, MUST BE AT LEAST 2, ONE FOR ME AND A FRIEND.

A NICE DRESS – LIKE MY GREY AMERICAN APPAREL ONE, BUT SLEEVELESS.

Pretty summery top – NOT a shirt, not a tee, must be pretty, show me what it looks like first.

Earrings – they must not be my main present though.

BIKINI – I MUST TRY THESE ON AND RECOMMEND TO YOU, SO BE PATIENT FOR LINKS.

Pants – from Topshop, VERY small present.

No piece of jewellery to be my main present as it's small and I don't wear jewellery.

Make-up – Possibly some foundation, but I must recommend colour, brand and type.

Spare money? Always acceptable.

For someone to paint my wooden desk for me – however this must be done well and cannot be my only present from this person.

To be allowed to have the whole cupboards and put the towels etc in the chest of drawers in my room and move that into the spare room. NO books unless requested.

FISH – MUST INCLUDE TANK, AUTOMATIC WATER CLEANER, 2 PRETTY FISH, AND DECORATIONS FOR INSIDE.

This is pretty much everything. Stick to this list and I will be very happy in the morning. To make me as happy as possible you will need to buy me at least three of my most desired things (in CAPS).

When my own teenagers are at their most unreachable and obnoxious, I think about this email and it cheers me up, not because they're necessarily less spoilt, but because the girl who sent that birthday list is now in her early twenties and is charming, considerate and in no way entitled. And I'm not just saying that because she may read this.

A few days after the 'Kevin the Teenager' incident, I'm driving my 14-year-old to his friend's house. A year ago I would have been in FUN DAD chat mode, making the most of an opportunity for a bit of one-on-one conversation time with one of my children, but a series of chippy exchanges during recent car journeys has encouraged me to scale back my ambitions. Now the AirPods nestled in his ears make it clear that, in case I'm in any doubt, conversation with his father is not top of the agenda.

Nevertheless, I can't help asking, 'What are you listening to?'

'Spotify,' he sighs, continuing to look out of the window.

'Yes, but I was wondering what actual music you were listening to?'

'Have you heard of Q-Tip?' he replies.

'Yes, I'm familiar with Q-Tip. He's very good. Joe always loved A Tribe Called Quest. Put it through the speakers.' Soon 'Breathe and Stop' fills the car and I try to imagine how exciting those sounds must be to him, even with his trying-too-hard-to-be-FUN DAD listening. I try to recall the most thrilling piece of music I heard when I was his age.

'Have you heard "Green Onions" by Booker T. & the MGs?' He shakes his head and starts tapping at his device. I look over, expecting to see him sexting or trading dank memes, but he's on Spotify calling up "Green Onions". Suddenly giddy with the joy of connection, I turn up the volume for the arrival of history's most exhilaratingly primordial Hammond organ figure.

When it hits, I resist the temptation to watch his face as he experiences it for the first time. At the first guitar solo he nods and says, 'It's really good,' and I take this as my cue to turn my head and see that he's trying not to smile.

'He's trying not to smile!' I say.

He smiles.

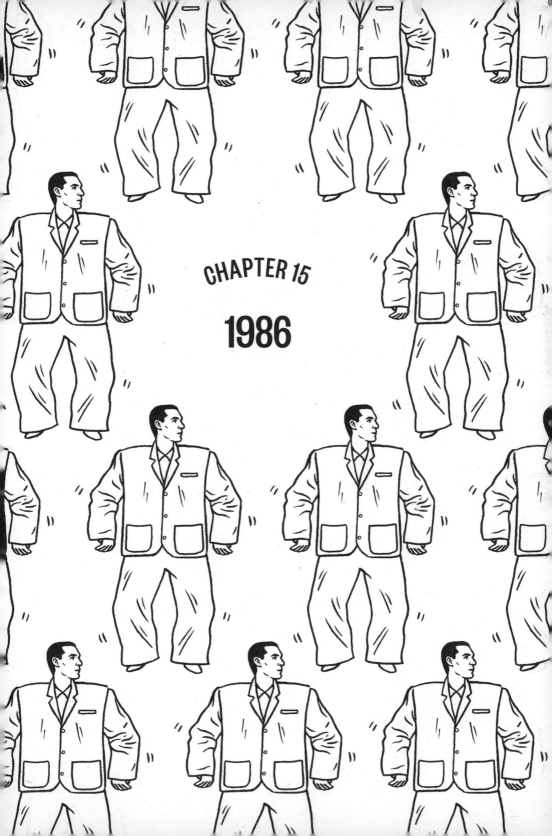

CHAPTER 15

1986

 started the new term in January 1986 nauseated at the prospect of having to see Lottie every day just a couple of weeks after she'd split up with me. It was my first experience of having to continue sharing a space, albeit a large space, with someone who had broken my heart, and every time I caught sight of her in Yard I felt poleaxed. How could she just be carrying on with her life? It was as if breaking up with me wasn't the worst thing that had ever happened to her.

If we found ourselves in the same room, Lottie would smile and do her best to be friendly, but I acted as though she'd executed my entire family in front of me, then danced around their corpses listening to Shakatak (for younger readers, Shakatak had a number of hits in the 1980s with airy jazz-funk numbers that sounded as if they'd been rejected from a commercial for feminine hygiene products for being too insubstantial – in other words, the kind of music that would not be an appropriate accompaniment for dancing around the corpses of my dead family).

Dad announced we could no longer afford the splendour of Earl's Court and Mum found a small terraced house in Clapham, South London. Initially sceptical, Dad perked up when he heard the area was becoming gentrified, but when he went to look round and discovered the gentrification hadn't yet spread to the area we planned to live in, he perked down again. To him, the house in Clapham was a step backwards, but I thought it was a bijou property with tons of character (my room used to belong to an 11-year-old disco-dancing champion and was covered in Barbie stickers), with excellent transport links to Joe Cornish (two Tube stops away in Stockwell) and convenient access to an up-and-coming metropolitan shopping hub (we were just a few hundred yards from a food, booze and hardware shop that also rented out videos).

Our new house was also a short walk from Clapham Common, where Lottie lived, and on several occasions on my way home from a night out with friends I'd spend a while sitting on a park bench opposite her place, listening to a compilation of sad songs, staring up at her bedroom window and thinking myself romantic rather than creepy. A couple of times I was joined on my Bench of Sorrow by men who'd identified me as a possible cruising companion, and they paid for their mistake by having to listen to my tale of lost love before making their excuses and rejoining the night. At least I got to talk to someone.

The thought of talking to my parents about anything complicated or emotional was too embarrassing, and I suspected their advice would be some form of 'Get over it', which I didn't want to hear. I was more in the market for 'Why don't you wallow in it for a very long time?'

Patrick was usually the person I confided in when it came to emotional matters, but he was stuck in his own romantic maelstrom and hadn't been around so much. I tried pouring at least part of my heart out to Joe and Louis, but their response was to offer some superficial reassurance, then start laughing. They weren't being callous; it was just unfamiliar territory for our relationship. I'm sure nowadays all teenage boys are sensitive, enlightened and always there for each other's emotional needs, but for the average 16-year-old male back in 1986, listening to detailed accounts of heartbroken misery was not considered fun or interesting.

It was around this time I started to become more interested in alcohol.

With the possible exception of Louis, who was still even fresher faced than we were, most of our gang were able to get served at pubs and off-licences despite being legally under-age. Booze, which had been gradually entering the picture for a couple of years, was now fuelling more and more of our get-togethers.

I should probably say right now that this isn't building up to me describing how I went completely off the rails and made the decision never to touch another drop. For the time being at least, I still enjoy alcohol, but I don't drink it for the same reasons or to the same degree that I once did, unless my mum's coming over or I have to drive the children to school.

Back in the sixth form, drinking on weekends made me feel as though I was taking a holiday from the awkward and anxious parts of myself I didn't like – but that's why most people start drinking, isn't it? I don't recall any of us standing round the *Track & Field* arcade game at Grafton's pub in Victoria Street and remarking on the delicate blend of flavours in their pint of Foster's. I knew it was naughty to be drinking in a pub underage, but that just made me feel like an outlaw and added to the fun. I didn't think about my health because, other than occasionally having to make myself sick if I got the spins and feeling a bit soft and blurry the morning after a drunken night, I didn't think it was doing me much harm.

For the next decade or so I had more or less the same attitude to alcohol that my parents and many of their friends did: that you only had a problem if you regularly started your day with eight cans of Special Brew on a park bench, talking to yourself and trying to punch people, but if the sun was past the yard arm, it was happy hour! And then there was smoking …

Mum and Dad had both smoked cigarettes but had stopped when I was still little, and by the time I was 15 I was a strident, self-righteous anti-smoker, loudly contemptuous of school friends who had begun to dabble, thinking them dreadful posers.

Then, on our family trip to China in 1985, I'd been wandering through a street market one day in Guangzhou looking for some edgy souvenirs to take back to school, when next to a display of lock knives a table filled with packets of cigarettes caught my eye. They were beautifully and intricately designed – all brightly coloured dragons and flowers – and in those days there wasn't a single warning or decaying body part in sight. I bought three packets for the equivalent of 15p and back at school I gave one to Patrick and one to Joe as a kind of joke.

Then late one night at school, in my single study at the very top of the house, I took a break from Bolsheviks and Mensheviks, crawled onto the low-walled, sloping section of roof outside my window and lit up my first cigarette while listening to 'The Funeral Party' by The Cure on my Walkman. It was completely revolting – the cigarette, not The Cure. I was relieved. 'I guess I'm not a smoker,' I thought. But the next time we had a weekend boozing session I took the pack with me as a prop, and after a couple of drinks I tried another. This time it wasn't so bad. In fact, when taken with alcohol the overall effect was rather pleasant and immediately made me feel complex and adult, which of course was the object of the exercise.

I still have a few minutes of home video shot around this time of a fairly typical Saturday-night excursion beginning with Joe and Louis messing about on a Northern Line train before getting off at Leicester Square and meeting Ben at Burger King for a Coke and a smoke while leafing through *Time Out* and deciding what film to see. That night it was Jean-Jacques Beineix's (*Bay-nex*) epically saucy drama of doomed romance, *Betty Blue*.

When the long, energetic sex scene that opens the film was finally over and our teenage trousers were beginning to slacken, most of the people sat in the smoking section (the right-hand side of the auditorium) lit up a cigarette. Everyone laughed because in those days it was common knowledge that after you'd had a bonk you had a ciggie. Though we were all virgins, we got the joke and sparked up, too, feeling very sophisticated for doing so, and after another scene in which Betty and friends drank Tequila Slammers, we stayed up late into the night at Ben's place in Kentish Town (his mum was away) and did the same.

RAMBLE

Part of me wishes I could go back and rescue the 16-year-old Buckles from a time in which so many self-destructive urges were normalised and glamorised, and set him on an altogether more salubrious path. But 16-year-old Buckles, once he'd got over the excitement of finding out time travel was real, would probably tell 50-year-old Buckles to stop being a hypocrite and fuck off back to his own far-from-perfect time and concentrate on doing a decent job with his own children, who as I type are probably busy finding their own ways to do the 'wrong' thing, as teenagers always will.

Can I blame my parents for not giving me better guidance when it came to love and other intoxicants? I'd love to, but they were busy with their own shit, and anyway, as one of my school reports once pointed out, I had the capacity to be 'sly and underhand' and was adept at keeping Mum and Dad in the dark when it came to most of my bad behaviour. But maybe I wouldn't have been so sneaky if I hadn't been sent to boarding school. Or if I'd never been born. One way or another, I'm pretty sure it was my parents' fault.

The Ghost of You Clings

As far as I was aware, Roxy Music were just old guys in dinner jackets who hung around with beautiful, much younger women at boring-looking parties on the French Riviera (where the DJ would probably be playing Roxy Music). 'You should listen to the early stuff,' said Patrick, so when the Bryan Ferry and Roxy Music compilation *Street Life* was released in 1986, I gave it a go.

Although most of the tracks catered mainly to the Yacht Roxy crowd, 'Love Is the Drug', 'Pyjamarama' and 'Virginia Plain' immediately jumped out as the kind of strange, arty pop that Bowie had encouraged me to appreciate. I also found myself enjoying some of Ferry's wonky covers, despite (or perhaps thanks to) not being familiar with the originals. I played 'A Hard Rain's a-Gonna Fall' over and over, thought 'Smoke Gets in Your Eyes' was lovely and 'These Foolish Things' was a hoot.

I made sure to bring my cassette of *Street Life* on the coach that had been hired to take a load of us sixth-formers to a party at our friend Guy Gadney's house in Cheltenham during summer half-term. I was still pining for Lottie, but she wasn't going to be at the party and there was an atmosphere of new sexy possibility, so I boarded the coach determined that by the end of the night I would be involved with kissing.

I asked the coach driver if he'd play my Roxy Music cassette and soon we were joining the A40 to the sound of Bryan

Ferry warbling, '*So me and you, just we two, got to search for something new*'. By the time 'These Foolish Things' came on I had drunk one of six large cans of Foster's I'd brought with me and was miming to the lyrics along with Patrick and a couple of other pals. Amazingly, a few of the girls laughed and joined in. 'Wow,' I thought. 'I think we might be the coolest, funniest people alive right now! If this coach journey is anything to go by, this is going to be the greatest party of all time, and kissing is definitely on the menu.'

Another can of Foster's later, I was desperate to urinate, but there was no toilet on the coach and we were on the motorway, so a quick stop wasn't an option. I'm not someone who can just ignore a full bladder and carry on with my life. All I can think about is when and how the discomfort will end. I asked the driver how much further we had to go and he said about half an hour. I was not going to last half an hour.

Rather than rejoin Patrick and the others at the back of the coach, I found an empty row, took the window seat, leaned forward and began making idle chit-chat with Boring Des McKenzie sat in front. Talking to Des was hard work, but I needed an excuse to lean forward so my long coat would disguise the fact that I was unzipping my flies and positioning myself to access the opening of one of my empty Foster's cans. As any willy owner who has ever done this knows, it's a very delicate procedure, fraught with aiming challenges and sharp-metal peril.

When I was confident that receptacle and nozzle were sufficiently well aligned, I began cautiously to proceed with the transfer. Waves of sweet relief washed over me as I tried to look interested in whatever Boring Des McKenzie was burbling on about, but when the can started to grow warm and heavy, my satisfaction turned to anxiety. I knew it must be nearly full, but the transfer was far from complete. I was able to strangle the flow before total catastro-pee, but as we took the exit for Cheltenham, I realised with great sadness that a significant amount of piss had missed the can entirely. There was now a large damp patch on the front of my jeans that would be hard to explain as anything other than a pee-pee accident, and that kind of explaining is low on the list of things you want to do when you're a teenager hoping to kiss someone at a party.

As the coach pulled up outside Guy's house, I draped my coat over myself to conceal my shame, then waited for everyone else to get off before I disembarked gingerly, carrying with me the warm beer can filled with my own amber nectar. I poured away the contents beneath the coach, then, determined to find a bathroom in which to deal with the situation ASAP, I made my way into the party.

Inside the bathroom I locked the door, lowered my jeans, sat down on the lavatory, folded several sheets of pink toilet paper and began rubbing away at the wet patch. This succeeded only in creating a collection of tiny pink toilet-paper sausages that I brushed despondently from the damp denim. Feeling the lighter in my jeans pocket, a great idea hit me: why not dry the pee-pee patch using man's red fire? I would need to apply the heat to the inside of the jean so as to avoid unsightly carbon deposits on the front, and I would need to keep the flame moving so as not to burn a hole, but it should work.

I had begun to take off my jeans when there was a loud knock at the bathroom door. 'Won't be long!' I called out. I had to move fast – there was no time to remove the jeans completely. Still sat on the toilet, I pushed them further down my thighs and spread my knees so as to pull the damp area taut, then clicked a guttering flame into life and carefully introduced it to the inside of the moist denim, but as I did so there was another loud knock and a female voice said, 'Are you going to be much longer?' Before I'd had a chance to reply, the hair on my inner thighs caught fire.

Patting out the flames, I hastily hoisted up my pee-pee jeans and flushed the toilet. The bathroom smelt of burnt hair as I threw open the door, making sure not to make eye contact with the girl behind it, and marched as quickly as possible to the darkest corner of the room, only to find it occupied by Boring Des McKenzie. Feeling we had bonded on the coach, Des unveiled his party piece: a recitation of Chapter 1 from *The Restaurant at the End of the Universe* by Douglas Adams, which he claimed to have memorised, insisting on starting again every time he made a mistake (which was often). There was no kissing for me that night.

Crosseyed and Painful

As a day boy, Joe was allocated a boarder's study that he could use as a base during school hours. The lucky boarder who played host to Joe (and everyone else who Joe invited to hang out during so-called 'private study' periods) was Paul Dales. A gifted musician and tech enthusiast, Paul always had some classic album playing through his expensive NAD amplifier and asked that visitors refrain from tampering with the configuration of his EQ sliders. We'd seen Tom Cruise's character Joel in the film *Risky Business* being asked the same thing by his dad, so being the impressionable arseholes we were, we did exactly what The Cruiser had done and jammed Paul's equaliser sliders up to the max whenever we got the opportunity. 'Sometimes you just gotta say what the fuck,' we said, quoting *Risky Business*. Paul sighed wearily.

Paul listened to music that I wasn't yet equipped to appreciate: Weather Report, Herbie Hancock and Miles Davis, as well as stuff that just sounded daft to me: Frank Zappa and early Genesis – full of madly complicated instrumentals played very fast at strange time signatures, occasionally pausing for some unfunny word bollocks. 'Not nearly as good as the Thompson Twins,' I thought. Then one day I went to hang out in Paul's study and he was playing an album that sounded even better than the Thompson Twins.

The songs were sparse and choppy, the singer odd and interesting. He sang in a strained high-pitched voice about his loved ones driving to the building where he worked and suggesting they should park before coming up to see him '*working, working*'. The singer said he would put down what he was doing because his friends were important. The strange formality of the lyrics made me laugh.

I realised this was the same guy who had done a song I remembered from boarding school, a song that had been in the charts when Patrick got angry with me for not caring that John Lennon had been shot: '*Same as it ever was, same as it ever was,*' it said. I looked at the cover of the cassette Paul was playing and saw that it was called *THE NAME OF THIS BAND IS TALKING HEADS*. All caps. Mmmm. Pleasing.

Paul let me make a copy of the cassette and I liked it more every time I played it, even though the music was less straight-forwardly poppy than most of what I tended to listen to, and despite the fact that it was a live album. I didn't get the point of live albums. The few that I'd heard always seemed much worse than the original studio recordings, but *THE NAME OF THIS BAND* ... was different. It was tight, sparse and solid, and I was beginning to realise that was how I liked my music (and, yes, my turds, too).

Once I was sure Talking Heads and I were getting on suf-ficiently well, I started buying their albums, beginning with *77* (that had the '*working, working*' song on it: 'Don't Worry About the Government'), then *More Songs About Buildings and Food* and *Fear of Music*. Scanning the inlays of those last two, I noticed they had been produced by Brian Eno and I thought I could hear what he added to songs like 'With Our Love' and 'Air': a weird mood somewhere between exhilara-tion and menace that I also heard on some of the stuff Eno did with Bowie – on 'Red Sails' or 'Sons of the Silent Age', for example (my editor's going to tell me to lose this stuff because it's too boringly muso. I won't argue if he does, so if it's still in it's his fault).

Paul had put together a few short-lived bands at school. One of them, The Generators, had played in the big main hall (known as 'Up School') a couple of years previously, with Joe singing 'What Presence?!' by Orange Juice. Paul's new band had just changed its name from Quadrant to Shady People and it included Patrick on guitar (Joe had quit by then due to creative differences).

I had watched Shady People rehearsing once or twice in the music centre and I'd entertained Paul and Patrick by grabbing a mic and singing Freddie Mercury's falsetto parts from 'Under Pressure'. I thought it would be great to be in a band, but learning to play an instrument seemed too much like hard work, so I was pleased when Paul suggested I provide guest vocals for an upcoming gig. I would be singing lead on Shady People's cover of the Talking Heads track 'Crosseyed and Painless'. A couple of weeks before the gig, Paul gave me a VHS of their concert film *Stop Making Sense* and I got to work learning the lyrics.

I bought *Remain in Light*, the album that has 'Crosseyed and Painless' on it, but other than 'Once in a Lifetime' (the '*same as it ever was*' song), I didn't like it as much as the more conventionally structured songs on their earlier albums. *Remain in Light* was more like dance music and I wasn't so keen on dance music. That was the preserve of sexy, unselfconscious people, not little hairy hobbit men. I would have preferred to sing 'The Big Country' or 'Pulled Up', but 'Crosseyed and Painless', being more of a rap, was probably better suited to my limited vocal talents.

By the day of the show I had worked myself up into a dangerous pitch of excited anticipation and mortal terror. When lessons were over I went up to my study and changed into my show clothes: a pair of Chelsea boots I'd borrowed from

My poster for the ill-fated 1986 Shady People gig at which I sang guest vocals. Sort of.

Patrick, my skinniest black jeans, a blue collarless shirt (with top button done up) and, to cap it all off, a big-shouldered white jacket that I had bought in Camden over the summer. It was intended as a nod to David Byrne's big square suit from *Stop Making Sense*, but what it said loudest was, 'I just stole this from a waiter.'

Patrick came into my study with a couple of the coolest girls from our year, Lottie's friend Julia, who was going out with Patrick, and Saskia, who only went out with boys from the year above. The guy in the study next door to mine saw them arriving and looked impressed. I flashed him a look that said, 'Yup, you'd better believe it,' and closed my door. Patrick had drafted in the girls to sing backing vocals at the gig, but they were as nervous as I was because they'd heard rumours that high-ranking members of the Lads were planning to come and disrupt the show. Patrick told us not to worry as he was friendly with some of the Lads and, anyway, he had a bottle of wine. We passed it round and within 10 minutes it was empty, whereupon we tottered off to the music centre.

Gigs like these were unusual at the school and the room was packed with curious onlookers from the years below sitting on the floor. I quickly scanned the room and there, leaning against the back wall in a line of statement haircuts and sarcastic grins, were about five core members of the Lads. Shady People started playing their set of unfashionably funky covers and clunky originals and, feeling queasy, I crouched to one side and waited for my guest spot, hands thrust deep into my big white jacket pockets, hoping that no one would snap their fingers and ask me for the bill.

Then I was up, and as I made my way to the microphone a few of the Lads began to chant, 'Talking Heads! Talking Heads!' while laughing to make it clear that they did not, in fact, appreciate Talking Heads. I glanced at Patrick. He looked stressed. Paul counted us in and the band started playing a ragged 'Crosseyed and Painless' as the Lads laughed and pointed.

In a film, this would be the moment where my character looked around the room as the din of the music and the hoots of derision faded beneath a loud, reverberating heartbeat. Then my character would find something in himself and rise to the occasion, delivering a performance that would leave the Lads nodding with reluctant respect.

But this being reality, it's the moment I fucked it.

I got through the '*Facts are simple and facts are straight ...*' rap, doing my best to ignore the Lads nodding, stroking their chins and cackling, then I caught Patrick's eye and with an exchange of cringing glances, we agreed to bail.

Stumbling my way through the audience to the door of the music centre, I looked back briefly to see Paul prodding away funkily at his synth and looking incredulous as he watched us leave. My response was to shrug, then grin at the Lads in spineless solidarity. Out in Yard we laughed. I went up to my study to change out of my waiter's jacket and we went to the pub. Rock and Roll.

In a long list of shameful behaviour from my Westminster days, that gig and the way we treated Paul is not at the very top, but it's certainly up there.

Despite the Shady People débâcle, my enthusiasm for anything related to Talking Heads continued to grow, though it took another few years for me to properly appreciate *Remain in Light* and to stop squirming with regret whenever I heard 'Crosseyed and Painless'.

America Is Waiting

As an A-level Spanish student I got to attend a three-week course in the Spanish city of Salamanca at the end of the summer holidays in 1986. I didn't learn much Spanish, but I loved exploring the bars and clubs of Salamanca with a group of friends that included Guy (of the Cheltenham pee-pee-patch party) and Theodora, a student from New York who invited me out to stay at her parents' place in Bayonne, New Jersey, during the Christmas holidays.

When I arrived in New York, Theodora kindly came to pick me up from JFK airport, but it wasn't long before we realised that the magical party chemistry we had shared in Spain had remained in Spain. After an awkward couple of days, Theodora mysteriously discovered she had prior family commitments and said regretfully that I had to find other lodgings. So I called Chad.

Chad was an American exchange student who had arrived at Westminster earlier in the year and had quickly become part of our gang. He was like an older brother, more worldly and physically mature than we were. He listened to grown-up music like Led Zeppelin and Little Feat, had a cryptic tattoo on his leg and planned to go into business making cannabis-infused beer. But, best of all, he was funny and American, like Bill Murray.

Chad said I could stay with him at his parents' place, a brownstone on East 93rd. However, as with Theodora, my friendship with Chad had been forged on neutral territory, and now on his home turf, surrounded by his family and friends, the relationship at first seemed less easy-going.

We went to a drinks party in an uptown apartment block that had marble floors and a doorman. The living room looked like a posh hotel suite and was filled with smart preppy types chatting and drinking champagne.

Graceland by Paul Simon was playing. Chad introduced me to a couple of the less preppy and more approachable people, but I was nervy and looked odd in skinny black jeans, scuffed Chelsea boots and my shabby over-sized black suit jacket. It wasn't long before I was perched on the arm of a Regency sofa smoking cigarettes on my own, missing Joe and thinking what a wanker Paul Simon was.

The next night we stayed in and had takeaway with Chad's dad who suggested we rent a film. Chad and his dad wanted to watch something classic, *Dirty Harry* or *Bullitt*, but I suggested *Dark Star*, confidently predicting that they were going to love it. By the time Pinback was battling the inflatable beach-ball alien, Chad's dad was asleep, Chad was smiling politely and I was feeling out of sync with the world.

Chad was off doing other things during the daytime, so I explored New York on my own. Each morning I took the Subway to Brooklyn and spent a few hours tagging and buying rare hip-hop records, then in the afternoon I'd skateboard to a few galleries before getting some food in Chinatown and catching something challenging at the theatre. Oh, hang on … sorry, I was thinking of someone more interesting. What I actually did on every one of the five days I was in New York in

1986 was walk down to Tower Records in Greenwich Village – New York was in the grip of a long crime wave at the time and I decided walking was safer than taking the Subway.

I liked walking around the city, my big overcoat pulled tight around me, stopping now and then to stick another cassette in my Walkman. I listened to Echo and the Bunnymen's greatest hits album, *Strange Days* by The Doors, *I'm the Man* by Joe Jackson, *True Stories* by Talking Heads and the soundtrack to a film I'd seen recently on TV: *Midnight Cowboy*. As I walked, I sucked in my cheeks and tried to affect the gaunt inscrutability I admired in David Byrne, but when I caught sight of my reflection in the windows of delis, dry-cleaners and department stores the little fellow peering back at me looked less like the Talking Heads lead singer and more like a plump Ratso Rizzo.

At Tower, I gazed at the giant handmade displays the art department had created for various new acts, then searched in vain for Talking Heads albums I didn't already own. Looking under 'B' for Byrne, I found *My Life in the Bush of Ghosts*, a collaboration with Brian Eno that I bought and listened to as I trudged back to East 93rd.

It contained what sounded to me like ominous ethnic robot music overlaid with recordings of people chanting, delivering monologues and ranting on radio phone-ins. It was very good, and the following day I bought *The Catherine Wheel*, an album of music composed by David Byrne for a theatre project by dancer and choreographer Twyla Tharp (a name that surely predisposed her to being either a dancer and choreographer or an ornery gold prospector with an idiosyncratic mule). *The Catherine Wheel* sounded like the midway point between *Remain in Light* and ... *Bush of Ghosts*, i.e. polyrhythmical, experimentalocious and samplerific.

By this time I was thinking David Byrne could do no wrong, and my final New York purchase was *Music for 'The Knee Plays'*, an album put together in 1984 as part of an avant-garde opera by experimental theatre maestro Robert Wilson. After the joy of discovering … *Bush of Ghosts* and *The Catherine Wheel, The Knee Plays* came on like indefensibly pretentious dog crap that threatened to make me think less of my beloved Mr Byrne. Every track featured mournful brass-band music with Byrne occasionally reading out lyrics that might have been written by a child on the least interesting part of the spectrum.

'*She turns on the tap and the water comes out, so she fills up a glass and drinks it. The glass is good for holding water. Other things that are good for holding water are bowls, bottles, and bags, but not jackets. Jackets are good for holding groceries …*' I made those lyrics up, but that's the sort of thing you're dealing with.

I played *Music for 'The Knee Plays'* a couple of times just to check I hadn't judged it too harshly, then, deciding that I hadn't judged it harshly enough, I put it away and forgot about it. Five years later, at art school, I stuck it on one afternoon out of curiosity. Suddenly, in an environment that lovingly nurtured indefensibly pretentious dog crap, *Music for 'The Knee Plays'* sounded magnificent; the brass-band music strange and hypnotic, and Byrne's lyrics intriguing and funny. It's still one of my favourite albums to listen to if I'm doing manual labour or working on a new installation that explores the tension between collective memory and farts.

Fubar

On my last night in New York Chad invited me to join him and his friends Ralph and Hank on a trip to see a new film everyone was raving about called *Platoon*. There was a big queue of people standing in the cold outside the cinema, but rather than join the line immediately, Ralph led the way round the corner and lit a joint.

Mum had told me that people who smoked marijuana ended up injecting heroin, and I knew from the 'Heroin

Screws You Up' public information campaign that heroin instantly gave you spots, made you ill, then killed you – three of my top Worsties. But Chad, Ralph and Hank were cool, funny and friendly, and I didn't want them to think I was uptight, so despite the risk of spots, illness and death, I had my first drag on a joint.

I started to feel dizzy almost immediately, but when Chad and the others headed back to the cinema I did my best not to let on and concentrated on putting one foot in front of the other as I followed them. Back in the queue for *Platoon*, with the edges of my vision darkening, I suddenly felt a sensation like water flushing from my head down through my body, and before I'd had a chance to warn anyone, my legs had buckled and I'd sunk to the Manhattan pavement (or 'sidewalk').

I was aware that Chad and the others were peering down at me with expressions of concern and amusement, but I was too spaced out to care. My only vaguely coherent thought was that one of New York's many muggers might be making a note of my defenceless state and adding me to their 'To Mug' list. However, I also knew that if I was helped to my feet, I would black out completely, so I sat cross-legged in the queue as Chad, Ralph and Hank kept me entertained doing impressions of Bugs Bunny, Daffy Duck and Elmer Fudd fighting in Vietnam. 'It's Loony Platoony!' said Hank, and everyone in the queue laughed, even Ratso having a whitey on the pavement.

By the time we were seated in the packed auditorium, I felt like Major Tom floating about my malfunctioning tin can and wondering if I'd ever make it back to earth. Then *Platoon* started.

Like Charlie Sheen's character, I felt I'd been dropped in the middle of an overwhelming nightmare and was struggling not to panic. My fearful confusion peaked about 15 minutes into the film, during a chaotic night-time jungle firefight scene in which *Star Wars*-style laser bolts appeared to be zipping between the soldiers. 'Why are there lasers in the jungle?' I whispered to Chad.

'Dude, they're tracer bullets. How you doin', man?' smiled Chad.

'I'm OK, I think.' I was no longer in physical difficulty, but every intense and upsetting scene was emotionally amplified and I was helplessly grateful for Willem Dafoe's kindness, scandalised by Tom Berenger's ruthlessness and in love with Charlie Sheen.

When *Platoon* was over we said goodbye to Ralph and Hank and began walking back through the sobering cold to Chad's place. My stomach was groaning so I bought a flapjack square from a convenience store and wolfed it as we walked. It was the best thing I'd ever tasted – like biting into eternal love. Chad laughed as I ran back to the store and bought another ten.

The next day I woke feeling foggy and sad. I liked the Buckles who had never smoked drugs, but now, with a single puff, he was gone forever. My consolation lay peeking out from beneath the pile of clothes on the floor by my bed: the Flapjack Squares of Eternal Love. I reached over for one, unwrapped it excitedly and took a bite. It was like sawdust from a hamster cage.

BOWIE ANNUAL

I didn't investigate Bowie's 1977 album *"Heroes"* for ages because I wasn't fond of the title track. My favourite Bowie songs were mysterious caverns in which nameless feelings were illuminated by lines like '… *it was midnight back at the kitchen door, / Like the grim face on the cathedral floor'*, but the sentiments in *"Heroes"* just seemed a bit obvious, triumphalist even. Blah blah, Kings, blah blah, Queens, blah blah, aren't dolphins brilliant? Yeah! Let's spend the day beating people.

I liked the *"Heroes"* album cover, though. The black-and-white shot of Bowie staring blankly with stiffly posed hands was exactly the kind of robotic sexiness I was after from Zavid, so, hoping there was more of that inside, I eventually dived in.

I'd never been to Berlin, but after listening to *"Heroes"* a couple of times I felt as though I'd been stuck there for months, talking to weirdos in a dark, rainy alley outside a jazz club where they keep the bins and all the jazz people do their wee-wees. With the exception of the title track, *"Heroes"* was full of music I couldn't imagine anyone else in the world listening to (especially 'Joe the Lion' and 'Sons of the Silent Age'), and I got into it much faster than I had any of his albums previously.

Side two contained more instrumental 'moodscapes'. Like *Low*, but bleaker. I especially liked 'Neuköln' (*Noy-kern*), which I thought of as the soundtrack to the rainy alley outside the jazz club, the desolate wails of Bowie's saxophone at the end sounding like someone who's just discovered their lover has been murdered. Or maybe they've just lost their wallet and missed the last bus home. Either way, somebody's having a shit evening.

One weekend late in 1986, while I was still in my sanctimonious pre-marijuana days, I found myself the only not-stoned person in a group of stoned people who wouldn't shut up about how stoned they were. Feeling fed up and left out, I put on 'Neuköln', turned out the lights, held a torch under my mouth and lip-synced to Bowie's anguished saxophone screams until one of the stoned people started to get the fear. The rest of them told me to stop being a prick and turn the lights back on.

RAMBLE

I bet some of you are still annoyed by what I said about the song '"Heroes"'. Perhaps I went a bit overboard. I always liked it perfectly well, but it took me another 30 years to properly appreciate it. In 1986 the thing I liked best about Bowie's Seventies music was that it made me feel like a member of an exclusive club, and the song '"Heroes"' felt like an anomaly, because, as with 'Let's Dance', the door policy was too slack. After he died, '"Heroes"' became a rallying point for broken-hearted fans and the remnants of my snobbery fell away. Every time I showed the video for '"Heroes"' at the end of the *BUG* David Bowie Specials I did in the years following his death, I got weepy.

The best bit about Bowie's cameo in *Absolute Beginners*, Julien Temple's stagey adaptation of Colin MacInnes's novel about late-Fifties London groovers released in April 1986, is a tiny moment when his advertising-executive character Vendice Partners is showing the film's protagonist Colin a model of a new housing development. 'It's lovely,' says Colin hesitantly, and for a moment Bowie drops the rotten American accent he's been doing and says in his own geezerish tones, 'No, it's not, son, it's 'orrible.' Then he goes back to being crap American again.

To me it seemed as though the real David, my David, the arty contrarian who just nine years before had released *Low* and *"Heroes"* a few months apart, was peeping through the Eighties and saying, 'What am I doing here? It's 'orrible!'

Now his musical output was a series of histrionic pop songs of variable quality tied to other projects: the brilliant 'This Is Not America' from the film *The Falcon and the Snowman*; the less brilliant but thoroughly amiable cover of 'Dancing in the Street' with Mick Jagger for Live Aid; one excellent and two so-so songs for the *Absolute Beginners* soundtrack; the blustering 'When the Wind Blows' for the depressing animated film of the same name and a good, uplifting theme song along with four other pieces of syrupy cat sick for Jim Henson's film *Labyrinth* (though I'm aware there are people who believe 'Magic Dance' to be a work of stone-cold genius).

Indeed, many fans will tell you *Labyrinth* is where their journey with Bowie began, but when Joe, Louis and I went to see it at the Odeon Leicester Square one Saturday night a few weeks after it was released in November 1986 I thought it was where my journey with Bowie might end.

At 17 I was too old to find *Labyrinth* delightful and too young to embrace it ironically. I didn't like the songs; I didn't like the middle-aged Goblin King's Kajagoogoo wig or the fact that his name was basically 'Gareth'; I didn't like Gareth's unsavoury obsession with a young girl, and I didn't like being able to see the outline of Gareth's genitals through his leggings – at least, not as much as you might expect.

CHAPTER 16

DOGFUN

y wife grew up around dogs, but our family never had pets. We travelled too often to make it practical, but it didn't help that my dad's antipathy towards the dog community was pronounced and legendary. Dogs offended his sense of order and he hated the chaos they could cause: the mess, the noise, the licking, the slobbering, the humping, the vandalising and, of course, the pissing and the shitting. If a dog turned up unexpectedly and began bounding across people and furniture, Dad would exclaim loudly, 'Get that bloody dog out of here!' even if he was in someone else's house and it was their dog.

I inherited this intolerance to a degree, but the older I got the more it was challenged by my animal-loving friends, and on one occasion my sister-in-law Harriet just came out and said it: 'You're a Dog Nazi.'

I parroted Dad's line that it was only the badly behaved dogs I didn't like, and when that didn't placate her I continued by saying, 'Look, maybe I *am* uptight, but if a friend came round and their six-year-old child took a big shit on the hall carpet, and there were no extenuating medical circumstances, I think it would be reasonable to at least be a little dismayed. And yet if I object to an animal running around the house depositing dog turds, which are, let's face it, some of the most offensive turds in the Turd World, I'm supposed to be some kind of Dog Nazi?'

'Not *some kind of*,' responded Harriet, 'an actual Dog Nazi. Yes. That's what you are.'

Though I did at least manage to stop myself mentioning that Hitler adored dogs, it was one of those arguments, conducted in front of friends, that started out as banter, then became uncomfortable and acrimonious and I was left wondering how much truth there was to Harriet's position.

My initial response was to do an impression of Harriet's dog on the BBC 6 Music radio show Joe and I were presenting at the time. I imitated her dog's tendency for loud panting and slobbery licking and also implied a fondness for farting and indiscriminate shitting (which wasn't at all accurate). Joe christened the fictional dog 'Boggins' and for a while Boggins was a semi-regular feature on the show.

Some people thought Boggins was funny, while others found him repulsive and offensively childish and, in an eerie prefiguring of Brexit, our listeners divided themselves into two distinct camps: 'Save Boggins' and 'Kill Boggins'.

At times, the Boggins debate became so heated that it was difficult to know how seriously to take some of the messages we received (examples below, both genuine):

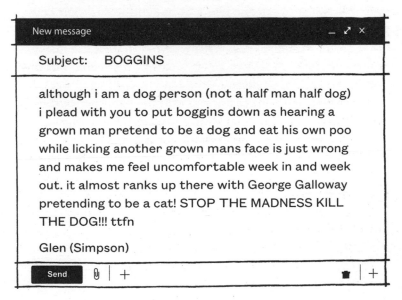

New message ⎯ ⤢ ✕

Subject: BOGGINS

although i am a dog person (not a half man half dog) i plead with you to put boggins down as hearing a grown man pretend to be a dog and eat his own poo while licking another grown mans face is just wrong and makes me feel uncomfortable week in and week out. it almost ranks up there with George Galloway pretending to be a cat! STOP THE MADNESS KILL THE DOG!!! ttfn

Glen (Simpson)

Send 📎 | +   🗑 | +

This message stung because it invoked one of the most excruciating moments in British TV history when in 2006 the outspoken Scottish politician George Galloway appeared on the reality show *Celebrity Big Brother* and with chilling enthusiasm threw himself into a task that required him to act like a cat. He could have just said '*miaow*' a couple of times and pretended to scratch something, but instead Galloway surprised everyone by crawling about in a bathrobe, licking his whiskery lips and nuzzling at the cupped hands of the actor Rula Lenska as she fed him imaginary treats and cooed that he was a 'Good pussy', a compliment that made him purr.

It was a moment I had watched with my wife when it was originally transmitted and we had squirmed on the sofa, stood up, sat down, held up our hands to block out the TV and beseeched, 'No, no, no, no, no, no, no, please, no, no, no, no, don't do that, no, no, no, no, no, no …' so painful was it to see another human being humiliating themselves to such a degree while seeming to think it rather fun.

Now, according to Glen, that's exactly what I was doing by pretending to be a dog called Boggins. I'm a comedian, not a politician, so humiliating myself is part of the job, but as George Galloway showed, there's a thin line between irreverent larking and cringe-inducing ignominy. Or maybe it's a big fat line, but Pussy Galloway and Boggins Buckles had bounded across it regardless.

I think a lot of the messages we got about Boggins were intended as banter, but a few appeared to be expressing genuine annoyance:

New message   _ ⤢ ×

Subject: BOGGINS IS RUINING IT

Whenever Boggins is around, my hands automatically reach for the 'stop play' button.
Not sure why but I can't stand him and he has been ruining my fun. It would really help if you had a warning that said 'this show features Boggins' then I would know that I can give the show a miss rather than stop half way through completely exasperated and frustrated. I have been a longstanding fan but this feels like the end of a beautiful affair and just because of a stupid dog? How could you.

Corinne
Department of International Development
University of Oxford

Send   ⎘ | +   🗑 | +

The final Adam and Joe 6 Music show was broadcast live from the Glastonbury festival in 2011 and it was then that we finally released Boggins into the mud, the filth and the stinks where he truly belonged. I'm told by regular festival-goers that he lives there still, hibernating in the base of the Manic Street Preachers' private Portaloo all year round and only emerging in June when he smells roadie musk, drug-infused urine and/or Goan seafood.

By early 2013 our youngest son, Nat, then aged eight, had been asking if we could get a dog for a while. I wasn't keen. With the children a little older and life at home becoming less messily unpredictable for the first time in a decade, I was reluctant to introduce a new agent of random disruption, but Harriet's upsetting accusations of dog Nazism still rang in my ears. I was also coming round to the argument that taking care of an animal would be good for the children, though I made it clear I would not personally be responsible for the dog's welfare and had no intention of ever picking up a single one of its turds.

A whippet-poodle cross would be easy-going and not too barky, said a friend. My wife looked online and found a litter of five being sold by a couple in Durham. She chose the smallest one and a week later Nat was stood in our kitchen with the three-week-old puppy in his arms. 'What are you going to call it?' I asked.

'Steve,' replied Nat immediately.

'It's a girl, Nat,' said his older brother. 'You can't call a girl Steve, it's ridiculous, you just can't do it. We should call her Rosie.'

'Who cares if she's a girl?' protested Nat. 'Steve's a cool name.' I was about to step in to mediate, but to everyone's surprise Nat continued, 'But Rosie's fine, too. Let's call her Rosie.'

Rosie was sweet, no doubt. Very sweet. She was as small, soft and light as my daughter's little black stuffed toy puppy (the distressingly named 'Puppalina'), but that was where the similarity ended.

Puppalina didn't get on the kitchen table and eat my scrambled eggs if I turned my back for more than four seconds. Puppalina didn't leave pools of lurid yellow piss on every inch of floorboard, carpet and bedspread.

Puppalina didn't drag out and chew each valuable item that was left accessible, including a brand-new pair of prescription glasses with expensive German varifocal lenses, a trendy coat I'd bought my wife in Sweden, which she said was the best present I've ever got her, and the first set of headphones I'd ever had that delivered properly punchy bass, smooth mids and detailed treble while always sitting snuggly in my ears, whatever the environment.

If everyone was out of the house, Rosie was left in the kitchen with all the chairs either stacked on the table or ranged against lower shelves in order to prevent further wanton destruction. My wife would leave Radio 4 playing, saying the sound of people talking would stop Rosie getting lonely, but I was concerned that the range of voices Rosie was hearing was not sufficiently diverse and that the political bias she would be absorbing was tantamount to 'in-dog-trination' (*pffffrrt*).

As the months passed and summer rolled round, it became clear that any fantasies I might have had about the children switching off their screens and going off on countryside adventures with their new best dog friend were not about to materialise. Instead (as usual) it was my wife who ended up doing all the work, and after a while my non-interventionist position, though clearly stated from the outset, became untenably arseholish. So one day I went for a walk up the farm tracks and between the fields behind our house and Rosie came with me.

The first few walks were not relaxing. Rosie, desperate to run free, would strain at her lead so hard that she would half choke herself, and a few times she nearly escaped by wriggling her small skull out of her collar. We invested in a harness. That worked OK for a while, but one foggy winter afternoon Rosie spotted a piggy muntjac deer across the frosty furrows of a ploughed field and with a couple of frantic contortions she slipped free of the harness and bounded after the deer, a hairy bullet disappearing into the mist with a diminishing volley of ecstatic yips.

I strode about, shouting for Rosie with increasing urgency as the light went, but when she still hadn't returned after half an hour I started to entertain worst-case scenarios. These were less about Rosie's fate and more about my family strongly disliking me and possibly even suspecting that I had deliberately lost her because deep down I was just a no-good Dog Nazi, like my dad.

Then suddenly there she was, loping towards me out of the gloom with her tongue lolling out and her black fur wet and slick against her whippet frame. She looked like a big black rat with spidery legs, grinning. A moment of sweet relief quickly gave way to anger and, taking hold of her skinny body, I roughly reattached the harness, then stomped home in silence as she padded along behind. 'It's enough to have my emotional welfare tethered to a wife and three children,' I thought hotly. 'Now I have to worry about a dog-spider who doesn't give a shit about anything except what she can possibly eat or destroy and expects a scritch-scratch on her tum-tum in the meantime? Well, fuck that.'

But that was five years ago. As you know, I don't feel like that any more.

It started to change when Dad moved in. Feeling that his own life was running out, my father's former extremism had been tempered by an appreciation for all living creatures. That included dogs, though Rosie was rather wary around Dad, as if she could still detect a faint Nazi whiff. Or maybe it was just the TCP. Either way, it was nice to see a softer version of Dad in Rosie's presence, as well as being somewhat satisfying to note that her affections were not entirely indiscriminate.

On particularly stressful days I found myself grateful for the opportunity to take to the farm tracks with Dog. By that time we'd decided that it was safe to let her off the lead, and though she would still disappear now and then, I usually got home to find her scratching at the front door. Out on the walks Rosie would bound about up ahead, looking back occasionally to check where I was, and while she gambolled and harassed the rabbit community, I got into the habit of recording voice notes on my phone.

I would talk about how things were going with Dad, my wife, the children, Rosie and work, and often I would get home feeling unburdened and more positive. Sometimes I'd record half-formed songs or jingles – things that a few years before I might have used on the 6 Music show and it made me miss those days. Joe was too busy with film projects to do a regular show any more, but it was on my walks with Rosie that I decided I should have a go at doing my own podcast, and get beyond the fear that continuing without Cornballs in that medium would just be too embarrassingly rubbish.

Instead, I decided I would talk to other people, and without the pressure of keeping things light and funny for live radio I thought the podcast would allow me to talk more seriously and honestly about the various hang-ups, insecurities and fears most of us grapple with every day. I was aware that for some of our old 6 Music listeners this might be less preferable than more reliable silliness, but I didn't see why the podcast couldn't accommodate both. Rosie agreed and *The Adam Buxton Podcast* became a phenomenal success, which in turn led to the commission of this extraordinary book.

To paraphrase the adage, I want to be the person I think Rosie thinks I am, though there are times when I suspect she may just think I'm the person who takes her for walks and sneaks bits of chicken into her food and picks the goosegrass balls out of her fur in the summer and scrubs the carpet when she pisses on it, in which case I'm already the person she thinks I am. I don't think she thinks I'm particularly nice, or kind, or clever, but if I sit down on the sofa in the kitchen she jumps up and lays her head on my lap anyway. What's more, when I'm feeling isolated or full of self-reproach, she holds my gaze with her amber dog eyes for longer than any sane human being would, and if it's not a meaningful connection, it's certainly a very skilful imitation of one.

CHAPTER 17

1987

t was easy to see the Beastie Boys as just three chancers from privileged backgrounds who had cynically hijacked the sounds and styles of working-class black hip-hop culture to promote their own frat-boy agenda. That wasn't true (not entirely), but whatever they were up to, by the spring of 1987 it was working very well.

The single '(You Gotta) Fight for Your Right (to Party!)' and the album *Licensed to Ill* had brought the Beasties to the attention of a massive audience, which included people like me, who felt threatened by 'real' hip-hop but were happy to buy into Mike D, Ad-Rock and MCA's whitewashed pantomime of obnoxiousness.

For me, Joe, Louis and our pals, this opportunity for mindless steam off-letting was perfectly timed. We were taking our A levels, after which the plan seemed to be to leave school and piss about for a while before getting back to making good on our parents' investment in our education. Joe was planning to go to film school and Louis had applied to Oxford. I knew they'd both get in and their lives would work out the way they wanted, and I envied them. I didn't have a clue what I was going to do. Apart from hanging out with Joe, the only thing I really enjoyed was drawing.

The one time I asked one of my tutors about art school as an option, it was explained to me that unless you were freakishly talented and got into the Slade or the Royal Academy, art school was a waste of time, somewhere thickos and slackers ended up if they couldn't get into proper university.

'Screw you and your conformist establishment sausage factory, Mr Tutor! Maybe I'll never be a great artist, but at least I'll be following my passion for doing passable drawings of robots and pop stars!' I didn't shout, having not jumped onto a table with a wild look in my eyes.

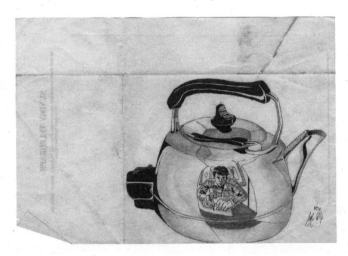

Breathtaking realism in this still life/self-portrait from the 15-year-old A. Buxton.

Instead, I glumly filled out the UCCA form, applied to do English at a selection of universities I was never going to get into, and tried to ignore the chasm of uncertainty that lay on the other side of the summer by fighting for my right to party.

Meanwhile the Beastie Boys had become tabloid fodder in the UK, with British journalists taking their shtick at face value and doing their best to spread moral panic whenever possible. Although I think moral panics should be treated with suspicion and would never advocate artistic censorship, I also have to acknowledge that the Beastie Boys' influence on me as a teenage man was almost completely negative. Their record gave me licence not only to ill, but to act on occasion like a massive prick when hanging with my homeboys. Apart from promoting a lame kind of ironic misogyny and homophobia, the Beasties were seemingly never without a six-pack of Budweiser, and that played a part in encouraging me to think of excessive beer consumption as entirely harmless man fun.

Throughout 1987 we'd often head out to a small hill in St James's Park and 'shotgun' cans of Budweiser, something we'd learned how to do from the film *The Sure Thing*, which starred another notorious corrupter of youth, John Cusack. 'Shotgunning brewskis' entailed holding the beer can upside down, punching a hole big enough for a finger to fit through at the side of the can near the base with a sharp object, covering the hole with your mouth, then raising the can upright and pulling the tab. Then you had to glug as fast as possible as the whole beer shot down your throat in a matter of seconds. This was followed by belching, can crushing, possibly some high-fiving and a sense that you were living life to its fullest.

There would have been shotgunning on the last night of the February half-term in 1987 after Louis, Joe, Zac, our American-exchange friend Chad and I went to see David Cronenberg's remake of *The Fly* at the Odeon Marble Arch.

RAMBLE

Unlike *Alien*, which frightened me in a fun way, the fear I got watching *The Fly* was altogether more disturbing, a nauseating dread of disease, disfigurement and physical decay, albeit leavened by Jeff Goldblum's top-notch handwork. The part I found most upsetting was the scene in the bathroom when Goldblum's scientist character Seth Brundle, having accidentally fused his DNA with that of a housefly after stepping into a teleporter together, was studying the progress of his physical transformation from Sexy Jeff to hideous Brundlefly with mounting alarm. There were groans of revulsion sprinkled with a few chuckles in the audience when he squeezed the tip of a finger and it squirted at the mirror like a popped zit, but as Jeff peeled away a rotten fingernail with a breathless wince, the mood became more sombre. And that was before the ear came off.

As I watched *The Fly* for the first time, the bathroom disintegration scene evoked the alarming indignities of going through puberty and the constant worry that my body was changing in ways that were not 'normal', let alone aesthetically pleasing.

Watching *The Fly* again more recently, the scene played out as an allegory for the physical process of ageing and the moments – increasingly frequent after my dad's death – when I catch sight of myself in the bathroom mirror and it's breathless wince time. Only the relatively slow pace of the deterioration prevents full-flailing panic, but essentially, I'm Brundlefly, except that instead of sharing the teleporter with a fly, I shared it, as we all do, with that stupid old bastard Father Time.

Sub-Ramble

Despite being Brundlefly, I've found the benefits of being older outweigh the disadvantages, and though my vanity is not deserting me at the same pace as my cowardly hair, it's not the source of frequent discomfort it would have been in 1987. So that's nice.

We emerged from the Odeon Marble Arch somewhat frazzled.

Chad announced that his grandad had a place about a 10-minute walk from the cinema and he was away. Good one, Chad's grandad! We stayed up all night at Chad's grandad's pad, listening to *Licensed to Ill* and drinking irresponsibly. Chad told us he'd had sex in the flat the night before with an actual woman!

They'd needed some lubrication, but all Chad could find was his grandad's Badedas, which unsurprisingly had led to copious pine-fresh genital foam production.

It was the most grown-up story I'd heard up to that point. We put on 'She's Crafty' one more time to celebrate and raided the ashtray to see if there were any smokable butts.

The next morning we staggered out of Chad's grandad's pad to get the Tube into school. Before taking the stairs down to Bond Street station, Louis asked us to wait a second, then, with commuters hurrying past, he leaned slightly over the pavement curb and nonchalantly let free an unbroken stream of puke that became known as 'The Column of Vomit' when recalled thereafter. Then he looked up, clapped his hands once and pointed the way down to the Tube. I admit that I was impressed. It took us all about three days to fully recover.

So yes, I'm adding the Beastie Boys and John Cusack to my list of people to blame for turning me into a little alcoholic dick, but Bruce Robinson probably played a part, too.

During the Easter break in 1987 Patrick and I went to see Robinson's film *Withnail and I*, a tale about two out-of-work actors trying to escape the squalor of their lives in 1960s London by drinking booze, taking drugs and going for a weekend in the country. Keen for something to take our minds off our respective teenage troubles and unprepared for how funny the film was going to be, Patrick and I got a bit hysterical as we watched, though Patrick was more expressive.

By the time an extremely inebriated Withnail was trying

to use a washing-up liquid bottle filled with child's piss to prove to the police he wasn't guilty of drink driving, Patrick had started rocking back and forth in his cinema seat until the whole row shook. The look of vacant, childlike confusion on Richard E. Grant's face when Withnail is busted using the pee-pee bottle then caused Patrick to flop right off his seat and begin literally rolling in the aisle (or, indeed, ROFL-ing).

Bruce Robinson presumably trusted that the audience for *Withnail and I* would understand that the film wasn't intended as a set of guidelines for a healthy and happy life, but for one 17-year-old short, hairy, overemotional audience member the idea of chemically blocking out an indifferent world with your best friend at your side was very appealing. Sure, the hangovers, paranoia and general sense of decay didn't look fun, but overall *Withnail and I* confirmed my growing suspicion that existence was more entertaining once you'd drifted into the arena of the un-sober.

When Paul McGann's Marwood character finally cleans up his act and breaks away from Withnail's disastrous, self-pitying orbit, I was thinking, 'No! Don't leave! Stay with your friend and keep boozing. That was the fun part.'

Bada Bada Bada Sa-wing Bada!

My anxieties about joining the adult world and being left behind by my friends were further tweaked by *Ferris Bueller's Day Off*.

There's an odd scene halfway through the film, out of step with the goofiness elsewhere, when Ferris, Sloane and Cameron visit the Art Institute of Chicago and tag along with a group of much younger children who are there on a school trip, holding hands with them as they're marched through the gallery by their teacher. The three friends break away to take in the art at their own pace as what sounds like library music from an advert for life insurance plays on the soundtrack (it's actually an instrumental cover of The Smiths' 'Please, Please, Please, Let Me Get What I Want' by The Dream Academy).

Ferris and Sloane kiss in front of some stained glass by Chagall while Cameron reckons with Georges Seurat's pointillist banger *A Sunday Afternoon on the Island of La Grande Jatte*. It's the one with all the people hanging out on a sunny day by the banks of the River Seine in the late 19th century. Top hats and long sleeves for the men, umbrellas and big-booty dresses for the women. Everyone together, everyone alone, see?

Cameron fixates on the little girl near the centre of the painting. She's the only figure looking directly at the viewer, making a connection the adults around her have ceased to make. Cameron hovers somewhere in between: no longer a child being looked after, not yet an adult in charge of his own life, but an interloper able to see the adult world for what it is: a place as superficial and absurd as the hand signals of stock-exchange workers, fathers who buy expensive cars then never drive them and dead-eyed teachers calling the roll like malfunctioning automatons: 'Bueller ... Bueller ... Bueller ... Bueller ...'

I could certainly relate to that sense of antechamber blues and couldn't understand why anyone would want to go through into that next big hall from which the sound of serious conversations reverberated, along with the noise of business being done, football crowds, fashion shows, political rallies and hospitals.

And yet Ferris uses all his guile to convince that Eighties movie staple, the snooty maître d', that he's Abe Froman, the sausage king of Chicago, just so he can gain access to the stuffy-looking adult playground of the Chez Luis restaurant. I mean, make up your mind. Is it superficial and absurd or do you love it?

I wasn't crazy about *Ferris Bueller's Day Off* on first viewing.

I thought Ferris was a bit of a smarmy git and his girlfriend Sloane was exactly the kind of person who would never have given me the time of day in real life, but in Ferris's friendship with the less adventurous Cameron I saw parallels to my relationship with Joe.

One summery evening during our last term, Cornballs, who had just passed his driving test, turned up at school in his parents' maroon Volvo 340 and we went for a drive round the West End listening to an Orange Juice compilation. '*Can you hear me calling from afar, / As you drive uptown in his daddy's car?*' said one of the songs.

'This is a very appropriate song,' I said.

'I picked it specially,' smiled Joe. Did that mean he had picked it specially or not?

It was exciting to be driving around with no adults in the car, but it was also disconcerting. Joe, six months older than me, seemed like the cockier, cleverer Ferris to my more timid Cameron quite often, and with him at the wheel of an actual car the contrast was more than usually pronounced.

'What do you think we'll be doing in ten years?' I said at one point.

'Well, I'm going to be making movies,' replied Joe.

'Yeah, but do you think we'll still be friends?' I asked, hoping the question didn't sound as heavily freighted as it was.

'I don't know, man. Probably not,' said Joe as we rounded Trafalgar Square and headed back towards Westminster.

Party Time

As the end of our time at Westminster loomed and the days grew longer and hotter, I was getting used to a strange new grown-up feeling: colossal anticlimax. The supposedly life-ending A-level exams I'd dreaded for so long finally arrived and people from our year drifted into school when they had a paper to sit, buggered off again afterwards and life just carried on. Gradually all the familiar groups I used to bounce between in Yard dwindled and disappeared.

The school organised a 'Leavers' Dinner', but word went round that only goony birds and tragic losers were planning to attend, so I bailed, along with Joe and most of our pals. It was a shame, as a lot of the goony birds were actually very nice and it would have been good to wish them well. Not the tragic losers, though. I couldn't be seen with them.

A little focus was restored when Mark announced he was planning a party at his parents' house in the Hampshire countryside where we had spent many overexcited weekends making stupid videos, riding up and down in the lift and licking famous paintings rather than reckoning with them. This was going to be the party to end all parties, an opportunity to draw a line under our Westminster experience with all the riotous abandon of *Animal House* and the emotional intensity of *The Breakfast Club*. That's how I was thinking about it anyway.

For weeks we discussed the guest list, carefully considering which sixth-form girls were cool and/or we still had a chance of snogging, and which boys should remain uninvited, either because they were too popular, not popular enough or just wankers.

The party was to take place around the pool house at the bottom of the big garden and we agreed it would be best not to invite too many people and instead keep it 'inner sanctum'.

Despite our efforts to enforce the social borders we'd observed at school, in the summery post-exam euphoria alliances shifted and Mark found himself at pub gatherings that included members of tribes we would have eyed with suspicion back in Yard. A couple of days before the big party Mark explained sheepishly that it was possible he may have got too caught up in the armistice spirit and invited a few members of the Lads who, he said, were actually much cooler than we'd

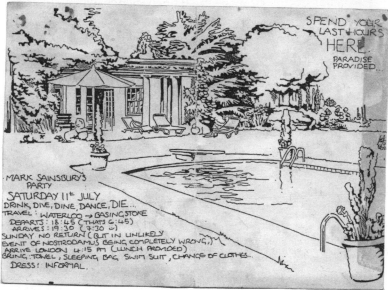

When sexism, privilege, John, Yoko and Hitler collide: the invite I made for the big post-A-level party at Mark's place.

given them credit for. 'But they're never going to show up,' Mark reassured us when we grumbled.

But of course they showed up.

As usual, helping Mark get the party set up with Joe and Ben the day before had been pure, uncomplicated fun, but as soon as guests started arriving the following evening the pressure to have a good time began to produce the opposite effect. I flitted about distractedly, smoking Marlboro Lights, making gin and tonics and shotgunning the odd can of Budweiser in between having conversations about how weird it felt to have actually left school, from which I would break off to check on the music.

Without record decks, we relied on tape compilations, and there was a lot of switching between Joe's selections of Orange Juice, James Brown, Haircut 100, George Michael, Prince and Sly & Robbie (whose song 'Boops (Here to Go)' had been a favourite in the build-up to exams) and my usual mixes of Bowie, Talking Heads, The Doors, The Cure and Joe Jackson.

Jackson's album *Jumpin' Jive*, which featured covers of swinging jazz numbers from the 1940s, was unexpectedly energising the dance floor when from the shadowy expanse of lawn we heard the sound of teenage boys trying to make their voices as low as possible, and moments later several figures in skinny jeans with indie-band haircuts swaggered from the gloom. The Lads had arrived. They'd even brought a teacher with them who they considered young and groovy. I mean, what the shit?

I nudged Joe and pointed. 'Lads at 12 O'clock, man.' Joe groaned, but when some of the more moderate Lads acknowledged us with self-conscious grins I wondered for a moment if Mark had been right and this was the night we'd leave school rivalries behind and celebrate our passage into the adult world together.

Nope.

Off went the Joe Jackson jazz and seconds later the bushes

trembled to the sounds of AC/DC's 'You Shook Me All Night Long' followed by much Sisters of Mercy. I looked around hoping for someone to object, but the tide had turned and within half an hour the girls were giggling with the Lads and flirting with the groovy teacher, and our gang was scattered. We had lost control of the pool house.

At one point there was a sudden flurry of activity and I saw Joe leaping Jesse Owens-like over loungers in order to avoid being pushed in the pool by several boisterously laughing Lads. 'This is like being bullied in my first term,' said Joe, uncharacteristically flustered.

We went looking for Louis and Ben and found them behind the pool house in a small thicket of trees and bushes, sitting on the ground with Zeb, one of the hippies with the most luxuriant hair.

They had just smoked a joint and were staring at a little boombox playing a song with the refrain 'Everybody must get stoned', which I thought made them look a bit too compliant. Joe and I sat down and listened for a while. 'Who is this?' I asked.

'Bob Dylan,' croaked Louis. It sounded like old-man music to me, but I liked 'I Want You'. It was a lovely tune and I thought it was brave of Bobbles to confess to stealing a flute from a dancing child with a Chinese suit. 'I wish every one of his songs didn't end with him getting his harmonica out, though,' Louis drawled. Zeb the hippy nodded and smiled.

And that was pretty much the high point of the party to end all parties.

Stern Lectures

Nineteen-eighty-seven was peak stern lecture year for A. Buckles.

Before my exams my house master had done his best to convince me of the need to apply myself more to my studies and less to socialising. 'You won't even know those people in five years,' he reasoned, trying to impress on me the value of thinking long term. It made sense, but try as I might I couldn't stop feeling that fun in the present was better than security in the future.

A shorter but no less sobering lecture was delivered at the end of the summer on holiday in Greece by the woman I lost my virginity to. A boozy night had ended with us alone on a moonlit beach where, thanks to my lack of experience and an excessively sensitive triggering mechanism, the entire process of one thing leading to another had been over in about 45 seconds.

She was a few years older than me and got impatient when afterwards I sat speechless with embarrassment, staring out to sea. 'Aren't you going to say anything?' she asked.

I looked at her arms in the moonlight. 'Your arms look nice in the moonlight,' I ventured.

That went down badly and she bristled. 'You know, you can't go through life with that fuck 'em and chuck 'em attitude.'

There was more to her lecture, but that was the headline. I wanted to explain that I didn't mean to be unfriendly, I was just temporarily immobilised by guilt and shame, though I realised hearing that might not make her feel any less used.

The next day we shook hands and parted on friendly terms, but her words played on a loop in my mind during idle moments for the next few weeks. Fucking followed by chucking was never part of my sexual repertoire thereafter. I was more likely to be guilty of knobbing followed by sobbing.

The next lecture came, unsurprisingly, from Dad.

My A-level results weren't good enough to get me into the universities I'd applied for and the school had advised sending me to a crammer where I might improve my grades, then reapply. That was going to cost even more money that Dad didn't have, so I needed to get a job.

The first person I knew who found gainful employment after we left school was Ben. For a few months before he went to drama school, Ben worked as a bartender at a Chicago-themed deep-dish pizza restaurant in a windowless, wood-panelled basement off Regent Street. I was impressed. 'I don't think I'm going to stay there very long, though,' said Ben. 'If you need money, you should get an interview, Ads. I bet they'd take you.' I went along the following week.

The restaurant's assistant manager eyed me as I filled out the application form. 'So you're Ben's friend. Another public school boy. Aren't you a bit *over-qualified* to work here?'

'Well, I did OK at O level,' I replied earnestly. 'I mean, I got As in English, art and history, but my A levels weren't very good. Apparently I'm going to have to re-take Spanish and reapply for university next year.'

'Right. Well, the good news is you're not going to need A-level Spanish to clear tables and wash pizza pans. The bar job's gone, but you could start next week as a busboy.'

'Great! What's a busboy?'

'You clear tables and wash pizza pans.'

'Oh, OK.'

I worked in restaurants off and on for the next five years.

BOWIE ANNUAL

On my eighteenth birthday Dad gave me some cufflinks and Mum got me a copy of Bowie's new album, *Never Let Me Down*. 'I didn't know if you already had it,' she said.

'Ah. No, I don't already have it, but that's because

it looks like such a terrible pile of old shit. Just look at the cover. He used to be Ziggy Stardust, Aladdin Sane, the Thin White Duke; now he's just Hobo in Theatrical Prop Store. And have you seen the video for "Day-in Day-out"? It's as if he fed the phrases "cool", "rock star" and "social problems" into Metal Mickey, then used the list Metal Mickey shat out as a treatment. How else does a rich, 40-year-old man decide the best way of dealing with urban deprivation is to tease his hair into a big quiff mullet, dress up like a Ramone that got fired for being too prissy and roller-skate (with elbow pads, of course) past dramatised scenes of homelessness, drug addiction and sexual assault in the mean streets of Los Angeles while pretending to play a no-neck guitar and belting out a single that can't decide if it's a protest song or the theme from a *Top Gun* sequel?'

'Blimey!' said Mum. 'Someone's been reading the *NME*. I thought you liked David Bowie.'

'I do like him, Mum. I love him. I just wish he'd do more of the things I like and less of this cheesy wannabe mainstream shit.'

'Says the Thompson Twins fan,' Mum shot back.

'I went off the Thompson Twins ages ago actually, Mum, but anyway, they were good at being mainstream. That was their job. It's not supposed to be Bowie's job.'

'But, Adam, surely part of the reason you like David Bowie is that he's always trying something different and taking creative risks? Sometimes those risks pay off and sometimes they don't. You can't just turn your back on him because he appears to be having some kind of artistic mid-life crisis. I think one day people will look back on *Never Let Me Down* and say that its reputation as Bowie's worst album has more to do with dated production and critical snobbery than it does with the actual songs, some of which – "Glass Spider", "Time

Will Crawl" and "Never Let Me Down", for example – are perfectly serviceable, despite lyrics that, I grant you, appear to have been written by a drunk fifth-former. You know, there were probably people who thought Ziggy was embarrassing back in 1972.'

'Ziggy *was* embarrassing, Mum. But all the daft costumes and make-up look amazing now because he was young and, more importantly, the songs were so good. They were good then and they'll be good in 1,000 years, but if he and the Spiders had come out with *Never Let Me Down*, not even Kansai Yamamoto, who as you know designed some of Ziggy's most striking outfits, would have been able to make Bowie look like anything other than an annoying theatre brat with a band.'

As I'm sure you realise (because I've used the same device a number of times in this book), what I actually said when I got the cassette of *Never Let Me Down* was, 'Thanks, Mummy, I can't wait to hear it.'

I ignored the cassette for a few days, then played it out of curiosity. 'Day-in Day-out' pretty much summed up the whole thing: noisy, overwrought and insipid. But in a bad way.

On holiday the previous year I'd made friends with another Bowie nut called Rick. A few days after my eighteenth birthday, Rick called saying he had a spare ticket to see Bowie playing live at Wembley Stadium as part of his Glass Spider tour. I didn't jump at the chance. I wasn't planning on listening to the studio version of *Never Let Me Down* again, and I wasn't keen to flog all the way out to Wembley to watch it being played live. I was also right in the middle of my A levels and my knuckles were supposed to be down, but Rick's invitation was so kind I didn't see how I could reasonably refuse it – and anyway, it was still David Bowie, even under the quiff mullet.

On a hot June afternoon, Rick and I weaved through the 70,000-strong crowd at Wembley Stadium towards the giant complex of vaguely arachnoid scaffolding at the far end. It was still broad daylight so the lighting that was meant to bring to life the 'spider' squatting over the stage wasn't yet noticeable and the overall atmosphere was genial but hardly electric.

As we shuffled past groups of people chatting about having seen Bowie at Live Aid or wondering whether he would play 'Let's Dance', I could feel my snobbery levels rising dangerously. 'How many of these "fans" regularly think deep thoughts and shed a tear as they listen to side two of *Low* on their headphones?' I wondered. 'Less than 4 per cent, I reckon. I imagine most of this crowd would probably prefer a football match to an audience with the man who sang "Letter to Hermione".'

There was a cheer as a figure arrived on stage and began playing a noodly, atonal guitar solo. The big video screens showed a close-up of the guitarist's face and I looked over at Rick. It was Carlos Alomar – along with Mick Ronson, Bowie's trustiest sideman. 'Carlos Alomar!' we grinned. Suddenly Alomar's atonal squeals were interrupted by a voice over the PA that shouted, 'SHUT UP!' Time to look at Rick again, because that was Bowie shouting 'SHUT UP!' the way he had over Robert Fripp's guitar at the end of 'It's No Game', the opening track from *Scary Monsters*. 'OK, maybe this show is going to be cool after all,' I thought.

That's when a load of extras from Duran Duran's 'Wild Boys' video dropped onto the stage on ropes and began walking over to things emphatically, striking poses and shouting lines like, 'We are the scum children! What have you done with our future?'

RAMBLE

I just watched some footage of the Glass Spider tour on YouTube and they didn't shout, 'We are the scum children! What have you done with our future?' Mainly they were shouting lines from 'Up the Hill Backwards' in a way that, at the time, made me hope we were going to hear 'Up the Hill Backwards', but no such luck. Also, they looked more like the Kids from *Fame* trying to be edgy than extras from the 'Wild Boys' video.

The show was full of references to parts of Bowie's career that he knew fans like me and Rick would pick up on. Unfortunately, it was also full of *Never Let Me Down*, all but two tracks of which were played that night. He threw us a few bones, though, and we were treated to solid versions of 'All the Madmen', 'Big Brother' and one of my favourite tracks from *Heroes*, the woozy, vaguely Middle Eastern-sounding 'Sons of the Silent Age'.

Perhaps worried that it was too weird for the 'Let's Dance' brigade, Bowie couldn't resist sprinkling some theatre dust over 'Sons of the Silent Age', and while Peter Frampton took over singing on the choruses, a woman stood in a pair of ski boots attached to planks, swaying forwards and backwards as Zavid pretended to be controlling her movements with magical hand gesturez.

What more could you want ... except maybe less?

My cassette of *Never Let Me Down* didn't re-emerge until Joe and I went travelling round Europe towards the end of that summer, when I stuffed it in my backpack, anticipating the fun of regaling Cornballs with choice moments of terribleness: the long spoken intro to 'Glass Spider' ('*Tiny wails, tiny cries*'), the song 'Too Dizzy', which sounded like the theme to a daytime TV interior decoration show, and the section on 'Shining Star (Makin' My Love)', in which Bowie and Mickey Rourke interrupt what sounds like a Pepsi & Shirlie B-side to exchange a series of raps about a hired killer who '*blew heads outta shape in the name of Trotsky, Sinn-Féin, Hitler cashdown*'.

But I hadn't realised how much of our Euro trip would be spent sitting outside toilets on packed, slow-moving trains or going out of our minds with boredom and hunger on overnight ferries, and when the conversation dried up the only thing that stopped me jumping overboard was my Walkman. With space at a premium, I had packed just a handful of cassettes, and when I'd overdosed on Van Morrison's *Astral Weeks*, the Stones' *Through the Past, Darkly* and my 120-minute compilation of Super Summer Sounds, I eventually turned to *Never Let Me Down*.

No, I didn't suddenly realise I'd been wrong about it. It was still shit, but it was like the shit of one of your children: somehow less offensive than other shit because it came out of someone you love. 'Shining Star (Makin' My Love)' started to sound like quite a good Pepsi & Shirlie B-side and rumbling through the outskirts of Rome on a hot coach I realised I was also enjoying the daytime TV bounce of 'Too Dizzy', despite an oddly threatening tone of jealous rage in the lyrics: '*I'm not trying to lose control, / But you're just pushing for a fight!*'

'Not very Zavid,' I thought.

RAMBLE

Bowie removed 'Too Dizzy' from subsequent editions of
Never Let Me Down and it's generally regarded as one of
the worst songs he ever recorded. I still like it.

Even 'Zeroes' – a song whose crap, sitar-soaked,
sub-Beatles sound was made especially offensive by the
'Heroes' pun – ended up being a song I love to this day.
Though it's possible I love it in much the same way as
I love scratching my nuts, picking my nose and smelling
my farts.

CHAPTER 18

RANDOM THOUGHTS CONCERNING OLD AGE

Towards the end of 2009 I returned home to Norfolk after a boozy night in London and, feeling every one of my 40 years, I decided it was time for a Special Bath. I turned the taps on full, lit a few candles, put on some Harold Budd and Brian Eno ambient music and squirted a thick green jet of Badedas bath 'gelee' into the tub as it filled, churning the water with both hands to build up a green mountain range of pine-smelling bubbles.

A few minutes later, finally luxuriating in my Special Bath, I decided I might like to switch from Eno and Budd's reverb-heavy piano minimalism to the *Blade Runner* soundtrack and I raised a hand through the bubbles to activate my smartphone. But once I'd wiped away the pine-fresh foam, I was shocked to see that my hand suddenly looked like an old man's hand: not just wrinkled, but papery and marked here and there with little brown dots and splotches over big knotty veins. 'Fuck,' I thought. 'I'm old.'

I started to imagine that I had lost consciousness as a 30-year-old and woken up to find myself aged 80, then wondered if that might be a good premise for a film. It struck me that it was a nice excuse to email Dad, then in his late eighties, and ask him for his observations about ageing.

My contact with Dad in those days was infrequent, and what messages we did exchange were usually short and to the point, but my email about old age must have caught him at the right moment, because the next morning there was a reply in my inbox entitled '*Random Thoughts on Old Age*'. It was filled with insights, observations and a few relevant aphorisms that he had collected over the years. He often talked of compiling these as an annotated book of quotes called *Words of Wisdom*, though that was another in a long line of money-making schemes that never quite came together – a bit like my film idea, which also got shelved in favour of less ambitious but more achievable projects.

I forgot about Dad's email until after he was dead. It popped up again when I was in the process of looking through old bits and pieces in the course of writing this book, and it struck me that it was probably the longest single communication he'd ever sent me, and in an odd way the most heartfelt. I was a decade older than I was when I first read it, and observations that had originally struck me as typically pompous were suddenly as grimly relatable as Michael McIntyre routines. See what you think.

> A very common phenomenon, even in middle age, I am
> sure, is the appalling moment when one realises that a
> large part of one's life has suddenly vanished without
> trace, like a mountain climber suddenly disappearing
> into a bottomless crevasse. I vividly remember such
> a moment in my own life (I was probably in my late
> thirties or early forties) when I actually exclaimed out
> loud, 'Where did it all go?' This is why one must always
> be on one's guard against that so tritely but so very
> aptly described danger of regarding one's days as if
> they were a rehearsal for the real thing, instead of being
> one's never-to-be-repeated LIFE ITSELF.

Yes, we should *carpe* the *diem* and take some time to watch C-beams glitter in the dark near the Tannhäuser Gate, because life moves pretty fast and if you don't stop to look around once in a while, you might find you spent most of it watching and rewatching films (and of course bonus features).

'You're as young as you feel' may be thunderingly trite, but it's also profoundly true. Health is not the prime conditioning factor here. Ill health and old age present their own syndrome, but a man can be perfectly fit in body yet behave as if he were verging on the geriatric.

Disbelief is probably the old person's most common condition of mind. He hears expressions such as 'the elderly', but only with difficulty associates himself with that company. Looking for cheap second-hand books, he explores a charity shop called Help the Aged, but does not for a moment see himself as an object of the requested benevolence. He has a bus pass, and values it, but is not entirely convinced of his entitlement to it (though it is obvious to him that the gent sitting across the way is a fully qualified holder of the same device).

This is why the admonition 'Oh, for heaven's sake, act your age!' can be so offensive and such bad advice. The intelligent senior citizen eschews the expression 'at my age' to preface a statement not simply because it is exceedingly pompous and boring, but because he knows that to get into the habit of acknowledging his years (or claiming them to gain advantage) is a sure way of accelerating the ageing process.

This reminded me of Joe when he was about 16 telling me about getting told off when he was pissing about on the Tube one day. An older woman told him to 'grow up' and Cornballs proudly reported to me that his response was, 'Why would I want to do that?' I remember feeling that I might have been on the woman's side.

> One doesn't 'feel' old 'in oneself' but is nevertheless
> all too often disagreeably reminded that the ever-
> youthful mind inhabits a mechanical contrivance that
> is not immune from mechanical wear and tear. It's a
> wonderful autumn day and one sees oneself taking a
> picnic lunch on one's back and walking the 17 miles
> from Lewes to Eastbourne over the Downs between
> early breakfast and 6 p.m., as one used frequently
> to do, then remembers that yesterday it required a
> considerable effort of will to complete a three-mile
> course (though much of it steeply uphill) in an hour
> and three-quarters.

Dad was always a keen 'hiker' and continued with his walks on the Sussex Downs until he moved in with us. Occasionally he'd bump into someone who would recognise him from his BaaadDad days and it always made him happy. There was one particular meeting Dad described to me by saying: 'I was out walking the other day and I met a fellow on a mountain bike. He stopped and said [does weird cockney accent], "'Ere, I know you! You're BaaadDad, in't ya?" I said, "Yes! That's right," and we had a very nice chat. But how strange that one should be recognised all the way out there on the Sussex Downs, don't you think?' I said I didn't think it was that strange. *The Adam and Joe Show* was a ratings juggernaut.

Years after Dad's death I discovered, through a series of minor coincidences, the identity of the cockney mountain biker. It was the Turner Prize-winning artist Grayson Perry.

According to Grayson, who it turns out used to watch *The Adam and Joe Show*, he had spotted my dad on the Downs twice and they chatted both times.

There are many ADVANTAGES to old age, provided that one has learnt one's lessons. PATIENCE is one of the most precious of these, though one of the hardest to acquire.

'He that can have patience can have what he will.'
BENJAMIN FRANKLIN

'Never think that God's delays are God's denials. Hold on; hold fast; hold out. Patience is genius.'
GEORGES-LOUIS LECLERC, *COMTE DE BUFFON*

To these I would add:

'Have another slice of chill cake.'
A. BUCKLES

FORTITUDE. It is quite comforting to know that one is capable of surviving the injuries inflicted by the slings and arrows of outrageous fortune without falling about, and that one is capable of doing so much more than may at first seem probable.

The key phrase here is 'without falling about'. Though Dad would never have referred to anyone as a 'snowflake', disparagingly or otherwise, he was never comfortable with people sharing every hang-up and anxiety and felt that to do so was to 'fall about'. If something was really wrong, a person should ask for help, but as for feeling scared, sad and hopeless now and then, well, what did you expect?

As Dad was so fond of reminding us, 'Life's a vale of tears,' but if you keep plodding on it'll generally brighten up.

I'm on board with some of that philosophy, but being able to talk about how you really feel now and then is useful, too. As long as the falling about is kept to an absolute minimum, of course.

INDIFFERENCE tends to come with old age. Not mindless indifference (which would preclude COMPASSION and consideration for others), but the NOT CARING about a whole host of things that used to concern one. (At the most trivial, for example: I used to be quite irritated by people I didn't know addressing me by my first name. I still think it's very bad form, but I don't care any more. I don't care where the knives and forks go or if a red glass is used for white burgundy; it doesn't affect the TASTE of the wine.

On the other hand, I don't care very much if people jump the queue as long as I'm not especially anxious to get back quickly from the supermarket or racing to the catch the train. And I don't care what people in general think about my writing; only about the opinions of those whom I happen especially to respect. The list is long and everyone will have their own.

I look forward to achieving a similar state of relaxed indifference, especially after all the time I've wasted worrying about negative opinions from disgruntled and even perfectly well-gruntled strangers on social media. But there'll be climate change in hell before someone uses a red glass for white burgundy without me fully losing my shit.

When I was reading back Dad's email I had just spent several weeks not only sorting through boxes filled with his old letters and photographs, but rereading my old diaries and notebooks to check memories and chronologies for this book. It was a process that started out fun but left me feeling shredded, the way I wished some of my diaries and notebooks had been. Then, when I read Dad's email, it was as if he was sat with me and sympathising – not something he had done since I was about seven and upset after some children teased me for being short and having small eyes.

> Literally and metaphorically, one goes into the attic, looking for reminders, and is overwhelmed by the accumulation of things, most of which have been completely or in Freudian analysis probably PURPOSEFULLY forgotten. It is dangerous stuff and can result in severe emotional distress. The mistakes one made; the wrongs endured or inflicted on others; the hopes shattered; the irreplaceable losses suffered; the projects of high promise unfulfilled ....! It is a bit like turning over a compost heap where discarded material has not yet had time to achieve a useful metamorphosis.
>
> Putting things to the back of (or out of) the mind is an indispensable aid to a salubrious existence and to disinter such things can be a noxious exercise. The odours of the past can be less than fragrant (the dead rat as well as the faded rose petals or the pressed gardenia).
>
> The attic can be a Pandora's box, among the most pernicious of all its contents being that of REGRET. Only a stout philosophy can save a man from this particular evil. Here are two aphorisms taken from *Words of Wisdom*: 'Your past is always going to be the

way it was. Stop trying to change it.' And, 'A prudent man will think what fate has conceded to him more important than what it has denied.'

At the same time, the old ought to remember that the last item in Pandora's box was HOPE.

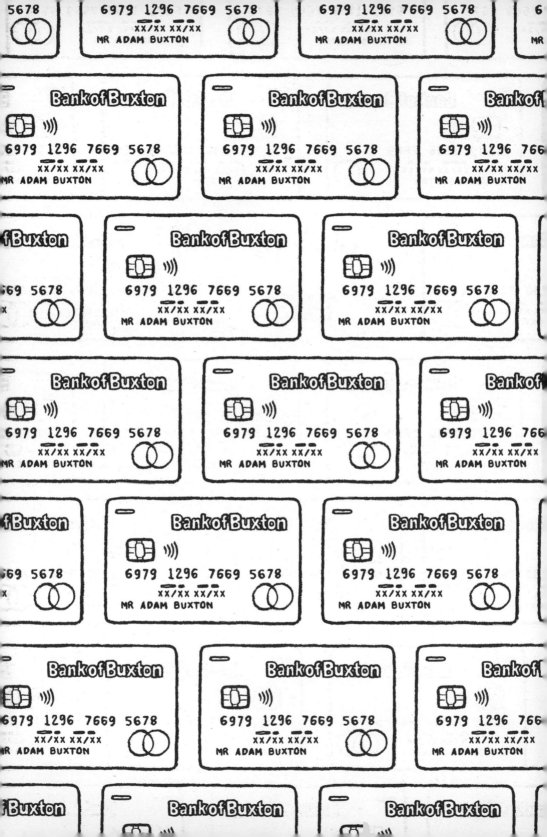

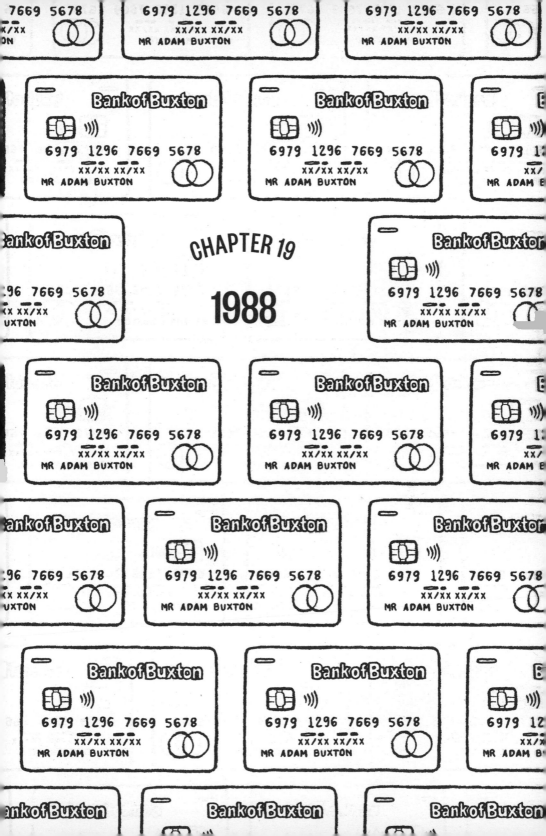

CHAPTER 19

1988

During my first week of training at the pizza restaurant, they put me on pot wash in the sweltering kitchen and I felt very sorry for myself. 'It's like *Down and Out in Paris and London*,' I complained to Cornballs. It was a relief when I was allowed out onto the floor with servers and customers, and I made it my mission to master the highly skilled art of the busboy.

At the beginning of each shift I was assigned a section of the restaurant where it was my responsibility to clear, clean and re-lay the tables. That meant piling dirty plates, glasses and cutlery into big plastic 'bus trays', taking those bus trays to the kitchen to be washed, then restocking the 'bus stations' in the centre of the restaurant floor with clean plates, glasses and cutlery in order to get tables ready for new diners as fast as possible.

The more efficient the busboy, the more tables a server could turn over and the more tips they would earn. At the end of the shift, if the server thought their busboy had done a good job, they gave them a split of the tips. But if you were slow, lazy or the server just didn't like you, you got 'stiffed'. On good nights I enjoyed the challenge of working as fast as I could, sometimes competing with other busboys to set up tables in just a few seconds. On bad nights I got non-stop shit from servers and kitchen boys and the only comfort was a 10-minute cigarette break that I took while listening to my

Walkman by the huge stinky cylindrical bins out the back. Poor, poor Buckles.

At the end of the night I was damp from the giant dish-washer, grimy from carrying teetering towers of pizza pans and my thighs were chaffing from having marched about at high speed for six hours, but I usually had some good tips in my pocket (in addition to the minimum wage for the shift) and I'd shuffle to the bus stop in Regent's Street, put on my headphones, listen to some Brian Eno and try not to fall asleep on the night bus back to Clapham.

It felt good to be making money. The first time I got £20 out of the cashpoint with my new debit card (nicknamed 'Jimmy Plastic'), it was one of the crowning thrills of my adolescence.

RAMBLE

I'd recently been introduced to the Cockney rhyming slang phrase 'Jimmy Riddle' meaning 'piddle' or urinate. I found it so amusing I decided it would be fun to stick 'Jimmy' in front of other words and phrases, despite there being no rhyming element. So there was Jimmy Plastic, Jimmy Fag Break, Jimmy Night Bus, etc. For some reason it never Jimmy Caught On, and by the Nineties I'd Jimmy Dropped It.

In autumn 1988 Dad's financial difficulties went critical when the new management at the *Telegraph* invited him to take compulsory retirement. By December he was borrowing money from me to keep up his mortgage payments, and when Mum found out she and Dad had another of their increasingly bitter rows. Mum didn't think an upper-middle-class father should be borrowing money from his son, but after a childhood of non-stop holidays, gadgets and *Star Wars* toys, not to mention the expensive schools, I thought it was fair enough.

Meanwhile, my further education was on hold. Warwick University had offered me a place to study English and American literature, but not until the following year. That suited me fine. After a few months of working at the restaurant I was enjoying the camaraderie and the drama. Who was sleeping with who? Who was on the fiddle? Who was clearly on drugs during their shifts? Yes, perhaps the job was less enjoyable if you weren't 18 and living with your parents, but for me it was like putting on plays back at school, except with a more diverse cast, and you got paid.

Before he went off to university, Patrick did a few months as a busboy at the pizza restaurant, too. We spent one of our first shifts together doing Derek and Clive impressions that came down to calling each other a 'fahking caaant' in a variety of styles, until an angry manager interrupted a 'CANCAN-CANCANCAN!' volley to remind us there were families around. We didn't get too many shifts together after that.

Around that time, Patrick and I were also deep in our enthusiasm for Van Morrison and Woody Allen. Van had been on our radar for a couple of years since getting into *Moondance*, then *Astral Weeks*, *Veedon Fleece*, *Saint Dominic's Preview* and everything else he'd done in the late Sixties and early Seventies. To me, Van was the sound of walking to warm pubs on cold nights with Patrick and his sister Eliza, who was reliably outrageous and funny. After the pub we'd go back to their house in Wandsworth and watch *Blind Date* while Eliza and I entertained Patrick with our very hilarious comments about Cilla and the contestants.

Until a few months previously I'd seen only two Woody Allen films and hadn't thought much of either of them. The first was *A Midsummer Night's Sex Comedy*. I watched it on

cable late one night on our trip to America in 1982, but it
had far less sex than I was hoping for (i.e. none) and far more
not-very-funny comedy. The second was in my first year at
Westminster when our housemaster took a group of us to see
Zelig. I was pleased to be at the cinema on a school night, but
I didn't get the point of *Zelig* at all. The guy wants to fit in and
be liked – and?

Then in November 1987, BBC Two showed a season of
Woody Allen comedies that, as well as *Manhattan*, *Sleeper*,
Take the Money and Run and *Everything You Always Wanted to
Know About Sex* (*But Were Afraid to Ask)*, included the first
ever UK TV showing of *Annie Hall*.

The film included the cleverest thing I'd seen (and
actually understood) up to that point: the moment in the
cinema queue when Woody Allen magically produces the
real Marshall McLuhan to humiliate a man pontificating
loudly about McLuhan's work before breaking the fourth
wall to say, 'Boy, if only life were really like this.' For a self-
absorbed young man who didn't understand women well,
finding ingenious jokes like these woven in with observations about the joy and pain of being in love left me feeling
I had a new best friend, and I hungrily devoured the rest of
Woody Allen's films.

I hate him now, though, obviously.

DJ Deep Dish

During opening hours, the restaurant PA would play tapes of
Chicago Oldies station Magic 104, so we would work to the
sound of DJ Dick Biondi playing Fifties and Sixties pop on
a loop.

When I arrived at the restaurant this was fun and I enjoyed
discovering tracks like 'Happy Together' by The Turtles,

'Runaway' by Del Shannon or Frank Sinatra's version of 'Chicago' (the restaurant chain's unofficial theme, which would play every hour). After a few weeks, however, songs like 'Concrete and Clay' by Unit 4 + 2 or 'Have I the Right' by The Honeycombs became the same kind of special torture that Bill Murray endures in Groundhog Day as he wakes up each morning to 'I Got You Babe' by Sonny & Cher (which Dick Biondi also played a lot). To this day, it only takes a few seconds of Old Blue Eyes singing 'Chicago' to bring on a feeling of grimy-pizza-pan-clearing exhaustion.

One of the managers at the restaurant was called Sally. She liked the compilation tapes I'd sometimes play when we were cleaning up at the end of the night. Sally agreed with me that the constantly repeating Oldies tapes were a significant threat to staff sanity, and she said next time I was working a quiet shift (Monday lunchtime was reliably dead) I could bring in one of my compilations to play while we worked. There were a couple of conditions: in line with company policy, the tape needed to have Frank Sinatra shitting on about Chicago every hour and the rest of the music had to be suitable for people to listen to while they ate revolting-looking pizza pies and garlic bread that was actually just stodgy pizza base brushed with buttery slop that looked and smelled like bile with bits of parsley in it.

The following Monday morning I turned up at work clutching my new compilation on a fresh C-60 cassette. Soon I would know the thrill of the DJ, the sense of power and connection that comes with controlling the mood of a group of strangers with a selection of music designed to surprise, delight and energise.

The restaurant opened and as the first few diners wandered in I pressed 'Play' on the tape deck and the room filled with Johnny Marr's opening guitar lines from '(Nothing But) Flowers', a favourite song on the new Talking Heads album, *Nude*. After the next few tracks it was clear my tape was a hit and servers nodded along approvingly to 'Can't Be Still' by Booker T. & The MGs, 'Love Me or Leave Me' by Nina Simone, 'I'm So Free' by Lou Reed and other selections entirely out of step with the rigidly prescribed restaurant theme.

Then came my curveball: a track from Joe Jackson's album *Night and Day*. I thought it would be too obvious to go for 'Steppin' Out', which had been a hit, so instead I chose an upbeat Salsa number called 'Cancer'.

Written as a sardonic response to the first flood of cancer scare articles in the late 1970s, the airily delivered lyrics are a litany of all the things that might give you the Big C (basically '*everything*', according to Jackson). I thought it was funny, but I was 18 and no one close to me had died of cancer. As the chorus of the song played (*'There's no cure! There's no answer! / Everything gives you cancer'*) I saw one of the servers over by the front-of-house desk scowling. 'What the fuck is this song?' she growled when I went over.

'It's funny,' I said.

'It's not fucking funny,' she replied and went to take an order.

My boss Sally emerged from the office, looked up at the speakers, hurried over to the tape player and hit stop.

It taught me a valuable lesson: it's one thing to playfully subvert an environment with music, but it's quite another to give it 'Cancer'.

'Follow the Leader – Yeah, Don't'

'Hey, man. Me and Ben are heading over to Lou's. His rentals are away so we're going to spoon,' said Joe on the phone. He was not suggesting that we go over to Louis's place and cuddle each other in bed, as nice as that would have been. We were in the habit of using the word 'spoon' to mean 'hang out' (origin: fool about – loon about – spoon about – spoon).

In a few weeks Ben would be off to drama school, Louis to university and Joe to film school, and I wondered if this would be one of the last spooning sessions we'd be having for a while.

Joe had just bought the 12-inch of 'Follow the Leader' by Eric B. & Rakim, and down in Louis's basement den he put it on and cranked it up. I liked the super-low bass, the spacey samples that I thought were the Mellotron from '2000 Light Years from Home' by the Stones (but are actually from 'Nautilus' by Bob James) and the mellifluous vocal and lyrics: 'Let's travel at magnificent speeds around the universe'.

We declared it a triumph and smoked a joint.

Either the joint was strong or we were weak, or both. Joe and Louis seemed to enjoy it, but Ben and I, who were more comfortable with lager, got the fear. Louis said he felt as though his head had been 'plugged into the National Grid'. The phrase made me think of *Tron* and I imagined light cycles zipping around my cranium. At first this was fun (the light cycles were my favourite part of *Tron*), but when I realised I was unable to control the random images tumbling through my mind, I got anxious and my heart started to pound alarmingly. I looked at the others to see how they were doing. They looked fucked. Suddenly Ben leaned forward and said, 'Oh my God, what if there's something in it?'

'There's marijuana in it,' said Joe.

'No, something else, something really bad,' said Ben. This was not what I wanted to hear.

RAMBLE

'Oh my God, there's something in it!' became a bit of a catchphrase for our gang after that night, but it belied a real terror I developed about being spiked and losing my mind. One of the servers at the restaurant would sometimes hand out microdots of acid to make shifts more interesting, but one of the other busboys told me she'd been known to slip them into people's drinks without telling them. Appropriately her name was Mickey (though I don't think her surname was Finn). I was terrified Mickey might spike me and that if she did, I'd immediately go full Syd Barrett in front of all the hen parties and city boys. From then on I only drank from a bottle I carried around with me, but this didn't prevent me from occasionally feeling a little faint during a busy shift and becoming convinced I was about to be dragged, hooting and howling, through the Doors of Perception and dumped in the Alley of Psychosis outside.

The idea there might be 'something in it' had made my heart start hammering so hard I assumed a coronary was inevitable. 'Shouldn't we call someone?' I suggested. Who could we call, though? We were filthy, illegal drug users, faced with just two choices: prison or death. So, cowering in my self-inflicted madness, I waited for death.

To kill time until Death arrived, I stuck on a VHS tape I'd brought with me that had the entire first series of *The Young Ones* on it. 'Is it still funny?' asked Louis.

'Yeah, man! It's amazing!' I replied as I inserted the tape. I knew more or less every line off by heart and the comforting familiarity of the show helped bring me gradually back down to earth.

RAMBLE

In the weeks after *The Young Ones* started airing in the winter of 1982, my friends and I weren't going into school and writing think pieces considering how this new sitcom about four student caricatures sharing a revolting house constituted a seismic event in modern comedy. Nor did we describe *The Young Ones* as 'anarchic', the way the announcer on BBC Two would before each new episode. That word was enough to make my dad start muttering darkly from the back of the sitting room. After a couple of minutes of Rick shouting and Vyvyan loudly smashing things, Dad would sigh heavily and stalk out, repeating, 'Anarchic ... God save us.'

Dad's disapproval made me wary of fully embracing *The Young Ones* at first, but I wasn't able to resist for long. It was fun to imitate the characters and there was something especially energising about talking like Rick. It felt great to curl your lip, widen your eyes, thrust your pelvis as if trying to have sex with every bit of air in the room and say, 'Right on!' (with a soft 'r') or to shout that someone was an 'UTTER BASTARD', before storming out wearing a look of gleefully furious indignation.

* * *

When Joe, Louis and Mark got back to London after the first term at their respective film schools and universities, they paid me a visit in the pizza restaurant a few days before Christmas. It felt like a long time since we'd been down in Lou's basement plugged into the National Grid and it was weird seeing them in there. I couldn't shake the suspicion that they felt sorry for me, clearing plates in a restaurant while they were in higher education, making new friends and preparing for the rest of their lives.

My response was to make it abundantly clear that I was one of the greatest busboys London had ever seen. I carried my bus trays at double speed, stacked my pizza tins perilously high and bantered with the much older servers ostentatiously. It was important to demonstrate that I was a vital and popular part of a group of actual grown-up women and men from a wide variety of backgrounds who didn't spend all their time pushing each other round in wheelbarrows dressed as babies, drinking lager and lime in the Nelson Mandela bar (which I assumed was what university was like). No, sir. We did real work in the real world.

When Joe, Louis and Mark had left, one of the servers teased me about my 'posh friends'. I complained that she was being snobbish and she laughed. 'Are you serious? They seemed all right but "Cakes" are always shit tippers, that's all I know,' she replied.

'Why do you call them "Cakes"?' I asked.

'Cos whenever we get a big party of posh mums with their kids and I take their drinks order it's always, "Yah, can we have 10 Cakes and three Diet Cakes, please?"'

BOWIE ANNUAL

Joe and Louis agreed with me that the best bit of *The Last Temptation of Christ* had been when Bowie turns up as Pontius Pilot and says to Jesus, 'Zo, you're the one they call Jeezuz of Nazzzareth.' The film was controversial. 'Some things should remain sacred or it's all meaningless,' said Dad. I still said the occasional prayer in those days and had been prepared to disapprove of seeing Jesus getting it together with Mary Magdalene, but I thought the film was moving and was especially pleased that most of Bowie's lines were generously drizzled with 'wuzz'.

For the next few days we said 'I wash my handz of thiz' a lot, and one evening Joe, Louis and I sat up late taping ourselves doing our respective Bowie impressions and running through favourite daft Bowie quotes.

These included: 'MTV. Too much iz never enough', 'Adolf Hitler wuz one of the world's first rock stars' and 'It wuz some pretty boy in class ... that I took home and neatly fucked on my bed upstairs.'

It was good to be reminded of the way I used to think of Bowie when *The Man Who Fell to Earth* was shown on *Moviedrome*, a new 'slot' on BBC Two in which Alex Cox, director of *Repo Man* and left-field movie champion, introduced some of his favourite cult films. I watched it nostalgically, remembering the weekend just before Christmas in 1981 when I'd seen *The Man Who Fell to Earth* listed in the *Radio Times*.

It was billed as 'a science-fiction film starring pop star David Bowie', thereby ticking two of my favourite boxes and immediately conjuring images of Zavid driving around alien planets in a hover car and exchanging wisecracks with robots (i.e. the perfect film).

Though it was showing late on a Sunday night, Mum had said I could stay up to watch it, and as it was starting she sat down with a glass of wine and said, 'I think I'll watch it, too. I like that "Space Odyssey" song of his.' Initially delighted that Mum was sharing in my Bowie enthusiasm, it turned out to be a very awkward occasion indeed.

Within five minutes it was clear we wouldn't be seeing Bowie battling baddies with a lightsaber (a shame, as he could have done the sound effects – 'Wuzzz, wuzzzz, wuzzzza wuzzz …' etc.). Instead, the tale of an alien disguised as a gauche Englishman called Thomas Jerome Newton trying to raise enough money to fly back to his family and save their planet from drought was less concerned with being exciting than it was with being oblique, impressionistic and at times nonsensical. I was keenly aware it was the kind of thing my mum was likely to dismiss as 'really weird', especially as it was really weird.

My discomfort turned to low-level torture during a long sequence in which a middle-aged college lecturer played by Rip Torn enjoys a boisterous shagging session with a young female student. This was intercut with Bowie eating noodles and watching some Kabuki theatre, all soundtracked with animalistic grunts, groans and increasingly noisy ethnic percussion. It's the first of several determinedly unerotic sex scenes in the film, and by the time Bowie's todger is on display while he and Candy Clark's character Mary-Lou get drunk and naked and fire a gun loaded with blanks at each other, Mum and I hadn't exchanged a word and I was looking forward to getting back to revising for my Common Entrance exams.

Although I didn't especially enjoy or understand
The Man Who Fell to Earth that night with my mum, I
had seen it twice more by the time I watched it again
on *Moviedrome*, and with each successive viewing I
had found more to like. As well as admiring Bowie's
legendarily spaced-out performance as the beautiful
alien, I enjoyed learning that his experience making the
film and tinkering with a soundtrack that was never used
ended up influencing (and providing cover images for)
two of my favourite Bowie albums: *Station to Station*,
made immediately after *The Man Who Fell to Earth* was
shot in 1975, and *Low*, recorded in 1976.

In 2012 I presented a screening of *The Man Who
Fell to Earth* as part of the BFI Southbank's Screen
Epiphanies series but came away feeling I'd misjudged
the tone of my introduction, which as usual was a

mixture of enthusiasm and piss-taking. The problem was that the audience, many of whom hadn't seen the film before, seemed to find it hard to shift gear when it started. There was much inappropriate laughter throughout, especially in the brief flashback scenes featuring Bowie on his home planet with his alien family waving him goodbye as he gets on a kind of train that looks like a big dog kennel covered in hairy turds.

While there is a fair bit of humorously mad stuff in it, *The Man Who Fell to Earth* still evokes for me all the wonder and weirdness of falling in love with Bowie when I was still a young man, cautiously beginning to open my mind to the possibility that there may be worthwhile things down the road less travelled, even though they may occasionally look like a big dog kennel covered in hairy turds.

Argument with Wife Log 3

SUBJECT OF ARGUMENT	TAKING THE TOWEL OUT OF THE BATHROOM SO AFTER I'VE SHOWERED THERE'S NO TOWEL
MAIN POINTS – WIFE	'You do so many things that are much more selfish.'
MAIN POINTS – BUCKLES	'DON'T TAKE THE TOWEL OUT OF THE BATHROOM.'
WINNER	BUCKLES

SUBJECT OF ARGUMENT	WIFE GETS RID OF LAVATORY BRUSH
MAIN POINTS – WIFE	'They're disgusting.'
MAIN POINTS – BUCKLES	'How do you propose keeping the toilet bowl free from faecal smearing?'
WINNER	BUCKLES

SUBJECT OF ARGUMENT	DOES A STANDARD FAN LOWER THE TEMPERATURE OF A ROOM?
MAIN POINTS – WIFE	'It's not air-conditioning. Fans just move the hot air around.'
MAIN POINTS – BUCKLES	'Fans make you COOLER. So the room must be COOLER.'
WINNER	WIFE

SUBJECT OF ARGUMENT	WHOSE FAMILY IS MORE DYSFUNCTIONAL
MAIN POINTS – WIFE	'Yours is.'
MAIN POINTS – BUCKLES	'Yours is.'
WINNER	BUCKLES

SUBJECT OF ARGUMENT	DISHWASHER DOOR LEFT OPEN
MAIN POINTS – WIFE	'I was still loading dishes.'
MAIN POINTS – BUCKLES	'If there's a ten-minute gap between the loading of each dish, the door needs to be closed to prevent tripping.'
WINNER	WIFE (but only because I stated my case with excessive tetch)

SUBJECT OF ARGUMENT	DOG SLEEPING ON OUR BED
MAIN POINTS – WIFE	'She loves sleeping on our bed and she's part of the family.'
MAIN POINTS – BUCKLES	'So is the plan for you and me to stop having sex completely?'
WINNER	BUCKLES

SUBJECT OF ARGUMENT	CONSTANT INTERRUPTIONS WHILE I'M WRITING THIS BOOK
MAIN POINTS – WIFE	'You're literally just writing down arguments we've had. It doesn't look that difficult.'
MAIN POINTS – BUCKLES	'You do it then. And don't say you don't want to because you've got a real job and you're not a dick.'
WINNER	BUCKLES

CHAPTER 20

1989

y extraordinary work in the field of table-clearing eventually led to me being invited to join the special forces of the restaurant world: the bartenders. Sure, the servers made more money, but the bar staff had their own separate domain that only they could access: an elevated section near the entrance where they stood protected behind their mahogany bulwark in smart shirts, bow ties and waistcoats, looking down over the restaurant floor.

Not long after I completed my training, Lenny the bar manager took his six-person team to see the Tom Cruise film *Cocktail* (or, as Joe referred to it, 'The Tale of a Cock'). Lenny was hoping *Cocktail* would inspire us to enliven Happy Hour at the pizza restaurant with the kind of bottle-flippin', glass-spinnin', high-fivin' 'flair' demonstrated in the film by bartenders Coughlin and Flanagan. We tried to incorporate a few of their moves, but the results, like some of the cocktails, were mixed, and left us, like some of the other cocktails, shaken.

Glass bottle shelves were smashed by flying tumblers, customers were lashed with arcs of cherry liqueur, and one busy Friday night an attempt to do a cool dance to 'Hippy Hippy Shake' while re-stocking glasses ended with me slipping and bringing down about 50 highballs. They shattered in a jagged heap and I landed palms down on the lot. I spent the rest of the evening getting stitches at St Thomas's A&E before meeting my workmates for a beer and a delicate high five at the end of the night.

The injury was one of several signs that it was finally time for me to leave the pizza restaurant and work elsewhere until it was my turn to be pushed around in a wheelbarrow while dressed as a baby, followed by pints of lager and lime in the Nelson Mandela bar at Warwick University. Despite the 'Cancer' and *Cocktail* incidents, my boss Sally gave me a good reference and I got a job behind the bar at another sub-terranean American-style hang-out, this time in Dover Street opposite The Ritz hotel.

Wave of New Relations

The Service Point was the section at the end of the bar where servers came to pick up drinks orders for their tables. Most of the bartenders preferred working on the main bar to working 'Point', because generally you got better tips from the customers than the servers. I liked the Service Point because it meant I got to see Miriam.

I had just celebrated my twentieth birthday. Miriam was 24 and seemed impossibly sophisticated. She was the first person I'd met who had taken Ecstasy, and after stressful restaurant shifts Miriam might head over to the Wag Club in Soho and spend the rest of the night weaving her long hands through the sweaty air to the sounds of Soul II Soul, Yazz, Inner City, Bomb the Bass and S'Express.

Other nights she'd come out with us non-ravers and we'd sit around in a late-night bar, drinking, smoking and talking about all the good stuff: restaurant politics, art and heartbreak. She was a good mix. Fierce and flaky. Concerned and carefree. Right on and non-judgemental. I heard my first dawn chorus after one of those late-night bar sessions. 'Look at me,' I thought on the night bus. 'I'm Jimmy Coming Home at Sunrise.'

Despite my fears that we were drifting away from one another, I still got to see my school gang whenever they were back in London. Joe and I went over to Louis's place one evening and I invited Miriam along, too. We'd all recently seen Spike Lee's film *Do the Right Thing* and rehashed a version of the conversation that all good *Guardian* and *Time Out* readers had to have about it. Then Joe put on Public Enemy and I wondered if Miriam thought we were trying a bit too hard.

As Cornballs and Louis started deconstructing the lyrics to 'Fight the Power', Miriam led me to another room and it seemed appropriate for us to get undressed. 'Ooh, Gustav Klimt woman,' I thought. 'She doesn't shave her armpits. Hope that means she won't mind my hairy back.' In fact, Miriam was more focused on my head. At one point in the proceedings she yanked my hair with such force I didn't know whether to cry out in pain or laugh at the over-the-top *Betty Blue*-ness of it.

Once we'd both stopped trying so hard, we realised we got on well and the rest of the summer was spent hanging around with Miriam and her grown-up friends. For a long time, my idea of a perfect Sunday had been waking up at midday and watching *Network 7* in bed with several bowls of cereal before my mum knocked on the door about 2 p.m. and asked if I was planning on getting up at any point. Now that Miriam was around, my routines got more highbrow. At least, there was a wine bar in Clapham that we went to quite a bit and we saw several exhibitions at the ICA and pretended we understood them.

I showed Miriam some of my drawings (though not the one of the JOEADZ corporate tower) and she was impressed. We went to some local life-drawing classes and sometimes we'd go back to her room afterwards and draw each other

– and yes, it was exactly like *Titanic*, but sometimes I was Kate and she was Leonardo.

When we were drawing together we were perfectly in sync, but our temperamental differences started to show when it came to the music we preferred. For Miriam, that was anything that sounded good on a dance floor where she could lose herself. For me, it was more likely to be music that soundtracked my angst. But in a fun way.

Intimidated by Pixies

I'd bought the first Pixies album, *Surfer Rosa*, when it came out the previous year, in March 1988. They were playing it downstairs in the King's Road branch of Our Price and I thought it sounded like music for tough people, so I asked the guy at the counter what it was. 'Pixies,' he grunted, probably surprised that a fresh-faced fellow in a pink collarless shirt with a lavatory-brush hairdo might be interested in such uncompromising music.

'Cool. I'll take it,' I said, sliding Jimmy Plastic over the counter.

I listened to *Surfer Rosa* as I walked home, but it sounded much less fun than it had in Our Price. Back in my room, I studied the cover photograph of a woman in a big flamenco skirt standing against a wall decorated with fairy lights, a crucifix and the broken neck of a guitar. I didn't register any of those things initially because she was also topless. As it was a cassette inlay, not a vinyl sleeve, which would have been better for studying purposes, I had to really squint to appreciate the impressive detail.

The sleeve gave no clue as to what the band looked like. The artwork and the harsh sound of the music made me imagine some druggy types in a dive bar on the Mexican border. I imagined Pixies probably wore tight, studded leathers and lit up strong joints between shots of Jack Daniel's and told straights like me to go fuck themselves. Well, I don't appreciate being spoken to like that, so the next day I walked back to Our Price and asked for my money back.

'Didn't you like it?' said the same counter guy.

'Not really my thing,' I mumbled, trying hard not to make it too obvious that I had been intimidated by Pixies.

A year later Pixies released their second album, *Doolittle*. I had seen the video for 'Here Comes Your Man' on *The ITV Chart Show* and the band performing 'Monkey Gone to Heaven' on BBC Two's culture programme *The Late Show* and I was surprised to find they didn't look intimidating at all. In fact, their female bassist, whose voice on *Surfer Rosa* had conjured images of an etiolated drug vampire, was actually adorably smiley and even looked approachable. OK, so in real life she did go through a bit of a drug vampire phase and she may well have told me to fuck off if I had ever approached her, but still, she seemed fantastic.

More important than any of that was the music, which was catchy, albeit with a hard-edged intensity that made it tremendous. *Doolittle* went round and round on my Walkman that summer and was the soundtrack to becoming friends with Miriam. The first time I cycled up to her place in Newington Green I had to keep stopping to rewind a song whose lyric celebrated being 'on a wave of new relations'. 'Like me,' I thought. I later discovered the song was actually called 'Wave of *Mutilation*'.

I went back and bought *Surfer Rosa* again, along with the first Pixies EP, *Come On Pilgrim*, which I could only get on vinyl. There was no topless flamenco woman on that cover, just a fellow with an unusually hairy back. The arrival of hair clumps on my own back was making me feel like Brundlefly, but the *Come On Pilgrim* man convinced me I didn't have anything to complain about. Pixies kept ticking all the right boxes.

In the years that followed it was gratifying to see their sound recognised as an important influence on rock luminaries such as Kurt Cobain, PJ Harvey and Radiohead, but I never thought they got enough credit for their brave, positive stance on hairy backs.

Gawain's World

After two years out of education, the thought of going to university filled me with gloom. I would miss my restaurant friends, and the prospect of seeing less of Miriam was a particular kick in the willy. I had made it through the whole summer without saying 'I love you' because I felt I'd said it too much in the past and now I was determined not to spoil the fun. But when Miriam told me tearfully that she'd miss me at a farewell get-together, I took it as my cue to be honest. Instant fun spoiler.

The following week I sat in my tiny halls-of-residence box room at Warwick University and resolved to give undergraduate life my best shot. But thoughts of Miriam, the ubiquitous funk of cheese toasties and the sound of *Green* by R.E.M. drifting out of every student dorm and every bar as if to declare, *Life of Brian*-style, 'Yes! We are all individuals!' was making it difficult to be positive. 'Try to be less superficial, Buckles,' I thought. 'Concentrate on the English and American literature.'

For some reason, possibly because I hadn't properly investigated the actual course, I thought the *English* literature part might be sidelined in favour of free-form discussions of groovy Americans like Kerouac, Kesey and Ginsberg. We'd argue about them animatedly over coffee and cigarettes, then continue the conversation late into the night in one of Coventry's many excellent bars.

As it turned out, the whole of my first term at Warwick was given over to studying *Sir Gawain and the Green Knight,* an alliterative poem written in fourteenth-century Middle English. At first, I found *Sir Gawain and the Green Knight* to be a fairly standard load of impenetrably boring old shit that reminded me of how much I'd hated studying Chaucer at school. However, after several tutor groups I started to think *Sir Gawain and the Green Knight* was actually the biggest load of impenetrably boring old shit I'd ever brushed up against in my life.

I knew the problem lay with me and that if only I could concentrate for long enough, the hidden joys of the ancient text would reveal themselves like images of leaping dolphins in a Magic Eye picture. But I was never any good with Magic Eye pictures (also, they weren't around until 1993). So I trudged about the concrete campus trying not to think of Miriam, and embraced every available opportunity for extra-curricular distraction.

After years of being terrified by the idea of psychedelic drugs, the drabness of university life emboldened me one night to say 'Yes', albeit nervously, when one of the people I'd started spending time with suggested we take magic mushrooms. My friend led the way to a remote part of the campus and in a messy, low-lit room I told the man in the Wonderstuff T-shirt with the ziplock toadstool bag, 'I don't want to get off my head. I just want to get a bit giggly.'

He handed me some toast piled with soggy mushroom flesh and said, 'That'll make you giggly.'

A couple of hours later I was wandering the university grounds with a group of fellow mushroom enthusiasts, marvelling at the details of leaves, lights, the roughness of brick and the smoothness of metal.

Occasionally there was a bit of giggling. When everything started to look drab again, I assumed the experience had concluded safely, so I said goodnight and went back to my study, ready to turn in. That's when things started to go wrong.

Lying in bed with my headphones on, I pressed play on my new Discman and, as the long opening track from *Astral Weeks* enveloped me in its familiar twinkling warmth, I smiled to myself. 'This is fun,' I thought. 'I took mushrooms and didn't have a terrible time. I'm Jimmy Psychedelic Drugs.' But halfway through the second track, 'Beside You', Van's magical musical forest began to darken.

There's a passage in 'Beside You' when the rambling poetry gives way to the more prosaic: '*You breathe in, you breathe out, / You breathe in, you breathe out, / You breathe in, you breathe out, / You breathe in, you breathe out, / And you're HIIIIIIIGH!!!!!*' and as if responding to Van's command, I began to breathe in and breathe out until by the end of the line I felt I was being yanked out of myself and lifted into airless space where images of faces began morphing into one another uncontrollably.

After a few minutes of trying to enjoy what looked like a CGI sequence from *Star Trek IV: The Voyage Home*, I found that the sheer relentlessness of the imagery was beginning to make me anxious, so I pressed stop on the Discman, sat up, turned on the light, went over to the sink and splashed water on my face. I looked up at my reflection in the mirror and my blood froze. There was someone else looking back at me.

I knew it must be me. He looked like me – handsome, intelligent, friendly but not ingratiating – but I didn't feel connected to him. It was like looking at a clone. Beginning to panic, I tried splashing more water on my face and opened my study window to let in the chilly October air, but when I turned back to the mirror the clone was still there. I didn't feel physically intoxicated, and the voice in my head sounded the way it usually did, but I knew the mushrooms had knocked an important cable loose and now I was frightened that it might never be repatched.

Pulling on some clothes, I went out to one of the communal toilets in the corridor, hoping the ordinariness of taking a pee would help snap me out of whatever I was experiencing, but when I went to fetch out the old chap I was very sad to find him shrunk to the size of an acorn. OK, so it was more like a large acorn, but still, my knob was smaller than it had been since I was about four. So now, in addition to fucking my mind, I had broken my Cøken.

In the end I went and knocked on the door of a friend's study and he let me sleep on his floor. It was uncomfortable for both of us, but I was grateful. I was just too freaked out to be alone.

The next day my penis returned to its regular size and I reconnected with my reflection, but my time at Warwick failed to improve. My grant application had been refused, but Dad was scrabbling around trying to keep my brother at Haileybury, so financially I was on my own. I had opened three bank accounts at the beginning of term and had been living off the £200 student overdraft they each offered, but now that money was gone. I could have found a job locally, but I told myself I'd make more money in less time if I travelled back to London on weekends and pulled a few bartending shifts, which meant I could also see Miriam and the rest of my friends, too. So that's what I did.

Miriam had been able to put the 'I love you' incident behind her and over the course of several weekend visits to London we picked up where we'd left off. The more fun I had in London, however, the harder it was to return to concrete Warwick, my tiny study and Sir Gawain.

Then one afternoon, working on the first big Gawain essay we'd been set, I had an epiphany. For several days I'd been struggling to write something that sounded scholarly and 'legit', when a passage in the book reminded me of a scene in *Withnail and I*. It was the bit in the flat near the beginning when Withnail's reading out an article about a shot-putter called Jeff Wode and he starts imagining what it would be like to be threatened by him: 'I'm gonna pull your head off.' 'No, please don't pull my head off.' 'I'm gonna pull your head off because I don't like your head.' There was something about the baldness of those lines I'd always liked, and I realised nothing was stopping me from writing my Gawain essay with a similar colloquial directness, as long as I stayed on topic, of course. I started the essay again and this time it flowed out of me in just a few hours.

A week later the essays were marked and our tutor was handing them back to the group. Overall, the standard was poor, she said. 'You're going to need to raise your game,' she told some of the other students, but I still hadn't got my essay back. 'Adam, would you mind staying behind?' she said. 'I'd like to talk to you about your essay afterwards, if that's all right.'

'Of course,' I said and waited for the other students to file out of the room.

'I didn't want to say this in front of the others because it wouldn't have been fair to them and I didn't want to embarrass you, but your *Gawain* essay was one of the most refreshing and insightful pieces of work I've seen since I've been teaching this course. You made all the relevant points, but you did it in a way that was funny, direct and genuinely surprising. So, thank you. In fact, I was wondering if you'd consider reading it aloud at our next tutorial. I think the other students would find it really useful.'

I swear to you, that's what I thought my tutor was going to say. Instead, she said, 'Have I done something to offend you?'

I asked her what she meant. 'Well, I assumed you were angry with me for some reason. Why would you hand in this essay otherwise?'

'Oh. I thought it was good. I thought you were going to say you liked it,' I replied, genuinely bewildered.

'This essay is an insult and I'm not going to mark it. I want you to go away and write a proper one now and hand it in to me tonight. Then we can forget all about this and move on.'

*   *   *

'Hey, it's good to see you, Adam,' said Mum when I got back to Clapham. 'How's university going? I want to hear all about it.'

'Actually, Mum, I've left university, and I'm not going back.'

My *Gawain* essay might well have been bad, even insultingly bad, but my tutor's reaction had convinced me once and for all that I was not where I was supposed to be. So, instead of plunging back into *Gawain* with a new attitude, which I considered doing for at least a couple of minutes, I went to see the dean of students and explained that life at Warwick had become unsustainable.

Mum wept. Dad sighed. Even Miriam looked a little apprehensive that I was back in London full time. Though she was pleased to see me, she knew I was liable to say 'I love you' at any moment and nobody wanted that. Miriam's big news was that she had decided to apply for art school and she suggested I do the same. 'It's weird you didn't go in the first place,' she said, and I realised she was right.

I got a portfolio together and applied to the most exciting-looking art schools I could find, including St Martins, where Zac was studying. I was worried about Miriam, though. I felt she lacked some of the formal skills and imaginative flair that characterised my work and it would be tough for her to get into the kinds of prestigious art institutions that would be begging me to attend. Needless to say, she got into her first choice while I was rejected by all but one of mine. I only needed to get into one, though, and my four years at art school set me on the path to doing everything I've done since then, for better or worse.

*   *   *

On New Year's Eve 1989 I cycled over to Louis's place where he and his girlfriend Sarah were hanging out with Joe and Zac and getting stoned. We sat about and sang along with Zac and

Joe as they played funny songs on the guitar. The Surprise Rhyme Song, The Robert De Niro Calypso and a country song about someone called Roscoe H. Spellgood who liked to go a long way in a short time. 'That's why I increase my velocity when possible, cos speed equals distance over time,' sang Zac, and the rest of us harmonised.

But I wanted to drink beers, not get stoned, so soon after 11 p.m. I decided to cycle into the West End where Miriam was doing a shift, thinking it would be good to be with her as 1990 dawned. But I misjudged how long it would take me to get there and in the end I was just entering the celebratory mêlée in Piccadilly Circus as the clock struck midnight and a drunk reveller pushed me off my bike. By the time I got to the restaurant where Miriam was working, she was having fun, I was pissed off and we ended up arguing.

Before I'd left South London that night, Sarah had taken a photo of Louis, Zac, Joe and me with my Instamatic camera. We look so positive and happy. It's strange to remember how

L to R: Zac Sandler, Louis Theroux, Joe Cornish and me at Louis's house, New Year's Eve, 1989.

much doubt and worry there was sloshing around. As for Miriam, we had a few more great months before I dropped my three favourite torpedoes and our boat finally went down.

Ten years after I asked Joe if he thought we'd still be friends in ten years, we were making *The Adam and Joe Show* together and Zac was helping us, contributing songs, models and cartoons. No idea what happened to Louis.

BOWIE ANNUAL

'David Bowie "back on course" with *Tin Machine*' said the cover of *Q* magazine in June 1989. I was reading the Bowie interview at the restaurant one afternoon before starting my bar shift and, though I didn't much like his new beard, Zavid was making all the right noizes.

He'd lost his way with his last three albums, he said. Yes, David, I agree! He wanted to pick up where he'd left off with *Scary Monsters*, he said. Yes, David, *Scary Monsters*! That's where we fell in love, back in the art room at boarding school, remember? He'd been inspired to return to a more stripped-down rock sound after listening to Pixies, he said. Fucking hell, David, YES! I love Pixies, too! Uh-oh … Looks like I'm excited about the new Bowie album.

I bought *Tin Machine* from Tower Records in Piccadilly Circus on my way into work the next day and when the shift was over I listened to it as I walked to Trafalgar Square to get the night bus. Two tracks in, I was thinking, 'Have I done something to offend you?'

Everything about the record struck me as an unwelcome exercise in trying to be one of the lads. Manly

men in suits playing manly blues rock with a manly nod
to the jagged guitar sound of the Pixies, but with none
of the vitality. The title track especially sounded like a
strange rock'n'roll nursery rhyme written by a grumpy
dad at a music festival. '*Tin machine, / Tin Machine, /
Take me anywhere, / Somewhere without alcohol, / Or
goons with muddy hair.*'

I wondered if the name 'Tin Machine' was inspired
by the Pixies song 'Bone Machine'? If so, that was the
problem in a nutshell.

What is a Bone Machine? A machine for crushing
bones? A machine *made* from bones? A machine *inside*
someone's bones? It's disturbing David Lynchy shit
whichever way you slice it. But a Tin Machine? That's just
a machine made of metal. A lot of machines are made of
metal. They tend not to be made of tin because tin is crap
and would make the machine more likely to fall apart.

But maybe I was being too hard on David and, not
for the first time, too literal. A couple of the songs on
Tin Machine were actually pretty good. 'Prisoner of
Love' had the same tone of grand, romantic desolation
that I heard in 'Because You're Young', a song I always
liked from *Scary Monsters*. 'I Can't Read' also stirred
the emotions with its drunk punk swagger and was the
closest the record got to being as edgy and interesting
as some of its influences. But that wasn't very close.

I really put in the hours with *Tin Machine*, but it
was competing for my valuable time with albums I'd
recently discovered by The Stone Roses, De La Soul,
Magazine, Grace Jones, XTC, Public Enemy, The Velvet
Underground and of course Pixies, so repeated wading
through po-faced rock sludge for two serviceable tracks
just didn't add up. Even The Traveling Wilburys had more
pep. Way more, in fact.

'I'm zorry you feel that way, son,' said imaginary

Bowie. 'But to be honest with you, I don't care any more. Or maybe I care too much and that's why I'm making a machine out of tin – a machine designed to collapse on itself, thereby enabling me to pop it in the rezycling bin and move on with my career without constantly being made to feel I'm dizappointing people like you. You and me have both changed a lot in the last ten years. We've had some good times. We've had some bad times. And we've had some really embarrassing times, but now I think it might be best for both of us if we zpent some time apart. You can check in on me now and then and see what I've been up to if you like, but if you see me in a corridor backstage after a show for BBC Radio 2 at Maida Vale Studios, don't be surprised if I make a beeline for a more zuccessful comedian.'

Fair enough.

My pre-ordered copy of Bowie's last album, *Blackstar*, arrived on 11 January 2016, just hours after I'd read the news of his death. I'd heard the singles and a couple of the older tracks already and thought they were good, but now that he was gone everything on the album sounded as mysterious, sad and uplifting as his music had back when I was a boy. For about two weeks *Blackstar* was the only music I could listen to. It gave shape to a confusion of feelings about Bowie, about Dad, about getting older, about all of it, but the final track, 'I Can't Give Everything Away', was the one I kept coming back to.

Mostly the song seemed to be a rumination on mortality, but as ever with Bowie, it contained little references to his career that catapulted me back to my study at school, not knowing how to feel about so many things and thinking as I listened to his records, 'Well, maybe I feel like that.'

'I Can't Give Everything Away' also seemed to be a final word on the game Zavid had played all his life.

A game that was part high art and part junk. Part truth and part bullshit. Part meaningful connection and part selfish isolation. Part original and part stolen (I'm just going to do a few more of these and then I'll stop). Part Hero and part Zero. Part one and part two. Part Glass Spider and part Sparse Glider. OK, you get the idea.

It couldn't always have been an easy or rewarding game for him to play, but I dare say he got more out of it than just money, back pats and blowjobs. I hope so.

CHAPTER 21

BAAADDAD

'o! Open up the doh, muthafucka,' called a voice through the raised flap of my parents' letterbox.

Dad bent down and loudly demanded, 'TRANSLATE.'

'Oh, sorry, Nigel, I thought you were Adam,' said Joe.

It was Christmas Eve 1993 and I was home from art school and looking forward to seeing Cornballs and Louis for what had become a traditional festive get-together at my parents' place in Clapham.

Though I was 24, my relationship with Dad was still very much closer to naughty student and stern teacher than adult son and father. Sitting around in the front room enjoying glasses of sparkling wine and Sainsbury's finest middle-class nibbles, Joe and I found it hard to keep a straight face when talking to Dad, but Louis was a master at supplying what my father craved: first-class Oxford-undergraduate banter with sprinkles of history, politics and current affairs, i.e. the kind of thing he was unlikely to get from his eldest son.

The Glenn Miller played, the sparkling wine flowed and Joe and I did our best to make Louis laugh as Dad regaled him with stories of his glory days at Worcester College, becoming more pompous and animated as the evening wore on. Despite our low-level piss-taking, it was great to see Dad showing off to Louis like this, money worries and rows with Mum temporarily set aside as he played the posh, worldly bon vivant for someone who actually got most of the references.

Three years later Louis was making a name for himself on both sides of the Atlantic as a reporter on Michael Moore's *TV Nation*, but whenever he was in town we'd get together, hang out and talk about what we were up to. When Joe and I told him about our pilot for *The Adam and Joe Show* Louis said, 'Ads, you should get your dad in it. He's funny. You could get him to review gangster rap records.'

RAMBLE

HOW WE GOT INTO TV

For the first half of the Nineties, Joe and I spent much of our free time pissing about and making videos.

We'd imagine we were the presenters of edgy youth TV shows – 'Today on *Interlog 10*, we talk to film director Marvin Gaye about his new film *Star Wars*' – we'd wander round galleries pretending to be critics, reviewing fire extinguishers, emergency exit signs and anything else that wasn't supposed to be art, and we'd make spoof commercials for invented products like Bigot Beer, Pro Labia moisturiser and Books – 'The words are all bunched up together! Try finding your way through them with a pen. Come on! It's time to Book!'

Meanwhile back at art school in Cheltenham, I was making more of my own videos in between half understanding books about post-modernism and the media, and getting into work by any artist who seemed to have a sense of humour, especially Nam June Paik, Cindy Sherman, Jeff Koons and William Wegman.

When a new local radio station called CD 603 opened up in Cheltenham, I sent in a tape of some songs and sub-Chris Morris news parodies I'd been recording. They gave me a job as the traffic and travel reporter for the breakfast show, cycling round Cheltenham dressed as a cowboy on a Sinclair battery-powered 'Zike'. I was also given a three-hour slot on Sunday nights between 10 p.m. and 1 a.m. where, without the pressure of anyone actually listening, I was able to play sketches and songs I'd recorded.

In early 1994, during my last year at art school, I saw an ad in the *NME* asking for 'weird, funny and original' home videos for *Takeover TV*, a new public-access-style clip show on Channel 4. I sent in a VHS of things I'd made with Joe as well as some of my own efforts, including a video for one of my songs about a fictional New York performance artist called Randy Tartt.

Back in Clapham that summer I got a call from World of Wonder, the production company that was making *Takeover TV*. Fenton Bailey, who ran the company with his American partner Randy Barbato, had seen my tape and liked it. In fact, he described my Randy Tartt video as 'genius'.

'Perhaps he's just fond of the name Randy,' I thought. When I met Fenton at World of Wonder's office above The Body Shop in Brixton, it turned out he was mainly fond of the word 'genius', which he used about everything from the coffee a researcher brought him, to the incredibly annoying recent chart hit 'Doop' (by Doop). I liked Fenton and it turned out that he and Randy had made several TV shows that I'd loved when I was at art school, so I was delighted when I was offered a job on *Takeover TV* as a researcher watching and logging tapes that people like me had sent in.

Takeover TV went out on Channel 4 in early 1995. My Randy Tartt clip was shown along with some videos I'd made with Joe. Fenton also invited me to present a couple of episodes, and when the show was recommissioned I got the job of presenting the whole series, though this time I tried to get Cornballs more involved.

One of Joe's ideas was to use our childhood toys (including my old *Star Wars* toys that Mum still had safely stored in the attic) to make parodies of movies and TV shows. Our first one was a two-minute version of *Apollo 13* featuring three stuffed toys in a bin (called 'Appallo 13'), and when it was finished we knew we'd hit on something incredibly special that would propel us into the very margins of cult micro stardom.

Peter Grimsdale, *Takeover TV*'s commissioning editor at Channel 4, suggested Joe and I come up with some ideas for our own show. After many false starts and tense conversations with Joe, whose frustration that he wasn't yet working on films I failed to properly appreciate at the time, we began putting together *The Adam and Joe Show,* and an incredibly small footnote in the annals of DIY television began to be written.

I wasn't sure I was up for having my dad as part of our show. After all, he'd spent the whole of my adolescence taking a series of dumps on every TV programme, film and piece of music I enjoyed, plus he was my dad, and aside from the odd booze-fuelled family get-together, I still found it hard to relax when he was around, but we needed material and Joe convinced me to give it a go. Dad agreed to help as soon as I asked and was only a little disappointed when I explained we didn't have the budget to actually pay him anything. 'I imagine there'll be other rewards when I become famous,' he reasoned.

On a grey day in August 1996 we loaded a mini DV tape into the Sony DCR-VX1000 camcorder (mandatory for every cheap TV production in the Nineties) and made our way over to the Olympia Exhibition Centre in West London where we were shooting the first footage for our pilot at the launch of the new-look Action Man doll. It was the first of many items we shot while we were still in the process of figuring out what the show actually was, and our producer Debbie would send us off to random events in the hope that they might provoke some solid-gold tomfoolery from me and Joe. The highlight of the Action Man launch was interviewing a human model who looked exactly like the new Action Man. We asked him to look surprised by something off-camera and then said, 'Nice reaction, man!' It didn't make it into the show.

From Olympia we headed over to Clapham and, with Dad sat in his favourite Christmas Eve pompous pontification chair, we recorded his first music review.

Feeling that gangster rap might be too narrow a remit, we'd given him a mix of genres to comment on, starting with 'Higher State of Consciousness' by Josh Wink, 'Men in Black' by Frank Black and 'Natural Born Killaz' by Dr Dre ft. Ice Cube.

Dad's initial response to the screeching techno of 'Higher State of Consciousness' was to recite from memory the poem 'In No Strange Land' by the Victorian writer and mystic Francis Thompson. It was a beautiful poem and Dad recited it movingly, but we were after something a bit pithier and a bit funnier.

'This isn't going to work,' I thought, but Joe persevered, asking Dad questions until he came out with something funny or interesting, at which point he'd ask him to repeat it in soundbite form. The finished piece with the soundbites appearing inside old-fashioned picture frames over the music videos went down well with everyone we showed it to. Back in 1996 it was still a novelty to see a plummy-voiced septuagenarian analysing youth culture in that way.

The name BaaadDad was a nod to another late-night Channel 4 show around that time: *Baadasss TV*, hosted by Andi Oliver and the rapper Ice-T, who proclaimed it a 'fly and funky' look at 'the idiosyncrasies of black culture'. So yeah, perfect for Dad.

When the first series of *The Adam and Joe Show* went out, it was the toy movie parodies and the BaaadDad segments that people seemed to respond to most enthusiastically, and the fact that he was my real father meant we ended up doing quite a few interviews together. These were fun. Dad liked the attention and I liked showing him that all those years of main-lining pop culture might not have been a total waste after all. 'Perhaps this is the moment when Dad and I start to become best pals,' I thought.

When *The Adam and Joe Show* was recommissioned in 1997 we decided that, as well as continuing with the music reviews, we should take BaaadDad out and about to explore various aspects of youth culture. Now that TV shows featuring comedians going on adventures with their parents has become a well-established genre, it seems odd that I didn't appear on screen with Dad in these segments. But back then I felt our relationship was too fraught to be entertaining on screen, and anyway, there was a danger it would have unbalanced things with me and Joe. Ensuring that one of us didn't get significantly more attention than the other was something we had started paying attention to after a few exchanges on the subject in which our breathing went weird and our voices got wobbly.

So Joe and I tended to stay behind the camera for Dad's segments and concentrated on getting the best out of him, something that Cornballs was particularly good at. In addition to his phenomenal, award-winning skills as a director, Joe had the advantage of being unencumbered by awkwardness around Dad and was happy to encourage him to do things on camera that I would have been too embarrassed or too protective to suggest.

We visited the Tribal Gathering dance music festival in 1997, and Joe got Dad to strike up a conversation with a woman in her early twenties who claimed to be tripping on acid (though as far as I could tell she was just Australian), and when she rolled a joint, Joe got Dad to take a couple of drags. I wasn't sure what to make of the footage when I watched it back. The sight of my 73-year-old father smoking drugs and turning on the charm with the young woman, saying to her at one point, 'You know, you're very beautiful,' made me uncomfortable, not least because he and my mum were getting on so badly at the time and I knew the footage would make her cringe.

Our editor Jon cut the piece so that Dad's 'you're very beautiful' line came immediately after his toke on the joint, and it worked well, as if being high (though he claimed not to have inhaled) had instantly made him talk like a hippy, rather than the line just being something a sleazy old guy might say. However, I worried that, in the course of trying to get the best out of Dad while managing the less palatable aspects of his personality, we were turning him into a caricature. Occasionally he, too, would sense that happening and resist. On those occasions, choosing between what was best for the show and what was best for Dad gave me a massive emotional wedgie.

* * *

In 1998 we flew to Ibiza to immerse BaaadDad in the island's culture of clubbing and hedonism. It was not a relaxing week. Dad spent half the time grumbling about how loud, loathsome and grotesque the music, the clubs and most of the people were, and the other half trying not to make it too obvious that he was ogling topless women on the beach. He was entitled to his opinion and perhaps even his ogling, but it had the effect of making me less protective and tolerant of him.

The tension between me and Dad came to a head early one morning in Trade nightclub. The music was particularly hard and loud, the lighting intense and disorientating, and he was in a bad mood. There was a muscly man in a loincloth dancing on a podium and Joe asked him whether he'd mind if my dad gave one of his glistening buttocks a quick kiss or possibly a lick. 'OK,' shrugged the muscly man over the din of the music and Joe leaned close to give my father the good news.

'Absolutely not,' replied Dad.

'How about you just touch his bum then?' said Joe. 'It's a beautiful bum.'

'No,' came Dad's flat reply.

'He'd be fine if it was a woman's bum,' I thought, somewhat redundantly.

When we got outside I told Dad he was being 'unprofessional'.

I was thinking this might be the wrong thing to say as I was saying it, and it turned out I was right. Dad got angrier than I'd seen him since I was 12 and I made my sister cry by excluding her from a game of Cheat with some children we'd met on holiday. And no wonder.

Whatever hang-ups I had about our relationship and his ogling tendencies, he was a man in his mid-seventies being asked to engage in buffoonery for the cameras from morning till late at night, often in an environment that was just about bearable if you'd had an E. The only pills Dad was popping were for his blood pressure. As if to prove how unfair I'd been, the next couple of days were spent filming Dad at a Club 18–30 resort where he joined in with activities that included go-kart racing, swigging Schnapps on a packed coach as the passengers cheered and a karaoke party that ended with about 100 semi-naked revellers chanting, 'BAAADDAD IS OUR LEADER! BAAADDAD IS OUR LEADER! LA LA LA LA! OOH! LA LA LA LA! OOH!'

The truth was that whether he was joining in with a plastic-bottle battle in the mosh pit for the Foo Fighters at V97, being taught to rap by Coolio or being coached to become a Young British Artist by Jake and Dinos Chapman, Dad never let us down and was 100 per cent professional. OK, let's say 95 per cent.

None of that changed his opinion of the show itself, however, or most things I did professionally from then on, which he referred to as 'pretty rubbishy, on the whole'. He disliked the bad language and the toilet humour, and it didn't help that whatever I did was usually stuffed with references he didn't get. Despite that, Joe and I managed to capture a few moments that supplied everything I'd hoped for when Dad started helping us with our TV nonsense.

*   *   *

We had a segment on *The Adam and Joe Show* called Vinyl Justice, in which Joe and I dressed up as policemen and 'raided' the homes of music artists in search of 'criminal records' in their collections. I always thought of it as an excuse to meet a few of my musical heroes and over the years we spent strange afternoons filming with Thomas Dolby, Nick Heyward of Haircut 100, Tim and Lætitia of Stereolab, Mark E. Smith of the Fall and, most exciting of all for me, Frank Black of Pixies, whose music, once I'd stopped being intimidated by it, had become as familiar and important to me as Bowie or Talking Heads.

We did Vinyl Justice with Frank at his Los Angeles home in late 1998, but earlier that year when he was in London playing some shows with his new band the Catholics I asked our producer if she could get us some time with him. It wasn't practical to do Vinyl Justice while Frank was touring, so we decided it might be funny if BaaadDad interviewed him instead, and ten years after I'd cycled round London listening to 'Here Comes Your Man' for the first time, Frank Black was sat opposite Dad in the front room of Joe's flat in Clerkenwell.

Frank and Dad got on famously, chatting about wine, Armagnac and their favourite stretches of road in France, which would have made a great segment for a show about indy music and European travel aimed at *Telegraph* readers, but it didn't fit in *The Adam and Joe Show*. I was just excited to meet Frank Black, so I didn't care, but I felt bad about wasting his time, so when we were finished we took him for tapas across the road at the newly opened Moro restaurant (then co-owned by our friend Mark). 'I wish all my interviews were like this,' declared Frank, beaming at Dad.

A few weeks later Frank got in touch and asked if Joe and

I would be interested in making a video for his new single 'Dog Gone'. Joe thought of doing an *E.T.* parody with Frank as the extra-terrestrial, munching Reese's Pieces in a garden shed, but Frank was still on tour, so we suggested using my dad somehow. 'Perfect,' said Frank, going on to explain that, whether or not it was useful for the video, 'Dog Gone' was written from the point of view of a meteorite on a collision course with earth. We decided that Dad would play not only the meteorite, flying through space as he sang, but a character a bit like Stanley Green, the man with the 'Less Protein' sign who we used to see wandering the West End of London in the Eighties.

I made a sandwich board for Dad that said '*THE END IS NIGH*' on the front, and '*I AM HERE*' on the back and printed out flyers with Frank Black's face on them for him to hand out. Then we spent a couple of afternoons filming around the West End and outside Brixton Tube where Dad fearlessly interacted with members of the public as they ignored, tolerated and abused him. Unfazed, Dad would look over to where we were filming from time to time, sing a few of the lyrics to 'Dog Gone' and get on with his Prophet of Doom duties, looking for all the world like just another crazy old irrelevant guy.

Chances are you haven't seen the video, and even if you look it up on YouTube you may think, 'I liked Adam's dad better when he smoked a joint at that music festival,' but the finished video for 'Dog Gone' is one of my favourite things Joe and I ever did together. I love the reactions of some of the people we filmed – the young woman in Brixton who takes a flyer from Dad then smiles sweetly at him; the wiry homeless man who dances round playfully taunting Dad with a toy dinosaur; even the bloke in the lift at Covent Garden Tube who responds to Dad's offer of a flyer by flicking a 'V' sign at him, a gesture Dad accommodated with a look of weary resignation. Mostly, though, I love seeing two worlds so important to me collide as Dad sings along to a song by the lead singer of Pixies.

Speaking of worlds colliding, in early 2016 I made a podcast about the way myself and others had reacted to David Bowie's death, and one of the people I spoke to was Dara O'Kearney, an Irish fan who had become email pen pals with Zavid. They corresponded regularly from the late Nineties onwards and would talk about what they'd been listening to, reading and watching. It turned out Bowie had watched *The Adam and Joe Show*. His favourite part was BaaadDad.

CHAPTER 22

CHECK-OUT TIME

'm not worried about death. There are times – when I'm arguing with members of my family, falling out with friends, watching the news or looking at Twitter – when non-existence seems rather appealing. It's the actual dying part I'm sadder about, and since my pa died I think about it a lot more.

Mainly I wonder how it'll come about, which makes me think of my health. In all likelihood, whatever is going to finish me off is lurking inside already; deadly sleeper cells radicalised by genetic scriptures or years of attacks from booze, biscuits and tobacco, waiting to bring down the short, hairy Tower of Buckles. I could wage war on these internal terrorists with exercise, self-control, cutting-edge diets, chanting, magnets, tea made from my own urine, etc., but even then, all it takes is a few disgruntled actors and it's curtains for my corrupted empire.

Or maybe the universe will clobber me another way and all the time spent worrying about my health will have been wasted. Perhaps I'll drive into a tree while attempting to pair the car stereo with my phone, or get pushed in front of a train during an argument with a rail official at Cambridge station, or the Russians will inject one of my Revels with a nerve agent, and in my last moments I'll be thinking, 'Oh no! I could have had *way* more doobies.'

One of my main worries about dying is the lack of control. Regaining a shred of autonomy is presumably one of the main factors when people consider voluntary euthanasia.

Arranging the exact time and nature of your exit has a lot of advantages from the point of view of tying up loose ends. I'm not talking about suicide here, by the way. As far as I can see that just creates a lifetime's supply of loose ends for the family and friends you leave behind. I'm talking about organising a nice farewell that eliminates the randomness, the surprise and the meaninglessness of so many deaths.

For example, when I felt the time was right, I could return to St Cuthbert's parish church in the cathedral city of Wells, Somerset, where in 2006 Edgar Wright directed my death scene in *Hot Fuzz*, and here, as part of a moving ceremony, someone I'd chosen specially (an old enemy I wanted to make peace with, or a competition winner perhaps) could topple one of the church spires and explode my head, as in the film. If Simon Pegg was experiencing a career slump, he could officiate. My family would probably not attend (unless they really hated me by that time), but for film fans, gore hounds and those who appreciate grand gestures that defy the arbitrary nature of existence, it would be a day to cherish.

* * *

My dad was determined to tie up as many loose ends as possible before he died. He didn't want us to be burdened with too much admin when he was gone. As he had no other assets to speak of, his hopes for leaving something behind for his children were pinned on selling his place in Newhaven where he'd lived by himself for his last 20 years, and he didn't want to pop off before the sale was finalised.

The house was eventually sold a few weeks before he died but brought in a fraction of the already modest sum my dad was expecting. He went full gloomy about it, as if cancer wasn't enough to be down in the dumps about. My sister, my brother and I never expected to inherit anything from Dad (other than some grumpy genes, a lot of books about the Second World War and various lengths of string), so we didn't care about the money, but he took it as another indication that he'd failed somehow. In his last days his face fixed into an expression of worry. I asked if he was frightened. 'No,' said Pa. What was he fretting about then? 'So many things,' he replied.

*   *   *

Watching TV with my wife and Rosie one night in mid-November 2015, my phone rang. It was Dad calling from his bedroom across the way. 'Adam? Something extraordinary's happened.'

'What's up?' I asked.

'I don't know who I am,' replied Pa.

My chest elevator dropped a few floors. I had been so focused on Dad's physical deterioration, I hadn't considered what might be happening to his mind.

Over in the flat I found him sitting up in bed looking worried. 'It's the strangest thing,' he said, all the hardness gone out of his voice. 'I woke up and I no longer had any sense of who I am.' I went and fetched a family photo album and found that he was able to recognise and identify everyone in it, so the problem wasn't with his memory. Instead, it was his sense of self that had short-circuited. It reminded me of my Warwick magic-mushroom experience and the clone I'd seen in the mirror. 'I bet you this is a side-effect of the morphine,' speculated Dr A. Buckles.

We went and sat in the living room. I made some tea and set it down for Dad with a couple of milk chocolate Hobnobs, hoping to refocus his mind on a simple pleasure. 'Have you ever dunked a biscuit?' I asked, prepared for him to tell me that dunking biscuits was vulgar, barbaric or grotesque.

'Of course I've dunked a biscuit,' he replied.

Dad dunked his Hobnob in the tea and for a moment I worried that he would fail to take it out before the submerged portion detached and sank, but luckily he withdrew it before it came to that. 'It's great to dunk a biscuit, isn't it?' I said.

'Yes,' replied Pa softly before continuing, as if to himself, 'Occasionally I feel that I'm absolutely irrelevant.'

OK. Time to shift to a conversational gear I hadn't used with Dad before.

'Who *is* relevant?' I asked.

'Ah, that's the big question,' said Dad, still not really looking at me. 'That is where it starts to be frightening.'

'Why would you be frightened by it?'

'Because we spend so much time and effort making sure that the state of our being is what it ought to be, and it becomes very unsettling if you start suspecting that it doesn't very much matter.'

'Well, it *doesn't* much matter. But that's why we make things and organise things, isn't it? Otherwise, of course it's all meaningless.'

'How are you feeling?' I asked after a while.

'I feel much better now,' said Dad weakly, 'but only because you're there.'

I didn't like to see him vulnerable and frightened. On the other hand, it was preferable to seeing him crotchety and impatient. At least I felt I could be of some use to him when he was in this state. Then he asked, 'What have you done with the black briefcase?' I told him it was safe. 'Do you know what's in it?'

I did know what was in it.

Several weeks earlier I'd complained to Dad about his commandeering of salad bowls for use as piss bottles (ignoring the carefully-washed fabric softener containers I'd provided for just such a purpose), and the conversation had escalated until he'd snapped, 'Perhaps it would be best for everyone if you just put me in a home then.' I said I'd look into it. Sat at my desk trying to regain my composure, my gaze drifted from the browser window where I had typed '*Norwich best care homes*' to the black briefcase on the corner filing cabinet. 'Screw it,' I thought. 'I'm going to take a look.'

It wasn't hard to get it open. I forced the catches with a screwdriver and they flipped up perkily as if to say, 'Hey! What took you so long?'

There was a gun inside. A Luger.

'It belonged to an SS officer,' said Dad, and I dunked a Hobnob. 'I took it off him when we liberated a POW camp on the outskirts of Hamburg. You would have known if you'd read my book.'

Copies of *The Road to Fleet Street*, the autobiography Dad had been working on in various forms for years and had finished just a couple of months before, had recently arrived in Norfolk, but between family, failed pilots and Dad commitments, there hadn't been the time to sit down and read it all. Also, at that point, I just couldn't face it. There were so many things I wanted to know about Dad, but, leafing through the book, I could see he hadn't written about them. As for what he *had* written about, I felt I'd heard most of those stories before. Maybe not the Luger story, though.

'I was thinking,' continued Dad, 'I might ask you to bring me the gun and I could just blow my brains out.'

I replied that I'd rather he didn't blow his brains out. Clearing up after the spectacular Code Brown in the bathroom last week had been bad enough. Dad ignored me and continued, 'I think the reason people shoot themselves is that they don't belong anywhere. They don't have any reason to be anywhere.'

'Or they've made such a mess of things they can't bear to think about it any more. Or they're mentally ill, but that's not the case with you, Dad.'

'The case with me is, I have no relevance. If it weren't for the fact that there would be a response from you, I wouldn't speak. Because that would remind me that I was the only person left in the world and that would remind me that I didn't exist.'

I asked him if he felt panicky. 'Of course. I'm panicky because I don't belong anywhere.'

'You belong here,' I said, and for a while neither of us spoke.

When I was confident that he was OK and through the worst of the morphine fugue, I asked if he'd like me to put on a film for him. 'What would you put on?' he asked. I tried to think what I would want to watch if I were in his position. 'Have you seen *Air Force One* with Harrison Ford?' Dad liked Harrison Ford. We watched *Raiders of the Lost Ark* one Christmas towards the end of the Eighties when Dad was beginning work on his novel, *The Proving Ground*. 'That's who should play me when they turn my book into a film,' said Dad. I put on *Air Force One* and headed back to Rosie and my wife.

*　*　*

After Pa's bad trip he made me promise I wouldn't let him wake up in the night feeling like that again. I told him if he took his sleeping pill every night, he should be fine, but that was easier said than done.

He'd stopped eating solid food by this point and was only drinking fluids with difficulty – an indication, said the GP, that the end was a few days away. His sleeping pills were tiny but getting one into his mouth and washing it down with some water had become like a *Mission Impossible* interrogation scene.

At the end of one particularly difficult day when I was looking forward to a beer, a podcast and a few hours of undisturbed rest, I placed the pill in Dad's mouth and offered him a glass of water to wash it down. He waved it away. 'Have you swallowed the pill?' I asked hopefully.

'I don't know,' he replied after a while.

'Well, have you or haven't you?' Pa opened his mouth and the pill fell out.

There followed around ten minutes of unsuccessful attempts to shift him into a position where he could more easily swallow the pill, every move accompanied by more of his blood-curdling groans and cries. It felt as though he was no longer helping me, even actively resisting my efforts to help him swallow the pill, but I refused to give in, reasoning that once it was down we could both get some undisturbed rest. After all, neither of us wanted a repeat of Lugernacht.

Exhausted and agitated, I was ready to throw up my hands and say, 'Sod this, I give up,' when I remembered the heavy little shot glasses I kept as souvenirs from my bartending days.

RAMBLE

I liked it when Dad would come into the bar while I was working. With a nod from my manager, I'd pour us a couple of shots of the most expensive Armagnac we had and Pa would beam at me. 'Golly, this is the really fancy stuff! I had a flask of this when I walked the Chilkoot Trail in Alaska and it saved my life on more than one occasion, let me tell you.' He had told me many times.

I crushed the sleeping pill into a powder and transferred it to the shot glass, which I topped up with water. Back in Dad's bedroom, I tipped back his skinny head and supported it as I lifted the glass to his lips and poured in the sleeping draught.

Once it was finally all gone, I told Dad I was heading to bed myself and wished him a good night. As I turned to leave, he murmured something I couldn't understand, except for the phrase 'sleep tonight with a clear conscience'.

'What's that, Daddy? Are you saying you don't have a clear conscience?'

To which he replied clearly, 'No, you!'

'Why wouldn't I have a clear conscience?' I asked, my heart beginning to thump.

'Because you're a bully.'

I considered this for a few moments, wondering if he might be right, thinking about times I'd been impatient with him, with the children, with my wife, with Rosie, thinking about all the ways there are to be a bully even if you think you're a good guy, a loyal son, a FUN DAD.

Then I thought, 'No, fuck that,' and said, 'Daddy, I am doing my best to keep you out of hospital and look after you here, as you said you wanted. You asked me not to let you wake up in the night again, which is why you need to take the sleeping pill. Now you call me a bully?'

A short pause, then he mumbled, 'I take it all back.'

'Hmmm. OK,' I said. 'Well, see you tomorrow.'

RAMBLE

Why am I telling you all this stuff? I suppose a selfish impulse to unburden myself is part of it, but people sometimes tell me they find it helpful when I discuss this kind of thing on the podcast, so I thought I shouldn't shy away from it here. Dad felt this sort of talk cheapened moments that were meant to be kept private or sacred. Maybe he was right.

Maybe I'll regret writing about all this one day. But for the time being all I can do is try to connect.

* * *

Dad didn't say much the day he died. I was sitting by his bed, still hoping he might rally sufficiently to deliver an inspiring farewell speech, have a crack at the meaning of life or just say,

'I thought your song "Sausages" was very good.' Instead, he drifted in and out of lucidity, occasionally gripping my hand softly or raising his rheumy eyes to meet mine, but obstinately refusing to get cinematic.

By the time the district nurses arrived to hook up an automatic syringe drive for his painkillers, he was no longer gripping my hand, there was a thousand-yard stare on him and his breathing sounded like a fucked coffee percolator.

'He should calm down a bit when the painkillers take effect,' said one of the nurses as they left, but half an hour passed and his chest was rattling so much it was freaking me out. I went into the living room and to distract myself I started playing a game on my phone, a Tetris variant based on numbers that I often played before bed while listening to a podcast to wind my brain down.

I jabbed away for a minute or two, then thought, 'Shit! I wouldn't want my dad to die while I was playing a phone game.' I went back in to find his breathing had become more jerky. I held his hand, called out to him, but he didn't register me. Now there were long pauses between sharp intakes of breath. 'Hey, Daddy! Can you hear me? I'm right here.' Then his face contorted and a single tear ran down his left cheek. Then he stopped breathing.

'Hey, Daddy!' I said for several minutes. 'Where are you? Are you there? Where are you?' Worth a try.

*　*　*

Earlier that day, just when I thought he had zoned out completely, Dad slowly reached out his arm, took my hand and brought it to his face. 'He probably wants me to wipe his mouth or scratch his ear or something,' I thought, but to my surprise he gave my hand a kiss. 'Oh shit!' I thought. 'This is it. Cinematic closure time!'

It didn't look as though he was going to die at that very moment, so I asked if he'd like me to read to him and looked over at the shelves filled with all the books that had made the trip from Newhaven earlier in the year. Dad gave me a trembling thumbs up. 'How about this one?' I said, picking out *Master and Commander* from a row filled with all the volumes in the same series by Patrick O'Brian. I remembered that Dad had once tried reading *Master and Commander* to me when I was very young, but I thought it was boring. I preferred the Mister Men books, which must have been painful for Dad, like one of my children turning their nose up at David Bowie only to get excited about Justin Bieber. I held up *Master and Commander* for Dad and he gave me another thumbs up.

As soon as I began to read, the moment felt over-burdened with significance. I tried my best to give the audiobook performance of a lifetime, but within a few lines I stumbled on some nautical jargon, and when I mispronounced the name 'Maturin' as '*Maturing*', Dad waved his hand emphatically for me to stop. I apologised and asked if he wanted me to continue. Feebly, he reached across and pushed the book out of my hands. I'd failed the audition for my own Moving Moment with Dying Dad scene, but, I reminded myself, he'd kissed my hand. That wasn't nothing.

* * *

It's supposed to be therapeutic to write a letter to a dead loved one, so here goes:

Dear Daddy,

How are you? I am fine. What's it like being dead (assuming it's anything at all)? I bet it's relaxing, like the feeling you get after cancelling a load of appointments and doing all your admin. Are there a lot of people playing phone games there?

Or maybe the afterlife is a perfect moment made eternal, like the Nexus in Star Trek: Generations (except without Whoopi Goldberg with a small coffee table on her head, trying to convince you to leave). If it's like the Nexus, I imagine you're sat on a picnic blanket outside a little log cabin on a snowy hillside somewhere in the Tyrol. There's a bottle of Moët chilling in the snow and you're with that ballet dancer who broke your heart before you met Mum. You remember? The one you would mention more often than you probably ought to have done.

Things are OK in Norfolk. Every few weeks Rosie and I walk over to visit your grave and make sure it's all in order. We don't want BaaadDad fans to cover it with graffiti, love locks, stickers, friendship bracelets and other trinkets, the way they did with Jim Morrison. None so far, you'll be relieved to hear. At Christmas I pour some Courvoisier down for you, but Rosie usually licks it up. It was good to see you and Rosie getting along in those final months, cos when we were little you used to be a real Dog Nazi, remember?

Sometimes I chat to your headstone and Rosie looks at me as if to say, 'You know he's dead and ghosts don't exist, don't you?' You certainly haven't sent me any ghostly signs since you've been gone, so I think she's probably right. If you were a ghost, I imagine you'd possess my laptop and start leaving comments about my bad grammar and striking through sentences you didn't like. And pretty much the whole of this last chapter would be out. I'd have to upgrade to the latest operating system to get rid of you, which I don't want to do because I'm worried it would affect the functionality of too many applications I rely on for BUG and the podcast.

I know we didn't have that much of a relationship in the last 20 years, but I wanted you to know, I thought you were the best when I was growing up. Funny and nice and clever and important. Remember when we went to New York and you said you'd forgotten to lock the safe where you kept all your expensive cameras, fancy bottles of wine and other priceless treasure? You decided to fly back to London on Concorde, lock the safe, then get the next Concorde back to New York the same day. We all thought that was pretty cool at the time. Now it seems to be the work of a madman, but it contributed to that feeling we had as children that as long as you were around, everything could be sorted and everything would be OK.

What a great feeling that was. I'm lucky to have had it, and I was always grateful for it, even when I eventually found out it wasn't real and you were as flawed as the rest of us. Even when you seemed disappointed by how everything turned out, even when you used to wear very short shorts and sit on your camping stool with your legs apart, so that one of your saggy old nuts popped out. Even then.

I do miss that feeling. I sometimes feel frightened since you left. Frightened I'm doing a bad job of bringing up my children, frightened I'm too weak-willed to be a better person and frightened of deteriorating and dying fretful. But that's just sometimes. Most of the time I'm all-round amazing – at least, that's what Rosie thinks. For example, I've been cooking some vegan and vegetarian meals. They're much nicer than I thought they would be, although it has meant I feel justified eating more cakes and biscuits. Also, I read a lot more books nowadays, though you'd probably think they were shit. There's other amazing stuff, but that's all that comes to mind just now.

Perhaps when I'm lying in my deathbed, I'll get one of my children to read to me, the way I did with you, remember? I won't ask them to read Master and Commander, though. They can read from Ramble Book by Adam Buxton. I hear it's great for deathbeds.

Anyway, thanks, Daddy. I love you. Bye.
Adam

ACKNOWLEDGEMENTS

Hey! Welcome back. You made it. Well done.

I've no idea why I didn't write a book years ago. It's so easy. Especially this kind of book. You just remember some funny things and a few sad things and write them down, then the editor (Jack Fogg) comes to your house after you've missed a few deadlines and says, 'These lists of your favourite albums and films are great, but maybe you could flesh them out a bit?' And that's it.

Nevertheless, there were times during the process of putting this book together when I started to wonder if it would join my failed TV pilots in the 'Didn't Quite Happen' bin. In those moments my special personality recipe of low self-esteem and high self-regard may have made me challenging to work with, be friends with, be related to and live with. I just checked with my wife and she's saying 'Nooo!' in a rather sarcastic and unbecoming fashion.

Anyway, in the hope of maintaining some of my relationships a while longer, I should probably thank some people who have helped with this book, directly or indirectly.

Here we go ...

Thanks to my mum, my brother and sister, who let me say what I wanted here, though I'm sure they could all tell you some very different stories about Dad, and about what

I was like to grow up with. Thanks as well to Aunty Jessica, my Californian cousins and my in-laws Harry, Sophy, Marilyn and Edward.

Thanks to my kind and generous friends, especially those who pop up in this book one way or another: Joe, Annabel, Mark, Zivi, Louis, Nancy, Dan, Garth, Woz, Lottie, Jo, Chris, Patrick, Zac, Ben W., Alison, Guy, Chad, Tom H., Ben H., Miriam, Bill Muggs, Jonathan, Jane, Emily, Edgar, Simon, Maureen and every member of The Best Band in the World.

Thanks to those who have helped me make an actual living from my ludicrous mouthings over the years: Chiggy, Emily, Becca and all at PBJ, Séamus, Matt, Anneka and all at Acast, Fenton Bailey, Randy Barbato, Peter Grimsdale, Stephanie Calman, James Stirling, all at Sue Terry, Louise Stephens, David Knight and the *BUG* team.

Thanks to everyone at HarperCollins, especially Holly Kyte for her insightful copy-editing, Isabel Prodger for her publicity skills, Orlando Mowbray for his mastery of marketing (sorry I came off Twitter just before the book came out, Orlando), Fionnuala Barrett for audio-book production, Terence Caven for book layout and Simeon Greenaway for cover design.

Special thanks to my editor Jack Fogg, who turned the torture into genuine fun.

Thanks to Luke Drozd for his magnificent posters and book plates.

Thanks to Helen Green for creating the artwork and the illustrations for this book with typical speed and professionalism. Helen draws the way I always wished I could draw. She draws Bowie the way I feel about him.

Thanks to the people that keep my fortunate life on the rails: Janice, Charlotte, Becca, Jonathan, Felicity and Ross. Thanks to great teachers everywhere, especially Mr Kendrick, Mr Field, Ms Miller, Mr Stewart and Mr Benenson. Thanks to doctors and nurses, especially in the NHS. Thanks to smiley train conductors, rubbish collectors, good cops, silly comedians, scientists working to save the planet … shit, this list is getting out of hand. OK, I'll wrap it up.

I hope that, despite my carping, my gratitude to my dad has come across. And Zavid, too, of course. Also buried inside this book is my love for my children, Rosie and my wife, without whom none of this would mean anything. Sitting around and laughing with you all is the happiest I get.

Right, that's enough of that.

I sometimes read books like this and think, 'How could they have possibly remembered all that stuff? Are they just making it up?' In my case I used a combination of diaries, videos and voice notes to recall specific details, though of course I probably got some things wrong or misremembered in the course of trying to make sense of certain incidents. The thing that proved almost magically effective when it came to unlocking many of the memories in here was music. I found that if I looked back at the UK charts for any given period in the Eighties, the songs would bring back a flood of precise details about what I was doing at the time.

For playlists containing a lot of the music mentioned in this book visit Spotify and search for therealadambuxton.

There are also videos and other bits and pieces on my website: adam-buxton.co.uk and on Joe's Instagram: mrjoecornish.

OK, now I really am going. Thanks. Bye.

Adam Buxton, March 2020